ALL ABOUT ISRAEL

by
Sara Schachter
and
Sol Scharfstein

KTAV PUBLISHING HOUSE, INC.

PHOTOGRAPHIC CREDITS

American Friends of the Hebrew University; Israel Department of Antiquities; Israel Office of Information; Palphot, Israel; Jewish National Fund; Jewish Theological Seminary; Magen David Adom; Zionist Archives and Library.

KTAV PUBLISHING HOUSE INC.
ISBN 87068-258-X
MV88

TABLE OF CONTENTS

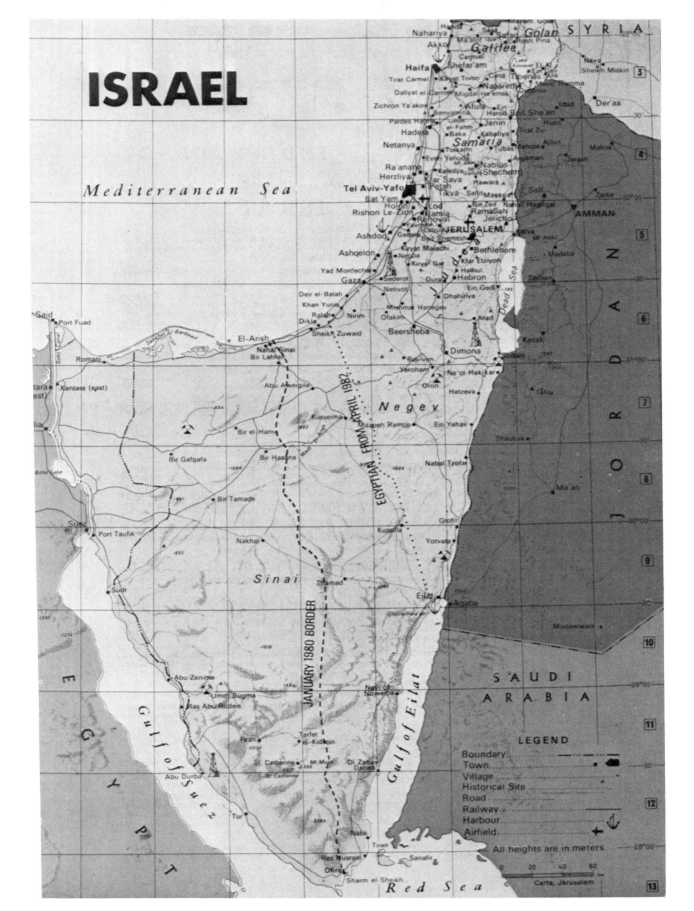

הכרזה על הקמת מדינת ישראל

DECLARATION OF INDEPENDENCE
OF THE
STATE OF ISRAEL

The Land of Israel was the birthplace of the Jewish people. Here their spiritual, religious and national identity was formed. Here they achieved independence and created a culture of national and universal significance. Here they wrote and gave the Bible to the world.

Exiled from Palestine, the Jewish people remained faithful to it in all the countries of their dispersion, never ceasing to pray and hope for their return and restoration of their national freedom.

Impelled by this historic association, Jews strove throughout the centuries to go back to the land of their fathers and regain statehood. In recent decades, they returned in their masses. They reclaimed a wilderness, revived their language, built cities and villages, and established a vigorous and evergrowing community, with its own economic and cultural life. They sought peace, yet were ever prepared to defend themselves. They brought blessings of progress to all inhabitants of the country.

In the year 1897 the first Zionist Congress, inspired by Theodor Herzl's vision of a Jewish State, proclaimed the right of the Jewish people to a national revival in their own country.

This right was acknowledged by the Balfour Declaration of November 2, 1917, and reaffirmed by the Mandate of the League of Nations, which gave explicit international recognition to the historic connection of the Jewish people with Palestine and their right to reconstitute their National Home.

The Nazi holocaust which engulfed millions of Jews in Europe proved anew the urgency of the reestablishment of the Jewish State, which would solve the problem of Jewish homelessness by opening the gates to all Jews and lifting the Jewish people to equality in the family of nations.

Survivors of the European catastrophe as well as Jews from other lands, claiming their right to a life of dignity, freedom and labor, and undeterred by hazards, hardships and obstacles, have tried unceasingly to enter Palestine.

In the second World War, the Jewish people in Palestine made a full contribution in the struggle of freedom-loving nations against the Nazi evil. The sacrifices of their soldiers and efforts of their workers gained them title to rank with the people who founded the United Nations. On November 29, 1947, the General Assembly of the United Nations adopted a resolution for reestablishment of an independent Jewish State in Palestine and called upon inhabitants of the country to take such steps as may be necessary on their part to put the plan into effect.

This recognition by the United Nations of the right of the Jewish people to establish their independent state may not be revoked. It is, moreover, the self-evident right of the Jewish people to be a nation, as all other nations, in its own sovereign state.

Accordingly we, the members of the National Council, representing the Jewish people in Palestine and the Zionist movement of the world, met together in solemn assembly by virtue of the natural and historic right of the Jewish people and of the resolution of the General Assembly of the United Nations, hereby proclaim the establishment of the Jewish State in Palestine, to be called Israel.

We hereby declare that as from the termination of the Mandate at midnight this night of the 14th to 15th of May, 1948, and until the setting up of duly elected bodies of the State in accordance with a Constitution to be drawn up by a Constituent Assembly not later than the first day of October, 1948, the present National Council shall act as the Provisional State Council, and its executive organ, the National Administration shall constitute the Provisional Government of the State of Israel.

The State of Israel will promote the development of the country for the benefit of all its inhabitants; will be based on precepts of liberty, justice and peace taught by the Hebrew prophets; will uphold the full social and political equality of all its citizens without distinction of race, creed or sex; will guarantee full freedom of conscience, worship, education and culture; will safeguard the sanctity and inviolability of shrines and holy places of all religions; and will dedicate itself to the principles of the Charter of the United Nations.

The State of Israel will be ready to cooperate with the organs and representatives of the United Nations in the implementation of the resolution of November 29, 1947, and will take steps to bring about an economic union over the whole of Palestine.

We appeal to the United Nations to assist the Jewish people in the building of its state and admit Israel into the family of nations.

In the midst of wanton aggression we call upon the Arab inhabitants of the State of Israel to return to the ways of peace and play their part in the development of the state, with full and equal citizenship and due representation in all its bodies and institutions, provisional or permanent.

We offer peace and amity to all neighboring states and their peoples, and invite them to cooperate with the independent Jewish nation for the common good of all. The State of Israel is ready to contribute its full share to the peaceful progress and reconstitution of the Middle East. Our call goes out to the Jewish people all over the world to rally to our side in the task of immigration and development, and to stand by us in the great struggle for the fulfillment of the dream of generations — the redemption of Israel.

With trust in Almighty God, we set our hands to this declaration at this session of the Provisional State Council in the city of Tel Aviv this Sabbath eve, the fifth day of Iyar, 5708, the fourteenth day of May, 1948.

THE SYMBOLS OF ISRAEL

The people of the State of Israel are intensely patriotic and deeply proud of their dual heritage as Israelis and as Jews. This pride is reflected in Israel's emblem, anthem, flag, and language, for all of these stand for Jewish ideals, experiences, and feelings dating from the earliest years of Jewish history, long before the modern State of Israel came into existence. Jews in all countries share the Israeli reverence for these symbolic expressions of Jewish peoplehood. They remind us, wherever we live, that we are members of one nation—of its history and its glory.

Emblem of Israel.

THE ISRAELI EMBLEM

Pottery lamp decorated with a menorah, third to fourth century, Israel.

There are many ways to tell stories. People can read stories out of books or remember them by heart. But another way to tell stories is without any words at all—through *pictures*. Pictures can tell stories just as *vividly* as words.

An *emblem* is a special kind of storytelling picture. It tells the story of a school, family, or nation so vividly that it comes to represent that school, family, or nation in people's minds. The emblem usually tells, in picture-form, something important about the history, goals, and values of the people it represents.

The emblem of the State of Israel shows the Temple Menorah, the ancient symbol of the Jewish people, surrounded by olive branches. Beneath the picture, the emblem has the word *Israel*. What story does it tell?

The Story Behind the Israeli Emblem

The Israeli emblem reminds us of a very sad story that happened many years ago, but which still remains sharp and painful in the memories of Jewish people. In the year

Roman coin with portrait of Titus, 79–81 C.E.

A panel of the mosaic pavement from the fourth-century C.E. synagogue of Hammat Tiberias. The panel shows a menorah, a shofar, and other Jewish symbols.
At the time of the synagogue's existence, Tiberias was the seat of the Sanhedrin.

70 C.E., a Roman general, Titus, captured the city of Jerusalem, and his armies savagely destroyed the Holy Temple which had stood at the heart of the Jewish capital. The Temple had been the proud, beautiful center of Jewish worship, but now Roman soldiers defiled its holiness. They seized the golden Temple Menorah. To shame their unfortunate Jewish prisoners, Roman soldiers forced them to parade in chains through the streets of Rome carrying captured Temple Menorah.

The Romans felt so proud of this triumph over the Jews that they pictured the event on a monument called the Arch of Titus, named after the general who had captured Jerusalem. Today, the Arch of Titus still stands in Rome, and the carved picture of the Jews carrying the shamed Menorah can still be seen. To the Romans, the story celebrated Roman might and triumph. But to Jews, the story told of the worst disgrace and humiliation for the Jewish people—the loss of independence in their homeland.

The Temple Menorah and the Dream of Independence

Finally, after almost two thousand years and much agony and bloodshed, the modern State of Israel reestablished the Jewish homeland. With pride, with faith, and with determination to survive, Jews had returned to Israel and, especially, to their capital, Jerusalem. Although the Temple and the Menorah were not actually rebuilt, the Jews felt that in a symbolic way, the Menorah had been saved from its ancient disgrace and restored to its original glory.

The emblem of the State of Israel, adopted in 1949, shows the seven-branched Temple Menorah. At first, this picture reminds us of the sad story of its Roman capture. But the Menorah also reminds us that the Jewish dream of independence and return has finally come true. At long, long last, we have restored the Jewish homeland to its former pride.

The Meaning of the Olive Branch

It is no accident that the emblem of Israel shows the menorah surrounded by two olive branches.

The prophet Zechariah lived in the sixth century B.C.E. after the tragic destruction of the First Temple. Zechariah had a vision in which he saw a golden seven-branched menorah flanked by two olive trees. The olive trees provided an unfailing supply of oil for the golden candelabrum.

Our rabbis interpreted this vision to mean that the Holy Temple and the State of Israel would someday be restored to their former glory.

What more fitting symbol could have been chosen for the modern State of Israel?

The Arch of Titus in Rome.

The Western Wall in the Old City of Jerusalem is all that remains of the Second Temple.

Israeli stamp with symbols of the twelve tribes encircling the Temple Menorah.

VOCABULARY AND CONCEPTS

Arch of Titus	שַׁעַר טִיטוֹס
Emblem	סֵמֶל
Menorah (Candelabrum)	מְנוֹרָה
HaKotel HaMaaravi (The Western Wall)	הַכּוֹתֶל הַמַּעֲרָבִי

13

THE ISRAELI FLAG

In 70 C.E., when the Roman general Titus captured Israel, the long night of Jewish homelessness began. Israel—which the Romans called Palestine—fell into the hands of foreign rulers. For years, foreign flags flew over the Jewish homeland and foreign governments ruled the Jews who remained there. Jews the world over prayed that someday they could return in pride and independence to their homeland.

In 1948, after nearly two thousand years of exile, the State of Israel was reestablished as the Jewish homeland. The new flag of the modern state was unfurled at the United Nations in 1949, and Jews everywhere felt their hearts fill with pride and joy. The flag was a symbol of the Jewish return.

A parade of flags at the opening of the Maccabiah in Israel. The Israeli flag is a symbol of the unity and independence of Israel.

Zionist leaders: Dr. Bodenheimer, Herzl, Max Nordau, and David Wolfssohn.

The meeting place of the Zionist Congress.

Parchment amulet bearing the Magen David, invoking God "in the name of the seal of Solomon."

How the Israeli Flag Was Chosen

Why was this particular flag chosen? What is the meaning of its design? Why two blue stripes on a white background, and why a six-pointed star?

David Wolffsohn, who attended the First Zionist Congress in 1897, tells the story of the birth of the Israeli flag:

> At the behest of our leader Herzl, I came to Basle to make preparations for the Zionist Congress, to assure its success and to avoid any opening for detractors. Among the many problems that occupied me then was one which contained something of the essence of the Jewish problem. What flag would we hang in the Congress Hall? Then an idea struck me. We have a flag—and it is blue and white. The *talith* (prayer-shawl) with which we wrap ourselves when we pray: that is our symbol. Let us take this *talith* from its bag and unroll it before the eyes of Israel and the eyes of all nations. So I ordered a blue and white flag with the Shield of David painted upon it. That is how our national flag, that flew over Congress Hall, came into being. And no one expressed any surprise or asked whence it came, or how.

The blue stripes above and below the Magen David (the six-pointed star) remind us of the *talith*. When we see the Israeli flag, we remember the faith and the prayers of the many generations of Jews who longed for the return to their homeland. We remember the prayers of Jews killed in the pogroms of Russia. We remember the prayers of the Jews murdered by the Nazis in the Holocaust of World War II, before the Jewish homeland had been reestablished. We can almost hear their prayers and see the suffering worshipers sway, dressed in their blue-and-white prayer-shawls.

The Magen David

The Magen David is a traditional symbol of Judaism. Look closely and you will see that the star is actually made up of two triangles, one right-side up and the other upside-down. One of them points upward—toward all that is spiritual and holy. The other one points downward—toward all that is earthly and secular. By leading a

15

A kibbutznik proudly poses beneath the flag of Israel.

life of Torah and mitzvot the Jew strives to bring together the worlds of the spiritual and the earthly, the worlds of the holy and the secular. The Jew tries to make the workaday world something holy, by following the God-given laws of Torah. Perhaps this is why the six-pointed star, with its two triangles pointing different ways but creating one beautiful form, symbolizes the Jewish nation.

Legend tells us that David, a great king of early Israel, adorned his shield with this six-pointed star. Thus the star is named the Magen David, which means "The Shield of David."

The Meaning of the Israeli Flag for Jews in Other Lands

Like the emblem of the State of Israel, the Israeli flag is a symbol of the unity and independence of the Jewish nation. We see the familiar blue-and-white flag in many places—in the classroom of our Hebrew school, in the synagogue, in front of the United Nations. The flag is a symbol of the proud return of the Jewish nation to its homeland.

An Israeli submarine unfurls its flag.

Israel stamp showing part of the Israeli Declaration of Independence.

You belong to this great Jewish nation. Your ancestors gave the world the Torah, which includes the Ten Commandments—the most important rules of morality that human beings possess. Your fellow Jews—thousands of them—have made valuable contributions to the world as scientists, historians, mathematicians, musicians, painters, writers, actors, teachers. Jews, in fact, have won more Nobel Prizes than any other people!

So when you look at the Israeli flag, stop and remember its special, symbolic meaning. It stands for the Jewish people—their faith, their pride, their return home. You are special, your people are special, and the blue-and-white flag that we salute is special, for it represents the glorious Jewish nation, Israel.

In the modern State of Israel, where Jews from all over the world have come to live, the age-old dream of Shivat Zion and Kibbutz Galuyot have become a reality. The waving flag proclaims our pride in the Jewish nation. Jews all over the world can see this flag and feel that all Jews are brothers. Even Jews in Russia, who lack our freedom to live and pray as Jews and to study the Jewish heritage, can see the Israeli flag and feel proud that their nation has returned home to its own land.

On a refugee boat. His hope of Kibbutz Galuyot has come true.

VOCABULARY AND CONCEPTS

Flag	דֶּגֶל
Magen David	מָגֵן דָּוִד
Tallit	טַלִּית
Torah	תּוֹרָה
Return to Israel	שִׁיבַת צִיּוֹן
The Ingathering of the Exiles	
	קִבּוּץ גָּלֻיוֹת

THE ISRAELI NATIONAL ANTHEM

An Israeli stamp issued in honor of the "Hatikvah."

Ever since you started Hebrew school, you have heard the singing of the Star-Spangled Banner and of the Hatikvah. You didn't know all the words to these songs right away. But you must have guessed that these two songs were special and important, for whenever we sing them, we rise and face the American and Israeli flags.

Each song is the special anthem identified with its nation. The Star-Spangled Banner is the American national anthem. And the Hatikvah is the national anthem of the State of Israel.

When we see the emblem of the State of Israel or the familiar blue-and-white Israeli flag, we sense the unity and brotherhood of the Jewish people. In the same way, when singing the Hatikvah, we feel a special oneness with Jews all over the world. We sing out our pride in the independent Jewish state that the anthem represents. We sing out our pride in the Jews of past days who struggled valiantly to restore the Jewish homeland to independence. We sing out our pride in the religious faith of Jews throughout the years of exile, the faith of Jews who never lost hope in the eventual return of their people to their God-given homeland.

Even if you do not understand all the Hebrew words, the beautiful melody of the Israeli national anthem hints at their meaning. The music begins at a slow pace and seems to express a deep, heartfelt yearning. The music builds up and becomes stronger and more powerful, ringing out finally with conviction and determination.

Hatikvah Symbolizes Hope

The title of the Israeli national anthem is *Hatikvah*, which means "The Hope." Written in 1878 by Naftali Herz Imber, a Galician Jew who later settled in America, the Hatikvah is about *hope*—the undying hope of the Jewish people, through the long years of exile, that they would someday return to independence in their homeland.

Why the Hope Began

In 70 C.E. Titus led his Roman soldiers in their destruction of Jerusalem. Most of the Jews were carried away as captives and scattered across the lands of the world.

But all through these long, difficult years of exile, the Jews never lost faith that someday, with God's help, they would return to Israel. It is this stubborn, miraculous *hope* that we sing about in the Israeli national anthem, the Hatikvah—The Hope.

How the Hope Came True

In 1948, with the declaration of the State of Israel, this long-held hope became a reality. In the Hatikvah, the Jewish yearning for return home has been given musical form. We can hear that undying Jewish hope in the melody, and we can understand it in the moving words of the national anthem.

Naftali Herz Imber, the composer of the Israeli national anthem, "Hatikvah."

In the Jewish heart
A Jewish spirit still sings,
And the eyes look east
Toward Zion.

Our hope is not lost,
Our hope of two thousand years,
To be a free nation in our land,
In the land of Zion and
Jerusalem.

כָּל עוֹד בַּלֵּבָב פְּנִימָה
נֶפֶשׁ יְהוּדִי הוֹמִיָּה
וּלְפַאֲתֵי מִזְרָח קָדִימָה
עַיִן לְצִיּוֹן צוֹפִיָּה.

עוֹד לֹא אָבְדָה תִקְוָתֵנוּ
הַתִּקְוָה שְׁנוֹת אַלְפַּיִם
לִהְיוֹת עַם חָפְשִׁי בְּאַרְצֵנוּ
בְּאֶרֶץ צִיּוֹן וִירוּשָׁלַיִם.

19

These are just a few of the prayers we offer for Shivat Zion, Israel.

Sound the great Shofar for freedom; lift up the banner to gather our exiles; and gather us from the four corners of the earth.

And to Jerusalem, Your City, return us in mercy, and dwell there as You have spoken, and rebuilt it soon in our days as an everlasting structure.

And let our eyes behold Your return to Zion in mercy! Blessed are You, O Lord, who restores Your divine presence in Zion.

The land for the settlements was purchased by the Keren Kayemeth Le'Yisrael, or Jewish National Fund, which was established in 1901 as the land-purchasing agency of the Zionist movement.

The Jewish National Fund depended on small sums of money collected throughout the Jewish world. The small blue-and-white Jewish National Fund box found a place in millions of Jewish homes all over the world.

How the Hope Was Kept Alive

During the two thousand years (two *millennia*) of exile, Jews settled down into communities in many, many different lands. But wherever they lived, they always kept a heartfelt prayer in their hearts for the return to Israel. They said special daily prayers for the return. These prayers are called prayers for the return to Zion, "Shivat Zion." They celebrated—and we Jews still celebrate—our holidays according to the Israeli seasons and calendar. We pray that the rain should fall at the right times and in the right amounts in the land of Israel, and we pray for a good, plentiful harvest there. A Jew may live in Portugal, Holland, Finland, Hungary, Canada, or South Africa—but the land which holds a special place in Jewish prayers and in Jewish hearts is the land of Israel. This is the message of the Hatikvah's first stanza.

Zion is another name for Israel and Jerusalem. In the synagogue, the Holy Ark where the Torah is kept always faces in the direction of Zion. As we pray along with the congregation, our eyes, our hearts, and our prayers are directed toward Israel and Jerusalem.

For so many long, painful years, the land of Israel was in the hands of foreigners. The Jews who lived in Palestine were not free; they could not own land, they could not build synagogues, they were not permitted to study Torah, and they were forbidden to pray at the Western Wall in Jerusalem. Yet their hope for freedom and independence never died. The second stanza of the Hatikvah recalls the undying hope of Jews through the generations, Jews who lived in other countries and Jews who had remained in Palestine.

The Importance of Israel

Now Jews are free in their own land. The miracle has happened. To make sure that all Jews feel welcome in their homeland, the Israeli Parliament (the Knesset) passed the Law of Return. This law guarantees that all Jews can become Israeli citizens, if and when they come

THE DIVINE PROMISES

God promised our forefathers, the first Hebrews, Abraham, Isaac, and Jacob, that the Jewish people would inherit the land of Israel and it would belong to them forever.

GOD PROMISES THE LAND TO ABRAHAM AND HIS DESCENDANTS

"Then God appeared to Abram and said: 'To your descendants I am going to give this land' " (Genesis 12:7).

THE SECOND PROMISE

"Raise your eyes now, and look out from the place where you are, north, south, east, and west; for all the land that you see I give to you and your seed [children] forever" (Genesis 13:14–17).

GOD REPEATS THE PROMISE TO ISAAC

"Reside in this land and I will be with you and bless you; surely I will give all these lands to you and your offspring, fulfilling the oath that I swore to your father Abraham" (Genesis 26:2–3).

According to the Torah, on his way to Aram, Jacob had a dream in which he saw a ladder reaching the sky and messengers climbing up and down the ladder.

"I am the God of your father, Abraham, and the God of Isaac. The land on which you are lying will be given to you and to your descendants" (Genesis 28:13).

to live in Israel. All Jews can return to the Holy Land where their ancestors lived and prayed, and where their ancestors Abraham, Isaac, and Jacob received God's promise that Israel would be the Jewish homeland.

When we sing the Hatikvah together, we are doing much more than just singing a nice melody. We are making a promise. We are promising ourselves and our people that we will never forget that undying Jewish hope for independence. We are promising that we will do all within our power to help the State of Israel prosper.

The Law of Return in modern Israel helped make the Jewish dream come true—the dream of Shivat Zion and Kibbutz Galuyot.

How We Can Help Israel

We can help. We can buy products made in Israel, and we can plant trees in Israel by contributing to the Jewish National Fund. We can support Israel Bond drives. We can study the Hebrew language, and we can spend time in Israel, as campers, students, tourists, and maybe someday as *olim*—new immigrants to the Jewish homeland.

We can also help by learning about Israel and the Israelis and by studying Jewish history. The more we understand the Jewish homeland, the more we will learn to love and value Israel, and the more we will be able to do to help the survival and the growth of our nation.

VOCABULARY AND CONCEPTS

National Anthem	הַתִּקְוָה
Zion	צִיּוֹן
Knesset	כְּנֶסֶת
Law of Return	חוֹק הַשָּׁבוּת
Jewish National Fund	קֶרֶן קַיֶּמֶת לְיִשְׂרָאֵל
Immigrant	עוֹלֶה (m) עוֹלָה (f)

THE HEBREW LANGUAGE

A Tel Aviv bus driver yells at a speeding motorcyclist. High school kids call out their orders for lunchtime falafel. A chic saleswoman in a Jerusalem boutique persuades a customer to buy an elegant leather jacket, and a professor of nuclear physics lectures at Haifa's Technion. All these modern-day activities take place in Hebrew—the oldest living language in the world!

Hebrew is both a very old and a very young language. It was spoken more than three thousand years ago. Yet it is so young that a radio program is needed to help people born in Israel to speak it correctly. How has the Hebrew language managed to survive for such a long, long time? How were the Jewish people able to revive this ancient tongue?

Hebrew in Ancient Times

Hebrew was spoken by our biblical fathers and mothers—Abraham and Sarah, Isaac and Rebecca, Jacob, Leah, and Rachel. The Torah is written in Hebrew. King Saul and King David, the great rulers of the Jewish people, spoke this tongue. And the Hebrew language set the Jews apart as a proud, independent people who ruled themselves in their own land.

But in the year 586 B.C.E., the Babylonians conquered Israel. Some Jews always remained in the Holy Land throughout the generations. But many were exiled in 586 B.C.E. to Babylonia, where a rich and important Jewish community arose. Here, Aramaic—not Hebrew—became the spoken language of the Jewish exiles. When the rabbis of the Babylonian community recorded the Oral Law, they wrote in Aramaic and compiled the great work known as the Talmud.

Modern Hebrew	Old Hebrew	Phoenician	Early Greek	Later Greek	Latin	English
א	ⲭ	ⲭ	A	A	A	A
ב	ⳢⳢ	Ⳣ	B	B	B	B
ג	ⲅⲅ	ⳝ	S ⳝ	ⳝ	C G	C,G
ד	ⲇ	ⲇ	Δ	Δ	D	D
ה	ⲏⲏⲏ	ⲕ	ⲕ	ⲕ	E	E
ו	ⲩ	Y	Y	Y	F V	F,V,U
ז	ⲍⲍⲍ	ⲍ	I	I	...	Z
ח	ⲏⲏⲏ	H	B	B	H	E,H
ט	ⲑⲑ	⊕	⊗	⊗	...	TH,PH
י	ⲕⲕⲕ	ⲍ	ⲍ	s	I	I
כ	ⲕⲕⲕ	Y	ⲕ	ⲕ	...	K,KH
ל	ⲗⲗⲗ	ⲗ	ⲗ	ⳞⲚ	L	L
מ	ⲙⲙⲙ	ⲙ	ⲙ	ⲙ	M	M
נ	ⲛⲛⲛ	ⲛ	ⲛ	N	N	N
ס	ⲝⲝ	ⲝ	ⲝ	ⲝ	X	X
ע	o	o	o	o	O	O
פ	ⲣ	ⲣ	ⲣ	ⲣ	P	P
צ	ⲧⲧ	ⲧ	ⲧ	M	...	...
ק	ⳠⳠ	Ⳡ	ⲕ	ⲕ	Q	Q
ר	ⲣⲣ	ⲣ	ⲣ	ⲣ	R	R
ש	ⲱⲱ	ⲱ	ⲱ	ⲓ	S	S
ת	ⲭⲭⲭ	X	ⲧ	ⲧ	ST	T

Table showing how the Hebrew and Phoenician letters passed through Greek and Latin forms to their present English form.

22

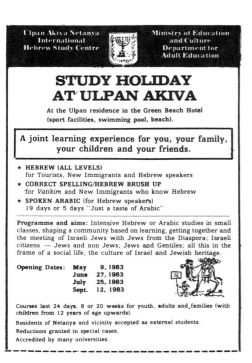

A newspaper advertisement for Ulpan Akiva in Natanya.

The Hebrew language is continually being updated with new words. The Hebrew Language Academy is the official organization that coins new words. Here are several new words.

Hebrew in the Diaspora

Many Jews, struggling to earn a living for their families, were forced to leave Israel in the years following the Babylonian exile. Soon large numbers of Jews lived in lands outside Israel—over a million in Egypt alone, for example. For these Jews, too, Hebrew was no longer a day-to-day language.

In the year 70 C.E., the Romans conquered Israel and forced more of the remaining Jews to leave. Some were taken as slaves to other parts of the far-flung Roman Empire. Others were able to seek refuge in the Jewish communities outside Israel, which were called collectively the *Diaspora,* a Greek word meaning "scattering" or "dispersion." To survive in their new homes in the Diaspora, exiled Jews had to master the local languages of the surrounding peoples—Italian, Spanish, Polish, Dutch, French, Romanian, Arabic, just to name a few.

The Importance of Hebrew in Jewish Life

One might expect that any nation scattered into communities all over the globe would lose its sense of national unity, forget the past, blend into the surrounding cultures, and lose touch with its heritage and history. But not the Jews.

The Jews never forgot Zion and the dream of Shivat Zion and Kibbutz Galuyot. They never forgot the proud independence of the Kingdom of Israel and their beloved homeland. And no matter what new languages they had to learn, one language forever remained at the heart of Jewish religious life—Hebrew.

Rabbis and scholars who wrote Bible commentaries and answered questions on *halacha* (Jewish law) had to know Hebrew very, very well. And even the simplest Jew needed enough Hebrew to say his daily prayers and to recite the blessings when called up to the Torah. Each boy on his Bar Mitzvah day was honored with the reading of the weekly Torah portion—in Hebrew, of course! In the synagogue, the cantor led the congregation in expressive, richly melodic Hebrew chants. Whether the Jews

עֶלִיעֶזֶר בֶּן יְהוּדָה

ELIEZER BEN YEHUDA
(1858–1922)

The father of spoken Hebrew

Eliezer Ben Yehuda was born in Vilna in 1858. He changed his name (originally Perlman) when he moved to Jerusalem in 1881. Aware that there were thousands of new facts and discoveries which could not be described in the vocabulary of ancient times, he devised words to fill the empty spaces in the Hebrew dictionary. His family, using his material, completed his undertaking after he died.

Eliezer Ben Yehuda achieved his goal: The revival of the Hebrew language as a living tongue.

had settled in sunny Italy or in the Russian Pale, in London or Lithuania, Paris or Pittsburgh, the language of prayer and Torah study was always the ancient tongue which symbolized Jewish peoplehood—Hebrew.

The religious life of the Jew kept Hebrew alive. Jewish prayer and Torah study kept the language vital—despite the loss of homeland and the dispersion of Jews into alien lands. And when the Jews finally returned to their beloved land in the late nineteenth century, the Hebrew language was restored as their daily language.

How Hebrew Became a Modern Language

In order to accomplish this, however, much hard work had to be done. The Jewish love for Hebrew was essential, but by itself love was not enough. First of all, Jews from all over the world, coming together in Israel, had to abandon the familiar languages they had grown up with and devote themselves to learning to speak a new one— often not a simple task, especially for adults. Second, there had been many developments in various fields in the thousands of years since the dispersion in Roman times, and if Hebrew was going to be effective as the language of a modern community, it had to be updated.

The process of updating Hebrew began with a man named Eliezer Ben Yehuda, who is considered the "father" of modern Hebrew. Arriving in Palestine in 1881, he established a school for Hebrew, prepared a dictionary, and issued a weekly newspaper in the strange, problematic language. Ben Yehuda invented new words for the many things Jews had to be able to talk about that were not around in the days of the Bible—electricity, ice cream, railroads, and democratic elections, for instance, and even modern methods of raising chickens. Some words were made from parts of old Hebrew words. Others were taken from other languages and given a Hebrew sound. Soon people were speaking and reading the new language. Hebrew became the living, spoken symbol of Jewish pride, unity, and independence.

The Role of Hebrew Today

Today, Hebrew connects Jews throughout the world. Modern Hebrew also helps Jews touch their roots. Anyone able to speak it can easily understand the Hebrew of the Bible. At once the oldest and youngest of languages, the reborn Hebrew language is a treasure to be cherished by all Jews.

VOCABULARY AND CONCEPTS

Hebrew	עִבְרִית
Oral law	תַּלְמוּד
Exile	גָּלוּת
Jewish law	הֲלָכָה

Young and old are eager to touch their roots. An adult Ulpan in New York City.

THE GOVERNMENT AND CENTRAL ORGANIZATIONS OF ISRAEL

A nation is like a very, very large family. All of its citizens feel a sense of identity and relatedness to each other, and together they share certain common goals and purposes, as well as a common destiny.

Just as the members of a family work together to achieve their goals, so must all the people of a nation. Every citizen pays taxes, and from this pooled income, the country works toward realizing the nation's goals— building the best possible schools, libraries, museums,

and homes, keeping towns and cities clean and safe, helping farms to thrive, establishing a strong defense force, taking care of new immigrants. Everyone agrees to keep the important rules that will ensure the happiness of the whole country—rules about honest business practices and respect for one another's privacy and possessions.

In a family, the parents establish rules and guidelines so that everyone can live together under one roof in peace and harmony. Like the parents of a family, the government of a country makes rules so that the country can run smoothly and its people can live together in peace and harmony. In a democratic country like Israel or the United States, the citizens choose the government leaders who make these rules, voting them into office at election time and voting them out of office if they do not carry out their jobs in a satisfactory manner. The government leaders are responsible and experienced men and women who create the best possible laws by which their country can be guided.

In Israel the head of the government is the Prime Minister. The main governing body is the Knesset. In addition, the government works closely with other large, important organizations. The Jewish Agency helps olim— *new immigrants to Israel—get settled into their new homes. The Histadrut helps them train for new jobs and arranges cultural programs—classes, films, shows, and concerts—to help the* olim *adjust to life in Israel. And the Israel Defense Forces—strong and brave—protect the land.*

THE KNESSET AND VOTING POLITICS

Voting in Israel.

This huge bronze menorah is in the Knesset courtyard in Jerusalem. It was a gift from the people of England to Israel.

There are two major political parties in Israel's government—the Likkud party, and the Labor party. Other parties in Israel are the Mafdal (the National Religious party), Agudat Israel (the strictly Orthodox religious party), and Rakach (the Communist party).

The Knesset (the name means "assembly" in Hebrew) is Israel's Parliament. This government body, which is similar in function to the U.S. Congress, makes and changes the country's laws and policies. The 120 *chavrei knesset* (members of the Knesset) represent all of the very different kinds of people who make up Israel's diverse population.

Political Parties

Naturally, different groups of Israelis have their own opinions about how their country should be run. These differences have resulted in the creation of many political parties, each one representing a group of people with distinct opinions.

28

Arab and Israeli Knesset members discussing a problem.

Israel is a democracy. Both Jews and Arabs have equal voting rights.

Elections in Israel

Unlike Americans, Israelis do not vote directly for specific candidates. They vote for the political party that best represents their ideas. Each party draws up a list of candidates, and the more votes the party gets, the more candidates on its list can become members of the Knesset. For example, if a party receives 10 percent of all the votes cast in an election, that political party is entitled to 10 percent of the Knesset seats. Since 10 percent of the total membership, 120, is 12, that party can send 12 candidates as representatives.

Voting in Israel

Every Israeli citizen over eighteen—man or woman, Jew or Arab—has the right to vote. Thus Jewish and Arab citizens have an equal say in deciding who will run the nation, and there are both Arabs and Jews in the Knesset. Most speeches in the Knesset are made in Hebrew, but Arab members may speak in Arabic, and they are provided with instant translations of Hebrew speeches into Arabic.

The Knesset building in Jerusalem. The Knesset is the legislative body of the State of Israel. Its 120 members are elected by a secret ballot.

VOCABULARY AND CONCEPTS

Elections	בְּחִירוֹת
Political party	מִפְלָגָה
Member of Parliament	חֲבֵר־כְּנֶסֶת

David Ben-Gurion, the first Prime Minister of Israel.

THE PRIME MINISTER AND THE CABINET

The leader of the Israeli government is the Prime Minister. He or she is elected by the Knesset. Naturally, the political party with the most members in the Knesset has the best chance of electing one of its own people to become Prime Minister.

The Prime Minister chooses the members of the Cabinet. The Cabinet ministers head the government's various departments and serve as the Prime Minister's special advisors, helping him to lead the country and make important decisions. Cabinet ministers are appointed by the Prime Minister and then approved by the Knesset. They advise the Prime Minister in the areas of defense, agriculture, health, education and culture, religious affairs, foreign affairs, and finance. At regular sessions every Sunday in Jerusalem, the Cabinet presents its proposals to the Knesset.

The President

Elected by the Knesset, the *Nasi*, or President,of Israel appoints judges and ambassadors and signs new laws into effect.

In Israel, the Prime Minister is the key leader of the government. In the U.S., the President of the country has far more power than does the President of Israel.

Presidential residence in Jerusalem.

גּוֹלְדָה מֵאִיר

GOLDA MEIR (1898–1978)
Fourth Prime Minister of Israel

Golda Meir was born in Kiev, Russia, where her father was a poor carpenter. In Russia, as a small girl, Golda Meir witnessed cruel, violent pogroms against the Jews. Later, Golda Meir said that her childhood memories of the pogroms influenced her to become an ardent Zionist. The little Russian girl was to become the Fifth Prime Minister of Israel.

When she was eight years old, her family moved to the United States and settled in Milwaukee. Golda Meir became a schoolteacher as well as a devoted Zionist. In 1921, she and her husband, Morris Myerson, moved to Israel (then called Palestine), joining Kibbutz Merchavyah. As a symbol of their dedication to the Jewish homeland, they decided to adopt a Hebrew name, changing Myerson to Meir, which means "Giver of Light."

An excellent speaker and a good organizer, Golda Meir became involved in politics, but her many activities began to take her away from the kibbutz. She worked with the women's labor union and then became a member of the Histadrut executive committee (the Histadrut is Israel's central labor union). Later she became the head of the Histadrut. In 1949, Golda Meir became a Knesset member and Minister of Labor. She began important programs, such as new housing projects and the building of good roads. She served as Foreign Minister of Israel between 1956 and 1965, becoming a famous international figure. In 1969, Golda Meir became Prime Minister of Israel.

After serving as Israel's leader during the Yom Kippur War, Golda Meir submitted her resignation on April 11, 1974, and retired from political office. When she died on December 8, 1978, an outpouring of grief came from all over the world for this great and courageous woman.

Israel's Prime Ministers

The first Prime Minister of Israel was David Ben-Gurion (1948–53); the second, Moshe Sharett (1953–55); the third, Ben-Gurion for a second term (1955–63); the fourth, Levi Eshkol (1963–69); the fifth, Golda Meir (1969–74); the sixth, Yitzhak Rabin (1974–77); and the seventh was Menachem Begin (1977–1983). In the election of 1984, to choose his successor, Israeli voters were sharply divided. Labor and Likud, the two largest parties, won about an equal number of votes. Since neither had a majority, they decided to join together in a national unity coalition. Under this arrangement, Shimon Peres, the Labor candidate, served as Prime Minister for two years, with Yitzchak Shamir, the Likud candidate, as Foreign Minister. In 1986 they changed places. Peres became Foreign Minister and Shamir became Prime Minister. Shamir was re-elected in 1988.

Elections are usually held every four years, but may take place sooner if the Prime Minister resigns, or the Knesset votes "no confidence" in its leaders, or the parties which joined together in a coalition are unable to resolve their conflicts. The newly elected Knesset in turn selects the country's new Prime Minister.

VOCABULARY AND CONCEPTS

President	נָשִׂיא
Prime Minister	רֹאשׁ הַמֶּמְשָׁלָה
Government	מֶמְשָׁלָה

President Richard Nixon of the United States with Prime Minister Golda Meir of Israel at the White House, 1972.

THE HISTADRUT

בֶּרֶל קַצְנֶלְסָן

BERL KATZNELSON (1887–1944)
Farmer and labor leader
Berl Katznelson's father was a
member of Hovevei Zion. Berl
grew up with dreams of *aliyah*
and like his father became a devoted Zionist. As a Hebrew teacher
and librarian in Russia, he influenced many children and teenagers with his Zionist goals.

When he was twenty-two, Berl
Katznelson moved to Israel. There
he became a farmer and a labor
leader. He helped form food cooperatives so that working people
could buy food at lower prices.
Katznelson helped start the Israeli
health-insurance fund, Kupat Cholim, so that everyone could afford
good medical care. He became edi-
tor of the Labor party's newspaper, *Davar,* and was a founder
of the Histadrut.

During the Nazi Holocaust,
Katznelson worked to save Jewish
victims. Under his guidance, Jewish soldiers parachuted into Nazi-
held territory to rescue survivors.

Sadly, Katznelson, who worked
so hard for Israel, died four years
before the Jewish State of Israel
was officially declared an independent nation.

HaHistadrut HaKelalit shel Ha'Ovdim Be'Eretz Yisrael
("The General Federation of Laborers in Israel"), as its
name hints, is a huge labor union which combines most of
Israel's workers. It was founded by David Ben-Gurion in
1920 to teach Jews how to become farmers and craftsmen.

All kinds of salaried workers belong to the Histadrut.
Lifeguards, secretaries, psychiatrists, and gardeners have
membership cards. Each member must pay dues, so the
Histadrut has a substantial budget. Thus the Histadrut,
next to the government itself, has become the most
powerful body in Israel today.

Health Care

The most important service provided by the Histadrut
is low-cost health care. If you belong to the Histadrut and
you or a member of your family need medical attention,
you will receive a doctor's full services at an affordable
fee. Medicines the doctor prescribes will also be available
to you at reasonable prices. This low-cost medical plan,
called Kupat Cholim ("Sick People's Fund"), is a great
blessing for the workers of Israel, who could not other-
wise afford to pay the high costs of medical treatment.
Kupat Cholim has a very large network of about a thousand local clinics as well as fifteen general hospitals.

Intensive farming is carried on in the Aravah Valley with the aid of water pumped in by Mekorot.

Other Activities

The Histadrut is also active in other ways. It owns a chain of department stores (HaMashbir HaMerkazi, or "The Central Marketplace") and it owns the major dairy company of Israel, T'nuva. It operates the Bank Ha-Poalim ("The Laborers' Bank") and a construction company called Shikkun Ovdim ("Workers' Shelter"). Mekorot is the Histadrut's water-pumping firm, which pumps water to the Negev. Solel Boneh, Histadrut's vast construction firm, builds roads and houses of every kind. And Egged is Histadrut's network of bus cooperatives, traveling all through the land of Israel.

Non-Jewish citizens are eligible for full membership in the Histadrut.

VOCABULARY AND CONCEPTS

Histadrut construction firm	סוֹלֵל בּוֹנֶה
"The Laborers' Bank"	בַּנְק הַפּוֹעֲלִים
General Federation of Labor	הִסְתַּדְרוּת
Health Care Medical Plan	קוּפַּת חוֹלִים
Bus company	אֶגֶד

THE JEWISH AGENCY

Immigrants to Israel Need Help

Imagine that you are a new immigrant to Israel from Russia, Iraq, Argentina, or the United States. You have just stepped off the boat or plane with your family; your arms are filled with packages of assorted belongings. "Thank God," you murmur to yourself, "We have completed our journey safely!" But when you take a long look around you, everything looks quite foreign. Suddenly you realize that you are going to need a lot of help adjusting to your new life in the land of Israel.

For one thing, everyone is jabbering at you in incredibly rapid Hebrew, a language which you probably do not understand perfectly. You are going to have to study Hebrew until you have mastered it fluently enough to make conversation and get a job. You and your family are tired and hungry after your long journey. You need a place to stay tonight, something to eat right now, and maybe even some money for day-to-day necessities until you are able to make your own living. You may need to

Immigrants from the Soviet Union being resettled in Israel. The immigrants are given apartments, help in finding a suitable job, and language training.

Immigrants attending a Hebrew Ulpan in Israel.

be retrained for a new type of work. You may need to learn new work skills that were never needed in your former home.

The Role of the Jewish Agency

Who helps you with all these needs? The Jewish Agency.

Founded in 1929, the Jewish Agency is the friend of the new immigrant to Israel. When newcomers arrive in the country, delegates of the Agency receive them with warm smiles and practical advice and assistance. The Agency provides new immigrants with living quarters and even gives cash grants when necessary. The Agency offers job-training programs and Hebrew-language courses called Ulpanim.

The Jewish Agency also has branches outside of Israel—in fact, it has offices in countries the world over. The Jewish Agency provides people everywhere with information about Israel. People interested in studying or settling in the Jewish homeland go to the Jewish Agency for advice.

The Jewish Agency During the Holocaust

During the 1930's, Hitler and the Nazis rose to power in Germany. Vicious anti-Semitic propaganda was a major part of the Nazi program, and under Hitler's leadership the Jews of Germany were persecuted and tormented. After the Nazis began World War II, they determined to kill all the Jews in the countries they conquered. Even before the war had begun, the Jewish Agency was working very hard to save as many Jews as possible from the Nazi Holocaust. In the year 1935 alone, the Jewish Agency helped 62,000 Jews reach Israel (then called Palestine). If these Jews had not left Europe, they would have been trapped in the tragic Nazi Holocaust, the terrible, irrational murder of six million Jews.

The Jews who were unable to escape in time suffered at the cruel hands of the Nazis. Whole communities perished. Concentration camps were built for what the Nazis called the "Final Solution" to the Jewish problem: suffocating Jews to death with poison gas, then burning their

35

הֶנְרִיטָה סָאלְד

HENRIETTA SZOLD (1860–1945)
Zionist activist, founder of Hadassah

Henrietta Szold was born in Baltimore, Maryland. Her father, rabbi of a wealthy Jewish congregation, made sure his daughter received a fine secular and religious education. After high school graduation, she became a teacher of Hebrew, Bible, and Jewish history.

She saw in Zionism a cure for the wounds inflicted by history upon the Jewish people. In 1909, she visited Israel and was appalled at the physical misery and disease suffered by many Zionist settlers. When she returned to the United States, Szold invited many important and capable women to join a group to help the Jewish settlers. The new group called itself Hadassah, and Henrietta Szold became its first president in 1914.

In the 1930's she was one of the main founders of Youth Aliyah. This great organization helped save tens of thousands of Jewish children from the Nazis. Children were brought by boat from Europe and placed in homes in Israel's farms and villages, where they could work to rebuild the land.

After her death in 1945, a fund she had started to coordinate youth activities was named Mosad Szold (Szold Foundation) in her honor.

bodies in ovens called crematoria. Before the Jews were murdered in this way, the Nazis took all their money and possessions, separated family members from one another, and worked all Jewish men, women, and children to exhaustion. Nazi doctors performed inhuman "medical experiments" on helpless Jews in concentration-camp laboratories.

How the Jewish Agency Helped the Survivors

Somehow, numbers of Jews managed to survive the horrible ordeal of the Nazi Holocaust and were rescued from the camps at the end of World War II. These survivors wanted to leave the European lands which had become so hateful to them, and yearned to go to Israel, the Jewish homeland, where they could finally feel safe. But the British government was in power over Israel at that time. The British refused to hear the pleas of the survivors, who longed to enter Israel. Only a tiny number of Jews were allowed by the British to immigrate to the country. The British refused to concern themselves with the fate of the homeless survivors, who had experienced years of suffering in Europe and who now hoped fervently for freedom in the Jewish land.

The kibbutzim of Ein Harod and Tel Yosef in the Jezreel Valley. The valley was a malarial swamp when the Jewish National Fund purchased the land in 1909. It is now one of the most fertile areas in Israel.

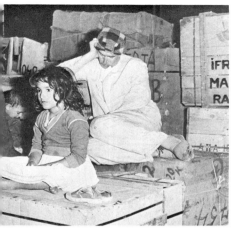

Moroccan Jewish immigrants and their baggage on a Haifa dock.

Israeli stamp dedicated to Henrietta Szold, the founder of Youth Aliyah and Hadassah.

The Jewish Agency stepped in at this point and helped many Jews reach Israel illegally, despite the British restrictions on immigration. By cover of darkness, ships full of European Jewish survivors sailed to Israel, often landing their passengers late at night in order to elude the British. These survivors were immediately taken by trucks to special centers, where they received clothing and housing from the Jewish Agency. By morning, there would be no sign on the shore that a ship had landed.

Frequently, before the Jewish survivors did anything else, they would stoop to the ground and kiss the soil of the homeland for which they had yearned so deeply. Thanks to the Agency's devoted workers, they found new homes in a land where they were welcome.

Youth Aliyah

In the 1930's, Henrietta Szold, an American Zionist leader, founded Youth Aliyah. This organization, a branch of the Jewish Agency, helped save tens of thousands of Jewish children from the Nazis and bring them to Eretz Yisrael.

Today, the Jewish Agency still works to help the newcomer to Israel in many ways—by teaching Hebrew, training for new jobs, and helping new olim find homes and work.

An overloaded refugee boat off-loads its illegal passengers.

VOCABULARY AND CONCEPTS

Hadassah	הֲדַסָּה
Hebrew-language course	אֻלְפָּן
Holocaust	שׁוֹאָה
Youth Aliyah	עֲלִיַת הַנֹּעַר
Illegal immigration	עֲלִיָה בֵּית

THE JEWISH NATIONAL FUND

The Keren Kayemeth Le'Yisrael, known in English-speaking countries as the Jewish National Fund, was founded in 1901 by members of the World Zionist Organization. Its purpose was to raise money from Jews throughout the world to purchase land in Palestine and to finance settlement efforts of Jewish pioneers. JNF contributions came from rich and poor, old and young—even schoolchildren did their bit, selling JNF stamps from door to door. By 1947 more than half the total amount of land owned by Jews in Israel had been bought with JNF

A forest planted by the Jewish National Fund in Israel.

Certificate of registration for land bought by the Jewish National Fund from the Arabs in 1943.

funds. The JNF has also helped in projects to improve and develop Israel's farmland. By the 1970's it had planted 120 million trees throughout Israel and had restored the fertility of 125,000 acres of previously barren land.

All of the forests planted by the JNF are in memory or in honor of a famous person who helped the State of Israel. One forest is in memory of Albert Einstein and another in memory of John F. Kennedy.

The JNF has paved over 1,200 miles of roads, built storage dams to store water, and opened new land areas for settlement.

A Jewish National Fund tree nursery. The saplings are being readied for replanting.

VOCABULARY AND CONCEPTS

Forest	יַעַר
Farmland	מֶשֶׁק
Jewish National Fund	
	קֶרֶן קַיֶּמֶת לְיִשְׂרָאֵל

39

ISRAEL'S DEFENSE FORCES

Israeli paratroopers on a training maneuver.

The Tsevah Haganah li'Yisrael, or Israel Defense Forces, includes the Army, the Air Force, and the Navy. The first letters of the Hebrew words in its name—*tsaddik, hey,* and *lamed*—together form the acronym Tsahal, which is what everyone calls the Israel Defense Forces for short. The word Tsahal in Hebrew means "triumphant joy"—the happy way you feel when you have won something important. Israelis are very proud of Tsahal. Since their country is constantly threatened by powerful enemies, they know that their safety depends on Tsahal, and they take pride in its achievements and victories.

Military Service

If there is a single common denominator in the land of Israel, it is the presence of Tsahal, the world's most amazing citizen army. Unlike the military forces in other countries, Tsahal is part of every aspect of the national life. Almost everyone does a tour of active duty in Tsahal and then continues in the reserves for years afterwards. Both men and women serve in Tsahal. In other countries people sometimes resent having to do military service. Israelis serve willingly, because in Tsahal they are directly involved in protecting their homes, their loved ones, their neighborhoods, and their nation.

Emblem of the Army

Emblem of the Air Force

Emblem of the Navy

Emblem of the Paratroopers

A unit of women in the Israel Defense Forces on parade

Almost everyone in Israel serves in the armed forces. At the age of eighteen young men are mobilized into Tsahal for a period of three years. After this they generally serve an average of forty-five days a year in the reserves until they reach age fifty-five. If war breaks out or there is a national emergency, all the reservists are mobilized to bring Tsahal up to its full fighting strength. After the age of fifty-five, many men continue to serve on a voluntary basis in the home defense guard.

Since the tiny country of Israel is surrounded by unfriendly Arabs, it needs the service of every single citizen. Thus women too receive military training, serving in the Women's Corps, or Cheyl Nashim—Chen for short, a Hebrew word which also means "charm." Most unmarried girls are drafted for a two-year period when they reach the age of eighteen. Women also serve in the reserves, but those who are not officers are released from reserve duty as soon as they become mothers. Many older women serve as volunteers in the home defense guard. In wartime Tsahal's women soldiers are generally assigned to work behind the lines, freeing men for the fighting jobs.

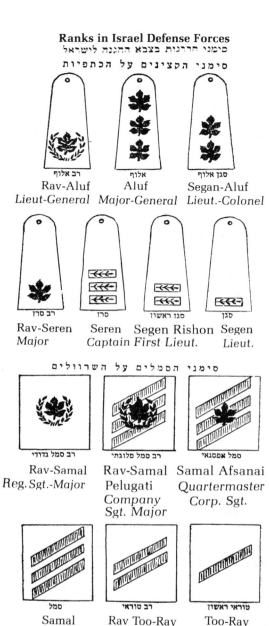

Ranks in Israel Defense Forces

סימני הדרגות בצבא ההגנה לישראל

סימני הקצינים על הכתפיות

Rav-Aluf
Lieut-General

Aluf
Major-General

Segan-Aluf
Lieut.-Colonel

Rav-Seren
Major

Seren
Captain

Segen Rishon
First Lieut.

Segen
Lieut.

סימני הסמלים על השרוולים

Rav-Samal
Reg. Sgt.-Major

**Rav-Samal
Pelugati**
*Company
Sgt. Major*

Samal Afsanai
*Quartermaster
Corp. Sgt.*

Samal
Seargent

Rav Too-Ray
Corporal

Too-Ray
Private

The symbols of rank for the non-commissioned and commissioned grades in the Israeli army.

Officers in the Israeli army wear the same kinds of uniforms as their soldiers and avoid "pulling rank." They earn their soldiers' respect by showing their intelligence, character, and dedication. These officers take the same risks that they expect their soldiers to assume. Marching ahead of their units in battle, they never command *Kadimah*—"Forward!" but rather *Acharai*—"After me!"

Tsahal does far more than provide military defense. A land of immigrants from varying backgrounds and cultures, Israel uses its armed forces to create one nation out of a diversified citizenry. Recruits who never knew the Hebrew language emerge from Tsahal three years later speaking, reading, and writing Hebrew. Boys of Yemenite origin mix with youngsters whose parents emigrated from Poland. History is taught in tandem with the intricacies of firing a mortar accurately. The army is a way of life for nearly every Israeli.

The Reserves

Military service is not over for Israelis until they have finished their full term in the reserves. Every man in Israel until the age of fifty-five and every childless woman until thirty-four must become a member of the reserves. Each year, reservists spend about forty-five days in training—a time of rigorous military drill in which reservists live as if the country were actually at war.

No other country asks so much of its people. The postman, the accountant, the professor, the silversmith, the plumber—all must leave their families and their jobs once a year to be with their reserve units.

Why is it so important for Israel's reservists to stay in constant training? So that Israel can mobilize a trained army which can match the regular armies of the Arabs. Without the ability to call upon her "citizen army" of the reserve units, Israel would not have a fighting chance against the huge numbers of Arab soldiers.

Gadna members practicing the art of rope-walking.

Emblem of the Gadna

Gadna

Training for the army sometimes begins before the army. Some Israelis have their first taste of military life while still in high school and start the army as teenagers! As early as the age of fourteen, Israelis can become members of Gadna, the Youth Corps. The name Gadna is short for Gedudei Ha'Noar Ivri. The movement, sponsored by both Tsahal and the Ministry of Education, is sort of a combination of army and school.

For several hours a week and a couple of entire weeks a year, Gadna members spend time at one of Israel's Gadna camps. Teenagers who grew up in different parts of the country meet together at Gadna camps and often become close friends. The day's schedule may include classes in the handling of rifles and grenades and an introduction to karate and jujitsu—as well as soccer games, arts and crafts, folk dances, and songs.

Gadna members hike cross-country all around Israel. Camping out, roughing it, singing songs around a campfire, laughing and talking to their friends and counselors, these teenagers have a great time. They also develop the cooperative spirit and the physical endurance that will make them good soldiers. As they hike, they often stop at new settlements and help out with whatever work needs to be done. The teenagers get a deeper, fuller knowledge of their country's land formations. Textbook knowledge about the Golan, the Negev, and the Hills of Gilboa suddenly comes alive with meaning when students can actually smell the fresh scent of pine trees and see the desert's tawny sand dunes. In the future these teenagers may find their close knowledge of the country useful, for as full-fledged soldiers they will have to defend the land from enemy invasion.

Gadna is such successful pre-army training that Asian and African countries send teachers and youth leaders to Israel to study and observe the operation of Gadna camps.

Soldier opening the valve of an irrigation pipe at a new *Nahal* (army) settlement in the Aravah, Ein Hazevah.

Emblem of the Nahal

Chen

Chen is the women's branch of the army. Women of Israel are not called upon to fight on the battlefield, but they help in many other ways—by fixing machinery and guns, running hospitals, and doing all the necessary work behind the scenes.

Nachal

Many Israeli farm settlements are located in remote areas on the country's borders, within easy range of Arab guns. Few people will risk moving to such a dangerous home.

After a few months of military training, recruits can choose to do their army service at one of these border settlements by becoming members of the army branch called Nachal—an acronym for Noar Chalutzi Lochem, "Pioneer and Fighter Youth." Nachal members lead a difficult, risky life. They are both soldiers and farmers. They till the earth, plant and harvest the crops, and guard the settlement against enemies.

Even after their army term is over, many Nachal members stay in border settlements. These brave men and women are willing to give up comfort and luxury and even to risk their lives and homes. They know that someone must protect the borders of the Jewish homeland, dangerous and risky as the task may be, and they are willing to assume this arduous responsibility. In wartime, the border settlements are the first to be attacked by the enemy. The pioneering farmers—former Nachal members—take the first blows, holding off the enemy while the rest of Israel mobilizes to the country's defense.

The acronym "Nachal" is also a Hebrew word related to the root meaning "heritage" or "inheritance." Nachal members treasure the land of Israel—all of it—as the beloved heritage of the Jewish people.

The Army Unifies and Educates

Jews in Israel come from Ashkenazic, Sephardic, and Oriental backgrounds. Tsahal helps to unify these people

44

In addition to their regular army duties, soldiers also help in many other ways. Here a corporal teaches two new immigrants to read as part of a campaign to wipe out illiteracy.

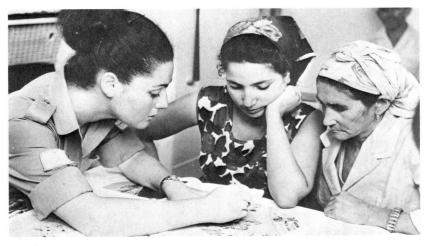

from diverse backgrounds into one Jewish community. The Persian jeweler, the carefree beachcomber from Tel Aviv, the studious Sephardic chemist, and the cheerful, idealistic young Canadian who made aliyah last year—all may become part of one army unit. Together they learn about one another's cultures. As the prayer for the new month goes, "Chaverim Kol Yisrael," which means "All Jews are friends." In Tsahal, many different kinds of Jews meet and become friends, and a land of immigrants becomes a strong and unified nation.

Many immigrants to Israel come from underdeveloped countries where not everyone learns to read and write. The army drafts these immigrants too, and provides them with the schooling they have missed. Thus illiteracy is wiped out in the young adult population of Israel. Other kinds of schooling are available too. The army teaches many skills that can be useful to soldiers when they return to civilian life—the operation and repair of radios and machinery, the use of electronic equipment, office work and laboratory skills. During military training, lectures, films, and classes are given which enhance the soldiers' knowledge of their country's history and geography.

Tsahal unifies and educates the Jews of Israel. This is what makes it so different from other armies throughout the world. It is one of the reasons why Israelis are so proud of Tsahal.

VOCABULARY AND CONCEPTS

Israel Defense Forces	צְבָא הַגֲנָה לְיִשְׂרָאֵל
Acronym for "Israel Defense Forces"	צַהַ"ל
"Follow me!"	אַחֲרַי
Parliament	כְּנֶסֶת
Youth Corps	גַדְנַ"ע
Women's branch of the army	(חֵ"ן)
Acronym for "Pioneer and Fighter Youth"	נַחַ"ל
"All Jews are responsible for one another"	כָּל יִשְׂרָאֵל עֲרֵבִים זֶה לָזֶה

45

NATURAL RESOURCES

A rich country possesses many valuable natural resources. If the country is well-watered and has fertile soil, it can produce a variety of crops. Minerals may lie beneath the earth's surface or underwater. But no country is truly rich unless it possesses the most vital natural resource of all—citizens who are skilled, talented, and hard-working. A country that lacks such citizens will not be able to utilize its resources; a country that has such citizens will be able to turn its raw resources into the many complex products that are needed in the modern world. Israel is by no means the richest of countries in terms of resources, but because its people are so able, it has a flourishing, prosperous, up-to-date economy.

WATER

The Importance of Water

Water is essential to life. All over the world, and in Israel too, people use water for drinking, cooking, washing, farming, putting out fires, making electricity, and running manufacturing processes. Your shirt and jeans were washed in a laundry machine that used many gallons of water. Yesterday's bath or shower used up some more. The plants that produced our fruits and vegetables had to be watered many, many times before they ripened and could give us food.

Water is vital to survival, but Israel's water resources are limited. Because of this, Israeli scientists have figured out just how much water is needed to make each specific crop grow, so that farmers will not waste one precious drop. Israel's largest crop, citrus fruit, takes 100 gallons of water to the pound. To produce just one pound of oranges, grapefruits, or lemons, the farmer must water his soil with a total of 100 gallons of water. Can you figure out how many gallons are needed to produce a million tons of citrus fruits, a typical year's crop?

How Israel Gets Its Water

Israel needs a great deal of water to survive, but the country has few sources of good, fresh water. The Jordan River and its tributary, the Yarkon, are the only important rivers, providing water to most of the country. The Sea of Galilee (also known as Lake Kinneret) gets its water from the Jordan; from this sea, a giant pipeline carries water down to the parched Negev soil, where it brings moisture and vitality and bloom to the desert land. Dams and cisterns all over Israel catch and store rainwater in the winter, saving it for use during the long, dry summer season.

The Nabateans were an Arab people who settled in the Negev in the sixth century B.C.E.

Though living in the desert, they were able to develop methods of water conservation and agriculture which are being studied in Israel today.

This is an aerial view of the ruin of the Nabatean city of Avdat.

A huge pipe which will carry water to the parched desert soil.

The Mediterranean Sea is also being tapped as a prime water source. Once the salt is removed from seawater in an expensive process called desalinization, it can be used just like fresh water. Israeli scientists constantly experiment to find new and better ways to turn the sea into a "bottomless well" of fresh, sweet water.

Dams and cisterns, pipelines, desalinization plants—all provide water to quench the thirst of Israel and to turn its wheels of progress.

Water in Israel's History

Want a drink of water? Just turn on the faucet, right? It's as easy as that.

But it hasn't always been so easy for the people of Israel to get enough good, fresh water. In ancient times, cities had to be built near ample water sources. Beersheva, a city in the Negev, was built near seven wells, and the city's name means "Seven-Wells." We can still view these seven ancient water-sources.

WATER AREAS AND RIVERS
  Lake Huleh—5.4 sq. miles.
  Lake Kinneret (Sea of Galilee)—63.7 sq. miles.
  Dead Sea—102 sq. miles.
  (The total Dead Sea area is 405 sq. miles, 303 sq. miles under Jordanian control.)
  The Jordan River's length is 186 miles, counting all the meanderings on the way to the Dead Sea.
  The Yarkon River near Tel Aviv—16.1 miles.
  The Kishon River near Haifa—8.1 miles.

The National Water Carrier from Lake Kinneret to the south was completed in 1964

Nabatean dams in the Negev hills still hold back the floodwaters. The lowermost dam was added under the British Mandate.

When water-sources were not close by, people had to save rainwater in special storage basins called cisterns. Deep holes were dug into the earth and waterproofed with clay or plaster. In the wintertime, rain was channeled into these cisterns and kept for use during the long, dry summer months. The city of Jerusalem, during the time of King Solomon, was provided with water from such cisterns. And today, the Pools of Solomon are still in use!

Even in the Negev, where rainfall was scarce, cisterns were used to store the small amount of rainwater. The Nabateans, an ancient non-Jewish people, were experts at this method of water conservation. Modern Israeli scientists have studied the remains of Nabatean cisterns in the Negev and have applied the wisdom of this ancient people to modern water conservation in the Jewish state. Today, with a pipeline from the Kinneret and special cisterns, the Negev soil is irrigated, and the once-barren wasteland blooms with fruit and flower.

Mekorot, which means "wells," was established by the Histadrut to pump water to the Negev and the other areas of Israel.

Water Rights

The 1995 peace agreement with the Palestinain Authority has brought the issue of water rights to the head of the peace table. No one, neither Israeli or nor Arab, is prepared to do with less water.

As the Palestinians are given autonomy, Israel will have to negotiate its access to the Jordan River and the deep aquifers under the Gaza Strip and the West Bank. Currently, Israel draws about one-third of its water from these aquifers.

Any peace treaty with Syria will have to consider the water supply which emanates from the Golan Heights. The water sources for the Jordan and Yarmuk rivers are in the Golan Heights.

VOCABULARY AND CONCEPTS

Sea of Galilee	יָם כִּנֶּרֶת
Jordan River	יַרְדֵּן
Dead Sea	יָם הַמֶּלַח

PLANTS AND ANIMALS OF ISRAEL

In ancient days, papyrus reeds were used to make a kind of paper. Several sheets were sewn together and formed into a roll.

Plants

The land of Israel contains a great variety of trees, plants, and flowers. Deep in the Negev, we find hardy desert trees and shrubs that are able to survive the dry heat. Here the tough saxawl tree lives for several hundred years; here grows the tree called Christ's thorn, with its white twigs and small, orange-colored fruits. Somehow flowers bloom, adding bright bursts of color to the desert landscape. The fragrant lavender, the violet-colored maria's iris, fuzzy yellow aaronsohnia bloom; white wormwood grows near sand dunes, its leaves giving a refreshingly scented oil.

Around Israel many different trees, plants, and flowers bloom, including over two hundred mentioned in the Bible. Olive wood was used to decorate the ancient Temple, and forests of this type still abound in modern Israel. Cypress, pine, oak, and laurel trees, too, date from biblical times in the Holy Land. Almonds, figs, grapes, apricots, and pomegranates are popular home-grown Israeli fruits. Flowers range from golden chrysanthemums, which often take over entire fields and roadsides, to bright red winter poppies, to the sinuous sea lavender, a coastal bloom. This plant, a real Israeli survivor, has tough roots which reach down for water even below the crumbly rock.

50

Ibex on the hills near Ein Gedi, a nature preserve in the Judean desert.

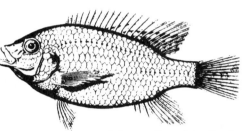

St. Peter's fish are found in fresh inland waters.

Every spring flocks of quail cross the Red Sea on their way to the Sinai Peninsula, where they land, exhausted, near the coast and are easily caught. This is how the Bible describes what happened during the Israelite sojourn in the desert.

Fish and Aquatic Life

There are three hundred different kinds of fishes in Israel's waters. The great variety exists because of the different climates near the different bodies of water around the country. In the tropical Red Sea, brilliantly colored fish swish through the colorful coral formations. Skin divers and visitors aboard glass-bottomed boats can view the porcupine fish, with its long spines that inflate when in danger, the imperial angelfish, with its elegant black and yellow striped body, and the fire fish, with its many slim fins that radiate out like flames. In the fresh waters of the Sea of Galilee, fishermen catch St. Peter's fish (so-called because tradition says they were eaten by Jesus' apostle) and catfish (which sometimes squeaks like a cat when caught). Carp is bred in artificial ponds and is a popular favorite around Israel.

Animals

Many different kinds of mammals live in the country. Wolves and leopards can still be found, just as in biblical times. The mongoose still roams the coastal plain. The Nubian ibex, a sure-footed mountain climber with keen eyesight and sense of smell, lives in protected herds near the Dead Sea. The camel, which can do without water for as long as a week and can travel over 100 miles a day, is kept by Bedouins throughout the Negev desert. Striped hyenas, whose howl has often been mistaken for laughter, prowl hilly areas and sometimes kill and eat domestic animals.

Birds and Insects

Since Israel is located in between Europe, Asia, and Africa, it is in the middle of the migration routes of many different kinds of birds. Some of these birds have been associated with Israel since the time of the Bible. Black ravens sound their hoarse "koarp" all over the country; white pelicans nest in the Huleh Valley; blue and red European bee-eaters catch insects in central Israel. The Arabian babbler is seen mainly around the Dead Sea. This bird's chatter sounds like human laughter!

51

Throughout Israel, there are more than 120 areas set aside as nature preserves in which landscape, birds, and animals receive protection.

These two stamps feature birds and gazelles which are protected species.

Diverse kinds of insects swarm through Israel too. Among the most common are scorpions (whose bite can be dangerous), butterflies, ants, crickets, praying mantises, beetles, centipedes, and bees. The scarab beetle used to be considered sacred by the ancient Egyptians, and an onslaught of the desert locust was one of the Ten Plagues that came before the Exodus of the ancient Israelites. These insects can still be found in modern Israel.

Nature Preserves

In ancient times, Israel abounded in plant and animal life forms which have nearly disappeared. During the generations of foreign rule, the land was burned and ravaged by invading armies. Alien rulers, who had little concern for the natural resources of the Jewish homeland, left only remnants of Israel's natural wealth.

Modern Israel is far more concerned with the preservation of her natural resources. Scientists have designed special areas called nature preserves where plants, fishes, and animals can thrive unharmed. No visitor may pick a fruit or flower here; no hunter may shoot an animal or bird. But anyone can come and enjoy the beautiful,

A crocodile sunning itself in the Biblical Zoo in Jerusalem.

Evaporation pans of the Dead Sea Works south of the Dead Sea.

Diamond cutting and polishing is one of Israel's most important export industries.

wonderous wealth of Israel's natural resources. Waterfalls sparkle, birds with bright plumage cry and call, unusual flowers grow, and the sleek, silvery fish swim the rivers and streams.

Many Israelis are members of Hachevra Le'Haganat Ha'Teva—"The Society for Nature Preserves." This society tries in every way possible to encourage people to keep the natural resources of Israel beautiful. They produce multicolored posters of Israel's flora and fauna. They lead tour groups through the nature preserves.

Minerals and Oils

Israel's mineral resources are valuable sources of revenue for the country. The government of Israel invests in the exploration of the land to help find and develop new resources of all kinds.

The Negev desert has become a profitable source for many different kinds of minerals. Phosphates, copper, manganese, feldspar, mica, glass sand, ball clay, bitumen-bearing rock, gypsum, flourite, chrome, sulphur, and kaolin have been discovered and mined for export. The Dead Sea produces tons of magnesium chloride, salt, potash, and magnesium bromide. Deposits of iron have been found in Galilee and peat deposits near Lake Huleh.

Oil has also been found in parts of Israel, but Israel's oil resources are much, much smaller than those of the surrounding Arab countries.

Natural Resources Become Exports

Because Israel makes good use of her natural resources, the country is able to benefit economically from them.

Israel exports vegetables, peanuts, chickens, eggs, fruits, wines, soup, jewelry, perfumes, furniture, electronics, munitions, and airplanes.

VOCABULARY AND CONCEPTS

Nature Preserves	הֲגָנַת הַטֶּבַע
Birds	צִפּוֹרִים
Animals	חַיּוֹת
Fish	דָּגִים
Biblical zoo	גַּן הַחַיּוֹת הַתַּנַכִ"י

53

HUMAN RESOURCES

A land's riches are its soil, its waters, its minerals, its crops—and its people! Without the bravery and ingenuity of Israel's soldiers, all the army's equipment would be useless. Without the energy and wisdom of the early pioneers, modern Israeli cities could never have been built. And without the Jewish people's undying faith in their nation's eventual return to their homeland, the State of Israel could never have been declared at all.

Israel's Jews come from so many distant places that sometimes it seems the only thing they have in common is their diversity! But all of Israel's Jews share pride in their people's survival and in the stubborn, miraculous, independent state that is their home.

Three times daily, through the centuries of exile, Jews had faced in the direction of Jerusalem to pray: "Sound the great shofar for our freedom, raise the banner for gathering our exiles, and gather us together from the four corners of the earth into our own land."

On May 14, 1948—the fifth day of the Hebrew month Iyyar, in the year 5708, according to the Jewish calendar—Israel gained its independence. On this great day, David Ben-Gurion announced, as if in answer to the familiar Hebrew prayer, that the new state would be open for the ingathering of the exiles. Israel opened her gates to Jewish immigrants from countries all over the world. In the years that followed, hundreds of thousands of Jews of different cultures, different languages, almost different worlds, streamed into the Jewish homeland—the first and only country open, without restriction, to any Jew who wished to come.

Today Israel's population has nearly 4 million Jews, and the diversity of its people makes the country almost like a miniature United Nations. In addition to its Jewish citizens, Israel also has 600,000 non-Jewish citizens, mainly Moslems, but also including Christian Arabs and Bedouins and Druzes. Israel's Jews try hard to live in peace and harmony with their non-Jewish neighbors and fellow-citizens. Under Israel's democratic system, all citizens, non-Jewish as well as Jewish, have full political and civil rights.

THE JEWS OF ISRAEL

Israel is the home of people from so many different lands that it is like a tiny world in itself, a "microcosm" of the globe. Its Jewish population includes baggy-trousered Kurds from the wild mountains of the Iranian frontier; trim, sophisticated Parisian ladies dressed in the latest chic silk fashions; ultra-pious Chasidim from Eastern Europe wearing round fur hats called "shtreimelach" and long, black silk coats called "kapotot" debonair Frenchmen sporting berets; American teenagers in jeans; and dainty Yemenite women from the edge of Arabia in embroidered, multi-colored trousers. Jews came to Israel from virtually every country. They came from Afghanistan, Abyssinia, and Libya, from Austria, Hungary, and Bulgaria, from Turkey, India, Poland, Germany, and Romania, from South Africa, South America, and any other place you can think of. Never before in the history of the world had so many people from so many different lands descended so quickly upon so small an area.

Ashkenazim

About half of Israel's Jews are the children and grandchildren of German and Eastern European Jews. They are called Ashkenazim, from the old Hebrew word *Ashkenaz,* the name for the area that is now northern France and Germany. Most of the Zionist settlers who built up Palestine were Jews from Eastern Europe. Many other Ashkenazim found freedom and security in Israel after the bitter sickness of the Nazi Holocaust in Eastern Europe. Many Ashkenazim speak Yiddish, a language which combines Hebrew and German words. Yiddish developed during the years of Jewish exile in European countries.

Sephardim

Sephardim and Oriental Jews make up the other half of Israel's Jewish population.

Refugees from Arab countries on their way to freedom in Israel. In Israel they were welcomed with open arms. They were taught Hebrew and were resettled on farms, villages, and in cities.

56

Spanish in Hebrew characters (Ladino). Title page of Bahya ibn Pakudah's *Duties of the Heart.*

Sephardim are descendants of the Jews expelled from Spain in 1492 by King Ferdinand and Queen Isabella. These Jews scattered to many countries, but since they were originally from Spain, they were called Sephardim, which in Hebrew means "Spaniards." Many Sephardim speak Ladino, a language which combines Hebrew and Spanish words, just as Yiddish combines Hebrew and German. Ladino developed during the years when Jews lived in Spanish-speaking countries.

Oriental Jews

Many of Israel's Jews are immigrants from Oriental countries, like Iraq, Yemen, Kurdistan, Persia, Afghanistan, Morocco, Libya, Tunisia, and Algeria. The special expertise of the craftsmen from these countries is renowned, and the souvenir shops of Israel are filled with jewelry and metal sculptures that capture the spirit of the Orient in their delicacy and precision. Many of the first immigrants from Oriental countries were not used to the technology and bustle of modern-day existence, and Israel had to help her new citizens adjust to the rapid pace of modern life.

Sometimes Oriental Jews are called Sephardic Jews, although in actuality their backgrounds differ, since unlike the Sephardim they are not descended from ancestors who once lived in Spain and Portugal.

Ashkenazic, Sephardic and Oriental Jews—one people

All Jews belong to one people. Our nation was scattered across the globe through the long night of Jewish exile—the Diaspora—but we all share one Torah, one heritage, one set of Jewish laws and holidays, one Siddur (prayerbook), and one deep, strong, heartfelt pride in the Jewish return to our homeland. But since the ancestors of Ashkenazic, Sephardic, and Oriental Jews lived many years in such different lands, each group naturally developed its own special customs and traditions.

Sabra fruits and Sabra soldiers.

The Ashkenazic, Sephardic, and Oriental Jews of Israel are not separated by geographical barriers the way their ancestors once were. They live side by side in Israel. Their children play together in the same kindergarten classes and attend the same high schools; they grow up together in the same neighborhoods and youth groups, and serve together in Israel's army regiments.

As the distinctions between the groups blur, Jews born in Israel no longer identify strongly as Ashkenazic, Sephardic, or Oriental Jews; instead, they are "sabras," native-born Israelis with their own Israeli culture—an amalgam of all three immigrant groups, plus a touch of something uniquely Israeli.

The term *sabra* is a nickname for Jews born in Israel. The sabra is a desert fruit that grows on cactus that is hard and prickly on the outside but soft and juicy on the inside. Israelis can seem very tough and abrupt when you first meet them. Once you get to know the sabra better, though, you will find the true tenderness hidden just beneath the tough exterior.

While all three groups have the same basic prayers, each has many of its own special, beautiful melodies and chants for certain prayers. Each group has created its own additions to the Siddur and the Machzor.

The different groups of Jews used to have their own ways of pronouncing Hebrew. This is understandable if you think about how different the English of an American sounds from the English of an Irishman or an Englishman or an Australian. Pronunciation differences exist even within the United States. The English of a New Yorker is quite different from that of an Iowan or a Texan! In modern Israel, the Sephardic pronunciation has become accepted as the standard way of speaking modern Hebrew. The children of all Jews—Ashkenazic, Sephardic, and Oriental—speak Hebrew in the same way.

VOCABULARY AND CONCEPTS

Sabra (native-born Israeli)	צַבָּר
Sephardic Jews	סְפָרַדִּים
Ashkenazic Jews	אַשְׁכְּנַזִּים
Oriental Jews	יְהוּדֵי עֲדוֹת הַמִּזְרָח
Yemenites	תֵּימָנִים
Germany	אַשְׁכְּנַז
Spain	סְפָרַד
Ashkenazic Jewish language	יִדִישׁ
Sephardic Jewish language	לאַדִינוֹ

58

THE RUSSIANS

ANATOLE (NATAN) SHARANSKY (1948-) Scientist, Activist, Refusenik.

Anatole Sharansky is a Jewish computer scientist who helped organize the Jewish refusenik movement in the USSR. In 1973, because of his activities, he was arrested and kept in solitary confinement for 18 months. He was finally placed on trial on the trumped-up charge of espionage. Despite worldwide protests Anatole was sentenced to 13 years of imprisonment.

After 11 years in prison and labor camps, he was released and immediately left for Israel. Anatole Sharansky, activist and refusenik, now leads the fight for the rights and welfare of new Soviet immigrants in Israel.

For about 2,000 years, the Land of Israel was in the hands of foreigners. In 1948 a miracle occurred and the land the Roman conquerors had renamed Palestine once more resumed its rightful name—Israel. To make sure that all Jews would be welcome in the homeland, the Knesset passed the Law of Return. Under this law all Jews, no matter what country they live in, have the right to become Israeli citizens if they come and live in Israel.

The Law of Return helped make the age-old dream of Shivat Zion ("Return to Zion") and Kibbutz G'luyot ("Ingathering of the Exiles") a reality.

As a result of the collapse of the Soviet Union, more than 500,000 Russians have made aliyah to Israel.

On the streets of Israel one hears almost as much Russian as Hebrew. Russian newspapers, magazines, books, plays, and music are very common. The country with the highest proportion of scientists and engineers in the whole world is slowly, but surely, on its way to becoming an economic Samson.

With all the problems— a new language and the military situation—the Russians keep on coming. Difficult economic conditions in Russia have accelerated anti-Semitism, and a desire to return to Judaism has kept the stream of olim coming.

Jews all over the world contribute to the resettlement and training of Russian Jewry. Above all, the Israelis have opened their country and their hearts to their Russian brothers and sisters.

The age-old talmudic saying "All Jews are responsible for each other" is the Israeli motto.

OPERATION MAGIC CARPET—THE JEWS OF YEMEN

In the hands of the skilled Yemenite craftsmen, gold, silver, and precious stones are transformed into a beautiful Torah Crown.

A Jewess from Yemen dressed in native costume.

VOCABULARY AND CONCEPTS

Operation Magic Carpet	מַרְבַד הַקְּסָמִים
Yemen	תֵּימָן
Yemenites	תֵּימָנִים

The Jews of Yemen, a backward Moslem country in southwestern Arabia, had lived since biblical times in a somewhat isolated community. The Jews of Yemen lived without the modern conveniences we take for granted—beds, chairs, toilets, trains, electric lights.

Despite their poverty, the Yemenite Jews remained clean, hard-working, and deeply religious people. They were so poor that a whole class of children had to study Torah from one book—so the Yemenite children learned to read Hebrew just as easily upside-down or sideways as right-side-up. Amidst the isolation and the bleakness of Yemen, these Jews created delicate, beautiful art forms and expressed themselves in song, dance, fine embroidery, and jewelry-making.

Groups of Yemenite Jews had settled in Israel after 1882. With the establishment of the State of Israel in 1948, a special airplane service was organized to bring the Yemenite Jews to their homeland, Israel.

Everyone wondered how the Yemenite Jews would react to the sight of an airplane, for these people had never seen anything at all like one! But the Yemenite Jews were not afraid to board the planes. They simply remembered that in the Bible, God had promised to bring His people back to Israel "on eagles' wings" (Exodus 19:4).

In the years 1949 and 1950 more than 50,000 Yemenite Jews were flown to Israel by this air service, which was known as Operation Magic Carpet. In Hebrew, Yemenites are called *Taymanim*.

60

Everyone wondered how the Yemenite Jews would react to the sight of an airplane, for these people had never seen anything at all like one! But the Yemenite Jews were not afraid to board the planes. They simply remembered that in the Bible, God had promised to bring His people back to Israel "on eagles' wings" (Exodus 19:4).

In the years 1949 and 1950 more than 50,000 Yemenite Jews were flown to Israel by this air service, which was known as Operation Magic Carpet. In Hebrew, Yemenites are called *Taymanim*.

VOCABULARY AND CONCEPTS

Operation Magic Carpet	מַרְבַד הַקְּסָמִים
Yemen	תֵּימָן
Yemenites	תֵּימָנִים

Taymanim waiting for the "Magic Carpet" to fly them to Israel and freedom.

61

THE SAMARITANS

Samaritans at prayer.

This small group of about five hundred people claims direct descent from the biblical Ephraim and Manasseh, sons of Joseph. Their religion is very much like Judaism, but the Samaritans believe the center of their worship should be on Mount Gerizim, behind Nablus, while the Jews consider Jerusalem their Holy City. And the Samaritans accept only the first five books of the Bible as Scripture, regarding the later writings as not divinely inspired.

Half of the Samaritan community lives in Nablus, at the foot of Mount Gerizim, and half in Holon, near Tel Aviv.

The Samaritan Passover

The Samaritans' most important holiday is Passover, which they observe just as it was observed in biblical times. The people leave Nablus to camp out on top of Mount Gerizim. In their mountaintop tents, led by their priests, this ancient sect resembles the Children of Israel on their flight from Egypt. The old prayers are chanted, the sacrificial lambs slaughtered, and the Passover ritual performed just as it was in ancient Israel, more than three thousand years ago.

The Torah of the Samaritans is housed in the synagogue in Nablus. It is written i ancient Hebrew and is extremely old.

VOCABULARY AND CONCEPTS

Samaritans	שׁוֹמְרוֹנִים
Mount Gerizim	הַר גְּרִיזִים
Passover	פֶּסַח

THE ARABS OF ISRAEL

The Koran is regarded by Moslems as God's word. The Koran consists of 114 chapters called surahs. This is a page from a very old Koran written in an early form of Arabic script.

Most Israeli Arabs are Moslems; the rest are either Christians or Druzes. All Arab citizens enjoy the same rights as Jewish citizens. This includes the right to vote and to be elected to all government offices.

Mohammed and the Islamic Religion

Moslems believe in the religion called Islam, which means, in Arabic, "submission" (to the will of God). Mohammed, a seventh-century merchant from the city of Mecca in what is now Saudi Arabia, founded Islam, and Moslems believe he was the prophet of God, called Allah in Arabic. Mohammed's teachings are recorded in the Moslem sacred book, the Koran.

At first, Mohammed tried to persuade the Jews to accept his teachings by showing that the Koran was in the same tradition as the Jewish prophetic works. Mohammed stressed the similarities between Islam and Judaism. But the Jews refused to accept Mohammed's teachings. After a while, Mohammed stopped trying to make Moslem rituals similar to Jewish traditions. Instead he emphasized

The holy city of Mecca and its mosque. Near the center of the mosque is a small shrine called the Kaaba. Moslems believe that the Kaaba was built by Abraham and Ishmael. Embedded in one wall of the Kaaba is a black stone. Moslems believe the stone was given to Adam by an angel. Each year thousands of Moslem pilgrims come from far away to kiss the sacred black stone.

Islam, like Christianity, is based on the Hebrew Bible. This old Moslem manuscript pictures Adam and Eve in the Garden of Eden.

THE DOME OF THE ROCK (MOSQUE OF OMAR)
The Mosque of Omar is a beautiful building faced with slabs of marble and multicolored mosaics. The mosque was built by CaliphAbd El-Malek in 691 C.E.

A Moslem legend claims that Mohammed ascended into the heavens from this very rock. Beside the rock is a box which is said to contain hairs from Mohammed's beard.

Inside the mosque, surrounded by a railing, is the sacred rock on which, it is said, Abraham offered his son Isaac as a sacrifice. Tradition has it that this rock is a foundation marking the center of the earth. Therefore, the Jews call it Even Hashettiya—"the Stone of Foundation."

King Solomon's Temple was built on this site.

the differences between Islam and Judaism. In place of the Jewish fast-day, Yom Kippur, Mohammed declared the Islamic fast-period, the fast of Ramadan. In place of the Jewish Sabbath on Saturday, Mohammed declared Friday as the Moslem day of holy assembly. Mohammed rejected most of the Jewish dietary laws.

How Islam Spread—The Jihad

After Mohammed died, his followers spread his religion to many different countries. They did this by conquering these countries by military strength and then forcing the people of these lands to convert to Islam. From Arabia, the followers of Mohammed converted pagan peoples to Islam—people in Syria, Palestine, Mesopotamia, Babylonia, Armenia, Persia, and Egypt, and later the followers of Mohammed reached as far as central Europe.

The Islamic name for such a military conquest is *jihad*, which in Arabic means "holy war." Some Arab enemies of modern Israel arouse the feelings of Arabs against Israel by speaking of the need for a *jihad* against Israel.

Moslems believed it was a virtuous act to force conquered pagan people to convert to Islam, offering them a choice of conversion or death. Christians and Jews were not forced to convert but were tolerated as second-class citizens.

'The State of Israel . . . will maintain complete equality of social and political rights for all its citizens, without distinction of creed, race or sex. It will guarantee freedom of religion and conscience, of language, education and culture. It will safeguard the Holy Places of all religions . . .

Declaration of Independence

Reading the Koran.

VOCABULARY AND CONCEPTS

Arabs	עֲרָבִים
Mohammed	מוּחַמָד
Allah	אַלָאהּ (אֶלֹהַּ)
Islam	אִסְלַאם
Moslem	מֻסְלְמִי
Koran	קוֹראַן
Mosque of Omar	מִיסְגָד עֹמֶר

Moslem Beliefs and Customs

Moslems believe that Allah is the one God. They revere Jewish and Christian figures like Abraham, Moses, and Jesus, and they include Mohammed as Allah's prophet. Religious Moslems pray five times daily. All over Israel, the Moslem call to prayer may be heard at these times. The worshiper kneels deeply to pray, with forehead touching the ground. He faces toward Mecca, the Arabian city where Mohammed was born.

Moslems are obliged to fast from sunrise to sunset during each day of Ramadan, the ninth month on their religious calendar. They must give a special yearly charity based on their incomes. Each Moslem is supposed to visit the city of Mecca at least once in his lifetime. This trip is called a *haj*.

Most of the Arabs living in Israel are not Bedouins. The majority live in cities and in farming villages. The Arabs are represented in the Knesset by several members. Arab workers are full-fledged members of the Histadrut.

Israeli Arab children, just like the Jewish children, receive free public education through high school.

Moslems at prayer in the El-Aqsa Mosque on the Temple Mount.

CHRISTIANS IN ISRAEL

Around 150,000 of Israel's Arabs are Christians, and in addition numerous Christians from North and South America, Europe, and other places come to Israel each year on religious pilgrimages, especially during the Christmas and Easter seasons. Christians view Israel as a Holy Land because Jesus was born there and lived there all his life. Christians believe that Jesus was the Messiah.

Jesus of Nazareth

Jesus was born in a small town in northern Israel called Nazareth, during the Roman rule over Israel. The young Jew became a popular preacher who spoke a simple, moral message to the humble villagers and fishermen who lived nearby. Jesus gathered around himself a small group of followers, called his *disciples*.

A view of the city of Nazareth.

Stone inscription of the name of Pontius Pilate, found in the ruins of Caesarea.

The Roman authorities ruling Israel at that time were suspicious of anyone who had a loyal following. They constantly feared revolution and worried that Jesus might incite his followers to rebel against the Roman government.

In the year 30 C.E., during Passover, Jesus came with his disciples to Jerusalem. During the festivals like Passover, when the city of Jerusalem was crowded with visitors, the Romans were most suspicious and most fearful of revolt. That Passover, the disciples of Jesus proclaimed him as the Messiah. Jesus was attracting more and more followers, and the local Roman official, Pontius Pilate, was getting more and more worried. Finally, Pilate ordered Jesus brought before him and condemned Jesus to be executed by crucifixion, then the routine form of Roman execution.

How Christianity Began

About fifty years after Jesus' death, his disciples began a written record of their preacher's life and teachings. As these teachings spread, Christianity arose as a religion in its own right, rather than just being a group of Jewish disciples following the Jewish preacher Jesus. Eventually, the Christian religion took hold in Europe and became a world movement. The written record of Jesus' life and teachings became known as the New Testament.

VOCABULARY AND CONCEPTS

New Testament	בְּרִית הַחֲדָשָׁה
Nazareth	נַצֶּרֶת
Jesus	יֵשׁוּ
Christianity	נַצְרוּת

THE DRUZES

The Druzes are a separate Arab people with their own religion. There are about 33,000 Druzes in Israel.

The Druze religion is monotheistic. That is, like Jews, Christians, and Moslems, they believe in one God. The Druzes believe that God operates in the world through a series of five cosmic principles, or "emanations," and that God chooses certain human beings as special representatives. According to Druze tradition, Jethro, the father-in-law of Moses, was one of God's special representatives. The supposed tomb of Jethro, near Tiberias, is a sacred Druze shrine.

The details of the Druze religion are known only to Druze priests, who must keep these details secret from outsiders. The religious sect is named after Ismail ad-Daiazi, who first preached the new religion in the surroundings of Mount Hermon, in the eleventh century.

Druze soldiers proudly welcome their leaders at the Tomb of Jethro.

A Druze member of the Israel Defense Forces proudly displays the flag of Israel.

The Druze People Help to Defend Israel

The Druzes settled in the Galilee area of Israel in the eleventh century, and they have been there ever since. During the War of Independence in 1948, the Druzes fought on the Jewish side. Today, young Druzes serve in the Israeli army in their own platoons under Druze officers. Since 1957, they have received official recognition in Israel as a separate religious community.

Although the Druzes speak the Arabic language, they have kept their identity separate from the rest of the Arab community. The Druzes do not accept converts to their religion, and they forbid intermarriage with people of other religions. They also have a strong, spirited sense of group solidarity and pride.

VOCABULARY AND CONCEPTS

Druze	דְּרוּזִים
Moses	מֹשֶׁה
Jethro	יִתְרוֹ

THE BEDOUINS

Bedouins, who are mostly Moslems, are the wandering tribesmen of the Middle Eastern deserts. It is hard to calculate just how many Bedouins live in the Israeli desert, the Negev, because they do not settle down long enough for an exact count. They are *nomads*, or wanderers. Bedouin caravans rove constantly. These hardy desert people pitch their tents wherever they find a good place to graze their sheep, goats, and camels.

The Bedouin Lifestyle

At first glance, time seems to have stood still for the Bedouins, the "lords of the desert," as they are called. Like their ancient ancestors, they live in goatskin tents. Bedouin women wear veils which cover them almost completely. Bedouin men, too, wear a traditional outfit that has not changed since the days of their forefathers. The Bedouin is clothed in long, flowing robes that can be

Moshe Dayan (1915–1980), seated with eye patch, was a famous Israeli war hero and diplomat; here he is being welcomed by the Bedouins.

An Israeli nurse treats a Bedouin child.

wrapped close for warmth in the winter or left hanging loose in the heat of summer. On his head, he wears a square white scarf called a *kafiyah* (keh-FEE-yah), tied on with a double coil of black wool or goat's hair. This headdress protects the Bedouin from the sun's burning rays and from the desert's stinging sands.

Thursday is the weekly market day for the Bedouins. Imagine the contrast of past and present on an early Thursday morning in the Negev city of Beersheva.

Some Bedouins, wearing their unusual desert garb, drive pickup trucks loaded up in back with sheep, goats, and donkeys. Other Bedouins weave their way through Beersheva traffic on their camels and donkeys. Once they reach the marketplace, Bedouins trade their animals and sell their farm products and handicrafts. Always, they bargain until they make the best possible deal.

How Bedouin Life Is Changing

In recent years, however, the Negev has become more and more modernized, and more and more of the desert land has become cultivated. Thus the Bedouin has more of a struggle each year to find open planting ground for

A Bedouin family dressed in their desert garb.

A camel caravan plods across the hot desert sands. The camel has been used for transport and work in the Near East for at least thirty centuries. The Bedouins of Israel still use the camel extensively.

his crops and grazing land for his animals. The day may come when once and for all, the "lords of the desert" will have to exchange their ancient ways for a more modern life.

Already there have been some changes. Many Bedouins now send their children to school, where they learn Hebrew as well as Arabic. The traveling health clinics are welcomed eagerly on their regular visits to the nomads' desert settlements. Some Bedouin tribes have even given up their wandering existence and have begun to establish permanent homes. These tribes accept the help of the Israeli government in buying land for farming and building homes. Several tribes have banded together to form a farming cooperative called Al Shalom.

Most of the Bedouins are loyal to the State of Israel. Many Bedouins serve in Israel's Defense Forces and some have distinguished themselves in action.

The old and the new. The "lord of the desert" and the "ship of the desert" greet a modern farm machine.

VOCABULARY AND CONCEPTS

Desert	מִדְבָּר
Kafiyah	קָפִיָה
Bedouins	בֵּידוּאִים

WOMEN IN ISRAEL

The Role of Women in Building Israel

In the pioneering days of the Jewish resettlement of Palestine, the women who came to build the land were courageous idealists. They had little patience with conventional "femininity," and they asked for no special privileges. Along with the men, these brave women worked and suffered, struggling to survive against all odds and hoping for the future of the land.

In cramped huts, without heat or hot water, these Zionist pioneers created modern Israel. They nursed the sick and wounded without adequate food or medication, they farmed the rocky or swampy soil, and they knew the constant threat of Arab terrorist attacks. Women learned to smuggle guns and grenades underneath their clothes. They learned to use firearms to defend themselves and

The first kibbutzim struggled to survive in a hostile environment. Bilu pioneers, men and women, laid down their lives for an ideal. These pioneers are happy with the results of their labors.

their homes, to guard the remote border settlements on which they lived. Women gave up their wedding bands to raise money for arms and medical supplies; they parachuted behind enemy lines as secret agents, risking their own lives for the sake of the Yishuv—the Jewish community in Palestine.

Israeli Women Have Full Equality

Thus Israelis have always believed that women are equal citizens, as capable and courageous as men. In 1969, Golda Meir, a former schoolteacher from Milwaukee, became the country's Prime Minister.

Women in Israel have complete freedom of education. They can study engineering and plan the bridges, buildings, and cities of their nation. They can study medicine and heal the sick; they can learn archaeology and art history, literature and law. Women in Israel own and operate businesses and restaurants, establish schools, direct traffic, organize museum showings, design clothing, draft blueprints for building construction, and serve in the Knesset.

Women in the Israeli Army

Women are drafted into Israel's Defense Force, where they become members of the Women's Corps, the Cheyl Nashim. Abbreviated, Cheyl Nashim is called Chen—which also means "charm" in Hebrew. Army women receive military training but are usually not assigned to fighting units in wartime. They learn to do the many crucial behind-the-lines jobs of war—the repair of rifles and equipment, and the operation of complex electronic devices. They learn to nurse the wounded and to teach Hebrew to immigrant soldiers. The women of Chen free many men for the fighting jobs in time of battle.

Some Israeli women cannot serve in Chen because of their religious beliefs. Strictly Orthodox, these women believe a Jewish woman's main role is in the home, caring for her family. They fear that the co-ed atmosphere of the army will not always be suitable for them. These Ortho-

In all of Israel's wars against the Arabs, women have always served in the army.

A stone quarry in Israel, in the early 1900's. The early pioneers had little patience with femininity. Their primary concern was building a land and a country of their own.

dox women serve their country in a special way. An organization called Sherut Leumi—"The National Voluntary Service"—places them in new development towns. Few professionals have settled in these towns, and the new immigrants there need a great deal of help. Sherut Leumi trains Orthodox women to work in these towns as teachers, nurses, social workers, and counselors. Without violating their religious ideals, the Orthodox women of Sherut Leumi do important work for their country.

The women of Israel serve their homeland in so many ways! The smuggler, fierce and proud in the difficult days of the War of Independence, hid a grenade beneath her long skirt and guarded her settlement through the dark nights of terrorism. A nineteen-year-old Chen lieutenant becomes a machine-gun expert. A woman doctor in a moshav clinic examines the eyes of patients; a biologist, in her quiet university laboratory, makes a breakthrough in the treatment of a dread disease. A hardworking schoolteacher in an isolated border town patiently teaches immigrant children and their parents how to speak the Hebrew language. A Tel Aviv businesswoman shakes hands with her banker as she finishes her investment

Women soldiers (Chen) on parade.

plans. A sunburned archaeology student stoops to examine a fragile pottery relic in the dust. And a tanned and smiling young woman smiles at a motorcyclist as she skillfully directs the traffic of a busy Haifa intersection.

Israel's women are more fully integrated into their society than are women in any other country of the world. They are truly full and equal partners with their n.enfolk in building and defending the Jewish state.

Arab Women

Arab girls and women in the Middle East, until very recently, stayed home as the "property" of their fathers or husbands. When they were allowed to venture out of the house, they had to cover themselves up with heavy veils and robes so that only their eyes were visible. They rarely went to school beyond the second or third grade, so they usually could not read or write. They were not allowed to earn their own living or vote. Their only work was taking care of the man and his home. In many Arab countries, this unfair treatment of girls and women still continues.

But Arab women in Israel have found new freedoms. They have come out from behind closed doors to get equal rights, catching up with their Jewish fellow-citizens. Many Arab women now attend classes and women's clubs, and their young daughters go to school alongside their brothers. Because elementary education in Israel is free and compulsory for Arabs as well as Jews, Arab boys and girls all over the country are learning how to read and write. Qualified boys and girls go on to high school and college in Israel's excellent institutions of learning.

Israeli army women repair the machinery vital to the succss of the IDF.

VOCABULARY AND CONCEPTS

National Voluntary Military Service

שֵׁרוּת לְאוּמִי

Women's branch of the army

חֵיל נָשִׁים (חֵ"ן)

76

EDUCATION IN ISRAEL

Jews are known as "the people of the book." In the poorest communities of Europe during the years of exile, Jews taught their children how to read and write. Most Jews could say their prayers and recite the blessings over the Torah, and in every Jewish community, the most learned rabbis and scholars were highly respected even if they lacked material wealth.

No wonder, then, that in modern Israel, education is the top priority of the government budget—so much so that every Israeli schoolchild can receive an excellent, free education from primary school through to high school graduation!

PRIMARY SCHOOLS

Israeli families can choose which type of school they prefer for their children, but all primary schools are free, compulsory, and cover the same basic subjects—reading, writing, and arithmetic. Both religious and nonreligious schools are available, as well as traditional yeshivot and Arab schools.

Primary school usually includes grades 1 to 8. But many schools now follow the American system in which primary school includes only grades 1 to 6. The student then continues in *chtivat beynayim*—junior high school—for grades 7, 8, and 9.

Bible Study

All Jewish schools teach Bible, with special emphasis on the prophetic ideals of brotherhood and justice. For all Israeli children, the places mentioned in the Bible are real, tangible places as well as words in books—Jerusalem, the Galil, the Negev desert. Religious schools teach the Bible and the Talmud in more detail and emphasize religious law. Strictly Orthodox Jews send their children to traditional yeshivot run by the Agudat Israel organization. In these schools, Bible, Talmud, and religious law are stressed.

Other Subjects

Farming, physical work, and home economics are taught in Israel's primary schools, for this land was built by the labor of the early Zionist pioneers, and much work of building still remains for the present generation of youngsters. Many of the nearly six thousand primary

Students in a religious school studying Talmud.

Can you find a clue to what time of year this photograph was taken?

schools in Israel have their own piece of farmland, where children can practice their new gardening skills. Some schools have their own wood and metal shops too. Children in the primary grades play sports together and learn how to cooperate and share. They paint, sing, and dance together, and they learn to read and write in Hebrew and in English.

The Weekly Sabbath Party

The highlight of the week is the Friday party in honor of the coming Sabbath day. All the children and their teacher join together to welcome the Sabbath. For a moment, everyone forgets the arithmetic test, the spelling quiz, the quarrel in the hallway, and the Jewish history midterm. Everyone is happy together, sharing a peaceful moment and welcoming in the Sabbath.

School in Israel usually starts at 8 o'clock in the morning and is over in the early afternoon. Children are able to go home for lunch with their families. Usually, they go to meetings of their youth groups in the afternoon.

79

Arab Schools

The Arab communities of Israel wish to teach their children in separate schools. The Israeli government provides the Arab schools with funding and assistance. At these schools, Arab children learn the Arabic language, culture, and religion. They learn the Hebrew language from the fourth grade on.

Sometimes, teachers in Arab and Jewish schools in the same neighborhood arrange for their classes to visit one another. The children make friends and get to know about their neighbors' customs, holidays, and traditions. Perhaps if enough Jewish and Arab children get to know and respect one another, peace in Israel can finally be achieved.

Arab children in an Arab school in Israel. These children will learn Arabic as well as Hebrew.

VOCABULARY AND CONCEPTS

Primary School	בֵּית סֵפֶר יְסוֹדִי
Junior High School	חֲטִיבַת בֵּינַיִים
Yeshiva	יְשִׁיבָה

High Schools

Before 1979, high school education in Israel was not free. Only students with high marks and whose families could afford tuition fees went to high school. Some scholarships were available, but competition was keen.

Since 1979, however, free high school education is available to everyone, for Israel's government has made education a top national priority. Academic, vocational, and agricultural schools offer high school educations to the young people of Israel.

Academic Schools

The Israeli student in an academic high school follows a rigorous course of classroom study. He or she learns the basic, required courses, as well as a choice of other subjects like calculus, French, dramatics, Arabic, botany, and physics. All students, in order to graduate from high school, must pass a special countrywide examination called the *bagrut*.

Herzlia High School in Tel Aviv, one of Israel's oldest and best schools.

A science laboratory in an Israeli high school.

The *bagrut* tests students on Hebrew (grammar, composition, and literature), English, mathematics, Bible, and history. Everyone studies long and hard for the *bagrut* exam, for all students who pass this special test are automatically admitted into college after they have done army service. The word *bagrut* in Hebrew means "maturity," and when Israeli students learn that they have passed the *bagrut*, they feel truly grown up.

Within the army, soldiers who never completed high school study can take courses toward the completion of the *bagrut* exam.

Class Trips and Outings

High school study in Israel is much more than classroom instruction. Every class goes on trips around the country, especially in the springtime. The class chooses its own destination. City kids usually want to visit a farm town, and farm kids long to see the big city!

Students at an agricultural school learn by doing.

VOCABULARY AND CONCEPTS

High school final examination	בַּגְרוּת
High School	בֵּית סֵפֶר תִּיכוֹנִי
Vocational School	בֵּית סֵפֶר מִקְצוֹעִי
Agricultural School	בֵּית סֵפֶר חַקְלָאִי

Before the students leave on their trip, they study the history and geography of the area they are about to tour. They examine maps and chart out their travels. They plan activities and they pack their knapsacks with enough food to last three or four days. Someone is sure to bring a guitar, so that the class can sing together around a camp-fire at night, accompanied by the soft music.

Vocational and Agricultural Schools

About half of Israel's students choose to complete vocational or agricultural high schools. In vocational schools, they learn valuable technical skills and become hospital assistants, mechanics, electricians, diamond cutters, printers, secretaries, and opticians. In agricultural schools, they learn how to run efficient farms. They study botany, soil science, and the care of poultry and livestock.

In Israel's vocational and agricultural high schools, students learn vital skills which prepare them to serve their nation in important ways.

An ORT vocational school in Israel. ORT, which stands for Organization for Rehabilitation and Training, prepares Jews for new employment opportunities. It has established trade schools and vocational workshops wherever Jews are found in great numbers. In Israel there are about fifty ORT schools with about 5,000 students.

HIGHER EDUCATION

In Israel many people continue their education after they are graduated from high school. Several different forms of higher education are available: yeshivot for religious studies, and colleges and universities for advanced academic, professional, and technical studies.

Yeshivot

Many of us think of education in terms of specific goals. We study hard to finish each school term with high marks. We finally are graduated from elementary school and junior high; then we enter high school and leave with a high school diploma. Then comes college graduation, medical training, a law degree, or a teaching license. We earn a degree and go out into the world to use it.

But Jews who decide to study at one of Israel's many yeshivot think of education in a different way. For them, learning the Bible and the Talmud is not something done just to earn a diploma. These Jews rejoice in studying the Bible for its own sake—*li'shma*. They study God's word in the Torah, or Written Law, and in the Talmud, or Oral Law, all day long. They revel in the holiness and the beauty of God's sacred works, and they seek to understand every single commandment.

The Special Yeshiva Atmosphere

The atmosphere of a yeshiva is very special and very exciting. The students generally live in one community, eating, praying, and studying together like one large family. All are immersed in the religious life of Torah and mitzvot. Yeshiva rabbis usually have a quality of special warmth and spiritual radiance.

A *yeshiva bachur* studies Talmud.

Some yeshivot in Israel are especially for Jews who do not know much Hebrew and who lack background in Jewish studies. To these schools come many serious young people who are searching deeply for answers to their religious questions. The rabbis at these yeshivot do their best to teach these young Jews and to guide them toward a good and satisfying Jewish life.

Universities

Though Israel is a small country, she has several excellent universities. Hebrew University has two modern campuses in Jerusalem, with a fine medical school. There is Tel Aviv University, and Bar-Ilan University in the suburbs of Tel Aviv. Bar-Ilan University, built by American Jews, is a university like Yeshiva University in the United States—a university which combines secular and religious education. Haifa University is located on

The new Hebrew University campus in Jerusalem.

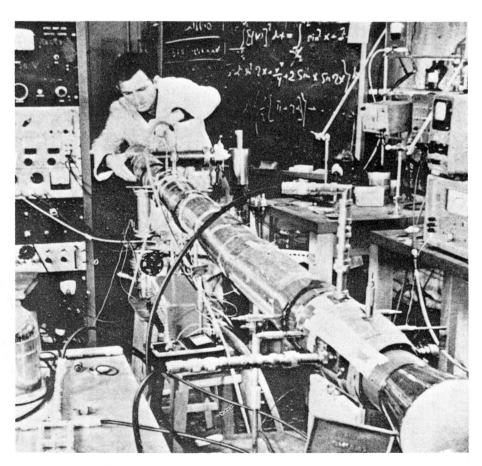

An Israeli scientist in the nuclear research laboratory of the Weizmann Institute, Rehovot.

The Ulpan program offers intensive courses in Hebrew to people of all ages, races, and religions.

Mount Carmel, and at the Technion, also in Haifa, students train in specialized scientific subjects. The newest Israeli university is Ben-Gurion University, in the heart of the Negev—Beersheva.

The American University System

American students generally go to college right after they are graduated from high school. Often, young students are uncertain about their future and need several years to "find themselves" and decide on a career. Their first years at college may include courses in such different subjects as physics, poetry, history, Bible, Greek, geology, theater, and art. Once they choose a major subject, they must take only about ten courses in that field in order to earn a college degree. Thus, American students with degrees in science or in literature have not had very many courses in their major subject, but they have had a wide variety of courses in many different areas of human knowledge.

Graduation day at Bar-Ilan University, Ramat-Gan.

The Israeli University System

The Israeli experience of college is quite different. Israeli young men generally serve in the army for about three years, and young women for two years, right after they are graduated from high school. By the time they enter college, most Israelis are twenty- or twenty-one-year-old army veterans. They must decide on a major course of study right away, as soon as college begins. Instead of sampling courses from many different departments, Israeli students take a full courseload in their major area: five courses in history, or five courses in science, or five courses in art. They do not have much choice about which courses they take, and they take few courses out of their own department. But when Israeli students are graduated from the university, they have a deep understanding of their own major field.

Which System Is Better?

The American system gives students a wide variety of many different subjects, but a rather skimpy emphasis on their major. The Israeli system gives students a very thorough knowledge of one major subject, but a limited acquaintance with the other university departments.

Which system do you think is best?

Ulpanim

Education is not just for children and teenagers. Many Israeli adults also attend educational courses of many kinds. The Ulpan program, which offers intensive courses in Hebrew language and Jewish culture, is one of the most popular.

Jews streamed into Israel from all over the world before and after the declaration of the independent Jewish homeland in 1948. How were all these people to learn one language—Hebrew?

To meet the language needs of these immigrants to Israel, the Ulpan program was created. The Ulpan has become an essential part of the immigrant's introduction

Students from many African countries come to Israel for both academic and technological training. A student from Ghana addresses his class on an aspect of electro-mechanics.

Synagogue on the Hebrew University campus, Jerusalem.

The Hebrew University advertises its summer courses for 1983.

to Israeli life. The new Israelis live at the Ulpan center, studying together thirty hours a week for about five months. The American dentist, the Russian physicist, the Iranian jeweler, and the Portuguese tailor—all are together in one Ulpan classroom. They learn the Hebrew words for grocery items, and together they pronounce such simple but important sentences as: *"Chalav* (milk), *lechem* (bread), *chemaa* (butter), *bevakasha* (please)." Together they struggle to read their first Hebrew newspaper and to understand the news report on the radio. Only Hebrew is spoken from the beginning of the Ulpan course, so the students are forced to learn the language of their new homeland.

There are over a hundred Ulpanim all over Israel. Some kibbutzim have a special Ulpan program at which new immigrants study for half a day and work a half a day at the kibbutz, in this way paying out the costs of their stay.

The Weizmann Institute of Science, founded in Rehovot in 1944, is one of Israel's foremost scientific institutions.

Today the Institute has numerous research departments which are occupied by hundreds of domestic and foreign research projects: lasers, computers, space, cancer, etc.

VOCABULARY AND CONCEPTS

Ulpan	אֻלְפָּן
University	אוּנִיבֶרְסִיטָה
Weizmann Institute	מָכוֹן וַייצְמַן
"For its own sake"	לִשְׁמָה
Good deed	מִצְוָה
Jewish day school or school for higher education	יְשִׁיבָה

YOUTH MOVEMENTS IN ISRAEL

In school, we sit at desks and listen to our teachers explain many different subjects—science, history, geography, art. We learn about plants and animals in colorful textbooks. On the blackboard, teachers write outlines that help us understand.

But the classroom is not our only place of learning. We can take class trips and discover things at first-hand. Instead of just reading about people and their cultures in a textbook, we can visit them, see how they dress, share their food, and join in their holiday celebrations. Instead of just reading about flowers in our science book, we can smell the fragrance of a rose garden and see the flowers' vibrant colors. In a real zoo we can pet and feed the animals we saw pictured in an encyclopedia. Much learning takes place outside of the classroom!

Youth Movement Activities for Fun and Learning

Israeli schoolchildren go to school each day, just like you. But after school and on holidays, they have another place of learning—their youth movements. Here they meet neighborhood children their own age, girls and boys. Together the children take hikes all over the Jewish homeland, seeing the vivid reality of many places they have learned about in history and geography and Bible classes at school. In school they studied about Masada—now they climb the rock fortress for themselves and imagine the plight of the trapped Jewish warriors who chose suicide rather than the disgrace of Roman slavery. They studied about the Hills of Gilboa, where King Saul fell on the battlefield—now they see the hills for themselves. They studied in science class all about the exotic flowers of the Negev desert—and now the children can see and touch and smell those very blooms.

A Zionist youth village in Israel. It was founded by Dr. Israel Goldstein.

The children celebrate Jewish holidays together too. On Purim everyone brings hamantashen, and on Chanukah everyone plays dreidel. Youth leaders explain the meanings of the holidays and customs.

At their youth groups, Israeli children make friends with children from their neighborhood whom they may not have met at school. In this way, the youth groups help Israeli children grow up with a wide circle of friends and neighbors.

Israeli Arab youths gather for an outing.

HaNoar HaOved Ve'HaLomed

The largest youth group in Israel is the Association of Working and Studying Youth (HaNoar HaOved Ve'HaLomed). Connected with Israel's huge labor union, the Histadrut, this youth group is sort of a junior labor union. Boys and girls who belong to HaNoar HaOved Ve'HaLomed can get job training and job placement through the group, in addition to hikes and trips.

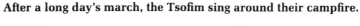
After a long day's march, the Tsofim sing around their campfire.

90

Tsofim

The Scouts (Tsofim) is the second-largest youth group in Israel. The Scouts take "no-frills" tours all over Israel, camping out and roughing it. The children learn all about Israel's terrain, plant life, and animal life.

Gadna

The Army of Israel organizes its own youth group for teenagers aged fourteen to eighteen, Gadna, which stands for Gedudei Ha'Noar Ha-Ivri "Hebrew Youth Corps." Gadna members learn how to handle guns and grenades as well as karate and jujitsu.

Bnai Akiva

The largest religious group is called Bnai Akiva. Bnai Akiva members often volunteer to help out on Israel's religious kibbutzim during their school holidays.

No matter what youth group the Israeli child belongs to, he or she is sure to tour the country on exciting and educational trips. After the schoolchild has grown older and is ready to enter the army, this knowledge of the land becomes useful. Now the soldier is familiar with Israel's terrain and can better defend the beloved homeland.

Both Jews and Arabs are members of the Tsofim.

VOCABULARY AND CONCEPTS

Masada (the last Jewish fortress during the first war with Romans)
מְצָדָה

Association of Working and Studying Youth
הַנֹּעַר הָעוֹבֵד וְהַלוֹמֵד

The Scouts   צוֹפִים

Religious Youth Movement   בְּנֵי־עֲקִיבָא

91

ARCHAEOLOGY IN ISRAEL

For two thousand years of exile, Jews learned the history of Israel by studying the Bible and books of Jewish history. Devout Jews read in the Book of Genesis about God's promise of the land of Canaan to the children of Abraham, Isaac, and Jacob. Medieval Jews, suffering under the oppression of Christians in European countries, read in the prophetic works about the glorious days of Jewish independence in ancient Israel. Jews in Poland, Peking, and Pittsburgh could read the Bible and rejoice in the ancient Israelites' conquest of Canaan. University students studied documents and history books about the days of foreign rule over Palestine.

But since the establishment of the modern state, Israelis have another way to study Israel's history—archaeology. The Bible and the history book are still invaluable guides to Israel's past. But there is also a new way to study the homeland's past—out of doors, wearing shorts, and shouting excitedly about a lucky find. The archaeologist's way to study history is to dig in Israel's earth for relics of the past.

ARCHEOLOGY AND HISTORY

Archaeology: A Guide to Israel's Past

The word "archaeology" is made up of two Greek words—*archaeo*, which means "ancient," and *logos*, which means "knowledge." Archaeologists delve in the earth for knowledge of the ancient past. They search for remains left by the ancient peoples who once inhabited Israel—bits of pottery called shards, scraps of letters, tattered shreds of Bibles and prayerbooks, and the decorated perfume-bottles and cosmetic cases of long-dead women. Like a detective, the archaeologist examines the silent evidence and tries hard to hear the story that each relic tells about the past.

Why Archaeology Is So Popular

Archaeologists find relics of the past in many countries. But only in Israel has archaeology become everyone's favorite hobby! University professors and government officials are always receiving letters from excited Israeli citizens who have found bits of pottery in their backyards. Whenever a dig is announced, hundreds of people show up at the site and volunteer their help. When a big find was made by archaeologists near Tel Aviv, the whole city declared a day of praying and celebration.

Perhaps archaeology is popular in Israel because Israelis can never ignore the fact of Israel's long, rich, and varied history—even if they would like to do so. Construction workers pouring concrete for the foundation of an apartment building in Jerusalem will suddenly hit the ruins of a centuries-old synagogue. All work on the new building must come to a standstill while the laborers gaze excitedly at their precious find. A schoolboy, idly toeing the ground near his Caesarea home, may find Roman coins, their faded inscriptions hailing Caesar. No wonder that Israelis are so conscious of their country's past.

The catacombs in Beth She'arim are decorated with reliefs, carvings, and inscriptions. This relief of the Ark of the Hebrew Law is found in one of the catacombs.

This stone seal belongs to the period of the Judean king Jeroboam. It was found at Megiddo. The line above the lion reads: "Shema." The line underneath reads: "Seal of Jeroboam."

Architectural fragment dated to the Hasmonean (Late Maccabean) Period. It was inscribed in the Aramaic language for the bones of King Uzziah of Judah (ca. 780–740), which were moved to a new resting place for some unknown reason. The inscription was found on the Mount of Olives.

Archaeology: Israel's Secret Weapon

Struggling to protect their homeland, the ancient Israelites battled many enemies: the Canaanites, Jebusites, Philistines, Amalekites, Greek-Syrians, and Assyrians, just to name a few. To win their many battles, the Israelites had to develop sound military strategies and a thorough understanding of Israel's land forms.

Modern Israelis are still battling to protect the Jewish homeland against many enemies: the Egyptians, Syrians, Jordanians, and Iraqis, just to name a few. The terrain of Israel to be defended is the same; only the names of the enemies have changed somewhat over the centuries. Because the land is the same, the strategies developed by the ancient Israelite generals are still useful to the modern Israel Defense Forces.

How Archaeology Helped Israel Win a War

In May 1948, when the State of Israel had just been declared, the Jews dreaded a Syrian attack from the north. But no one knew exactly how the Syrians would invade Israel. Then the Israeli general Yigal Yadin, an avid student of the Bible and of archaeology, had an idea. He knew the route that the ancient Syrians had used 2,300 years ago to attack Israel. Yadin reasoned that the modern Syrian general would see the same military possibilities on the map as had his ancient counterpart. General Yadin sent out Israeli troops to prepare for the Syrian attack. Yadin's guess of the Syrian's route turned out to be right, and the Syrian "surprise attack" failed, for it had been no surprise at all.

Later in 1948, Yadin used his knowledge of archaeology to rediscover a long-forgotten road that had been built by the Romans across the Negev desert. By using this ancient road, an Israeli striking force was able to outflank the Egyptian army and attack it from the rear.

Archaeology Adds to Israel's Wealth

Though the Bible mentions Israel's mineral resources, the modern settlers found no mines. An American

NELSON GLUECK (1900–1971)
Rabbi and archaeologist

As director of the American School of Oriental Research in Jerusalem in the 1930's and 1940's, Glueck carried out extensive archaeological work in Jordan and Israel. Concentrating on the Negev from 1952, he discovered and excavated many ancient sites, including King Solomon's copper mines at Wadi Arabah and King Solomon's port city of Ezion-Gever near present-day Eilat. From 1947 to his death, Rabbi Nelson Glueck also served as president of Hebrew Union College.

rabbi and archaeologist, Dr. Nelson Glueck, kept searching for copper deposits in Israel. "If the Book of Deuteronomy describes Israel's copper mines, then the remains of those mines must still be around—somewhere!" he said to himself. Finally, Dr. Glueck found copper deposits at Timna—and the remains of these mines were dated back to the days of King Solomon himself!

Today, copper from Timna's mines is a great source of wealth for Israel.

Archaeology and the Negev Settlements

Israelis once sent a sample of Negev soil to Washington for scientific advice. "Substandard," replied the American agricultural experts. "Don't try to grow anything there!" But today, the Israeli Negev blooms with fruits, flowers, vegetable gardens, and the proud, happy, shining faces of new settlers and their children. Archaeology helped make all this possible.

Archaeologists discovered the remains of farms in the desert that had belonged to an ancient people, the Nabateans. The Nabateans had succeeded in growing rich crops in the Negev, in the same soil that the American experts had declared hopeless!

The tell of biblical Lachish. This tell is being actively excavated.

Slowly, the Israeli scientists studied the remains of the ancient farms and learned about the complex system of water irrigation and terracing developed by the Nabateans. Modern agricultural experts learned many lessons from the ancient Nabatean techniques. Today's Negev is watered by special cisterns and pipelines that were created partly because of the wisdom gained by archaeologists who studied Nabatean farms.

Archaeology and Jewish History

Some modern scholars are skeptical about our Bible. "Nice stories," they say, "but did any of this really happen?" Archaeology has proved the Bible's accuracy in many, many instances.

We read in the Bible of how Joshua conquered Hazor, a Canaanite city, and of how King Solomon rebuilt it three hundred years later. Modern archaeologists found the remains of a destroyed Canaanite city and of a rebuilt Israelite city at exactly the place given in the Bible, and dating back to exactly the right period of history. At Megiddo, archaeologists have found the immense stables for the horses of King Solomon's chariot forces, just as the Bible described them. And archaeologists in Jerusalem found relics which confirm the Bible's description of the Holy Temple.

Archaeology also fills in many gaps in our knowledge of Jewish history. The recently discovered Dead Sea Scrolls teach us a great deal about the life of the Jewish community around the time of Jesus. The letters of Bar Kochba, found in a cave at Ein Gedi, teach valuable details about this great Jewish warrior. This general so inspired his brave warriors that they chose to die by their own swords rather than bear the disgrace of Roman slavery.

Archaeology is important to Israelis for so many reasons! It is a special help to the army general. It boosts Israel's economy when it leads to the discovery of important resources, and it has helped in the development of the Negev. Archaeology has been a valuable way of

THE SILOAM TUNNEL AND INSCRIPTION

In order to bring water within reach of the inhabitants of Jerusalem in time of siege, King Hezekiah of Judah cut a horizontal water tunnel in the bedrock from the spring of Gihon to the valley west of the Ophel Hill. The water flowed through the tunnel (below) and passed into a stone-covered cistern and reservoir.

Archaeologists have found the major portion of an inscription describing the moment when the tunnel was completed. It was cut into the wall inside the entrance: Height of tunnel about 6 feet and over.

"... and while there were still three cubits to be cut through, [there was heard] the voice of a man calling to his fellow, for there was an overlap [?] in the rock on the right [and on the left]. And when the tunnel was driven through, the quarrymen hewed [the rock], each man toward his fellow, axe against axe, and the water flowed from the spring toward the reservoir for 1,200 cubits, and the height of the rock above the heads of the quarrymen was 100 cubits."

Some of the famous Dead Sea Scrolls were found in these ancient jars in caves at Qumran. The scrolls may have been written by a sect of Essenes living under Roman rule.

enhancing the study of Jewish history and of confirming the truth of the Bible.

No wonder that everyone in Israel is so excited about archaeology!

Israelis and the Bible

To children from New York, Paris, or London, Bible study always seems a bit removed from daily life. The religious holidays, religious truths, and Jewish history of the Bible are all important parts of their lives. But the Bible is in Hebrew, and American, French, or English children must learn a new language in order to understand the original Hebrew text. And they live in cities that have little to do with the people and places named in the Bible—Isaac, Isaiah, Nehemiah, Sinai, Jaffa, and the Hills of Gilboa.

The Bible Comes Alive for Israelis

Israeli children have an entirely different feeling about the Bible. They cannot help but feel the closeness of the

The archaeologist Jean Perrot at an excavation site near Beersheva.

Fragments from the Nash papyrus, one of the oldest known Hebrew manuscripts, containing the Decalogue and the Shema. It was discovered in Egypt and dates from the late Maccabean period.

Bible to daily life. The Book of Samuel teaches about King David, the poet-king who made Jerusalem the capital of ancient Israel; the Israeli child is immediately reminded of modern-day Jerusalem, capital of the nation and home of the Knesset, Israel's Parliament. Many Israeli children have toured the Knesset on class trips, and have visited older brothers or sisters in their dormitory rooms at the Hebrew University. When Israeli children learn about the destruction of the Temple in the prophetic books of the Bible, they remember the Western Wall, the few remaining stones of the ancient Temple. When Israeli children study Genesis and learn about the journey of Abraham and Sarah to Beersheva, they may recall a camel ride taken there last summer, while on a visit to cousins in that bustling city called the capital of the Negev.

The Language of the Bible

The Hebrew of the Bible, the language in which God gave Israel the Ten Commandments and in which the prophets spoke their words of burning poetry, is very close to the Hebrew that Israeli children use to learn the multiplication tables and to order a falafel on the streetcorner. If Israeli schoolchildren could go back in time to the biblical period, they could understand Moses!

Thus Israeli children grow up with a special feeling of the Bible's closeness to their daily lives. The places described in the Bible are places where many modern Israelis live, work, and study, and the Hebrew language of the Bible is the language of the modern state.

VOCABULARY AND CONCEPTS

Archaeology	אַרְכֵיאוֹלוֹגְיָה
Holy Temple	בֵּית הַמִּקְדָּשׁ
Dead Sea Scrolls	מְגִילוֹת יָם הַמֶּלַח

HOW ISRAEL LIVES

To function properly, a nation must take care of the basic, everyday needs of its citizens. People and goods must be able to move quickly from place to place. Citizens must be able to use their nation's money. And everyone must be able to find a suitable home and work.

Israel needs good transportation and a strong economy. The cities and farms of Israel must remain strong and healthy in order for the nation's citizens to find good homes.

TRANSPORTATION IN ISRAEL

Without good transportation, Israel could not have become the strong and healthy nation she is today. Good transportation is vital to Israel's economic and military well-being.

Israel's raw materials—minerals, wood, chemicals, and so on—must be shipped quickly and cheaply to where they are needed, so that buildings can go up and industry can flourish. Fruits, vegetables, dairy products, and other foods must be moved to the markets and ports with all possible speed, so that nothing spoils. University students, many of whom hold part-time jobs, need good transportation to move quickly to and from work and school.

During wartime, Israeli soldiers must be able to get to the battlefront. Supplies and ammunition must be transported to the fighters who need them. Israel's Defense Force uses the country's buses, cars, and trucks to help in the defense effort. Israel's transport planes and ships bring war materials from other countries, to help Israel protect herself from her enemies.

Good transportation to and from Israel may even help bring peace. The great speed of modern planes has made all the people of the world neighbors. People of all nations can visit Israel. Tourists and native Israelis can meet each other face to face and get to know each other's customs, ideas, and ideals. They can learn from each other, and the hatreds born of ignorance can vanish in the light of mutual understanding. Perhaps people can learn to live together in the world with greater peace and harmony.

The first bus (1920's) serving the Haifa–Beirut route.

Inside Israel there are four major forms of transportation: the bus, the railroad train, the truck, and the car (including taxis). Traveling to and from Israel can be done by sea or by air.

Buses

Most people in Israel get to and from work or school by bus. So if you ride a bus in a major Israeli city on a typical day, you are sure to see many different types of Israelis. Imagine a dusty Tel Aviv afternoon in early summer. You have just climbed onto a crowded, swerving bus. In front of you sits a bearded Chasid, reading intently from a yellowed book of religious commentaries written hundreds of years ago. From time to time, he strokes his beard as he concentrates. He doesn't seem to hear the lively laughter of the university students, who are talking with gusto about their professors, friends, vacation plans, and music collections. A young mother sits contentedly, clutching her infant son and several big grocery bags filled with fresh fruits and vegetables. Sturdy, tanned little sabras swing their green bookbags and chatter in rapid-fire Hebrew, while an elegantly dressed business-woman tries to ignore them and read her newspaper. In front of the bus, the driver keeps a portable radio blaring so that he can hear the news.

Egged

The largest bus company in Israel is called Egged. Egged bus drivers are more than just employees. They are part-owners in the company's stock. Partly for this reason, Israeli bus drivers have earned a reputation for being rather strong-willed and impatient when dealing with their passengers. Frequently, a bus will pull out just as an unfortunate Israeli has reached the station, leaving the man or woman to shout after the driver in frantic Hebrew: *Re-gah! Re-gah!* ("Just a minute! Just a minute!").

Buses in Israel move people from place to place not only within the individual cities. Buses also move people

A traffic jam somewhere in Israel.

A diesel train in Haifa.

A truck-assembly plant in Israel.

from one part of Israel to another. Each major Israeli city has a central bus station, called the *Tachanah Merkazit*. There, people check time schedules and buy tickets for buses that go almost all over Israel. Each ticket costs a different amount of money, depending on the length of the trip.

No Transportation on Shabbat

On Friday afternoon, schools, offices, and stores close up early, so that everyone can have time to prepare for Shabbat. The Egged buses are particularly crowded on this afternoon, and the bus driver's temper may be particularly short! Everyone wants to get on the bus, finish the errands, and do the shopping, so that they can be ready at the proper time to welcome the Shabbat.

Since Jewish religious law forbids travel by car on the Shabbat, most Egged bus lines in Israel do not operate on Shabbat.

The Railroad

Another very important form of transportation in Israel, the railroad, is owned and operated by the government. This railroad line connects the three major cities in Israel—Tel Aviv, Haifa, and Jerusalem—and gradually is being extended down to the Negev.

One of the thrilling sights to visitors is that of a great diesel engine bearing the emblem of Israel winding speedily through the countryside, pulling behind it a long string of freight and passenger cars. These modern "ships of the desert" play a very important part in Israel's continued growth.

Trucks

Israel has a thriving truck transportation system. Huge trucks speed over the highways, hauling cement and sand, and loads of copper from King Solomon's mines. Refrigerator trucks rush crisp, fresh vegetables and fruits to markets for domestic sale and to airports and seaports for export. Tanker trucks filled with oil and chemicals ride the roadways night and day.

Small "tricycle trucks" can also be seen on the roads of Israel. These are small wheeled trucks mounted behind cycles. The tricycle trucks can carry surprisingly large loads and are very convenient for traveling the narrow streets in the ancient quarters of the cities.

The Sherut

The *Sherut* ("service" in Hebrew) is a public transportation service with a spirit all its own. The *sherut* is a shared taxi that moves along a fixed route; for instance, one popular *sherut* route is from Tel Aviv to Jerusalem. Each seat costs a little more than a seat in a bus. At the special *sherut* stop, the driver waits until enough people going to the same destination have gathered. These five or six strangers all get into the same *sherut*. Usually, by the end of the ride, everyone has introduced himself, and some may even have told their life stories, if the trip has been long enough. A proud grandma may have passed around photographs of her kibbutz grandchildren, some matchmaking may have been begun for the handsome, single law student in the front seat, and a heated political debate may have been sparked between two excitable businessmen in the back. A tourist traveling by *sherut* may get invited for the coming Shabbat to the homes of all the other passengers.

Other Vehicles

Private taxis are also available in Israel, and you can hire one to take you alone to your destination. But the *sherut* is a special part of the Israeli experience.

There are also many private cars, motor scooters, and bicycles on the crowded Israeli streets. Stand on a corner in any major city in Israel, and you can watch the cars of the world roll by. Fords and "Chevies" from the United States, Datsuns from Japan, Italian Fiats—Israel's roads know them all.

An automobile factory in Israel.

Israel has a long seafaring tradition going all the way back to biblical times. This is an ancient Israeli galley on a commemorative stamp issued by the Israeli Post Office.

The Merchant Marine

The Israeli merchant marine, with over 150 ocean-going ships, helps the country grow and prosper. Special refrigerator ships carry perishable Israeli food exports to faraway places. Fishing boats haul in catches of delicious seafood for the dining tables of the nation. Cargo ships import and export merchandise to and from Israel, a free flow of trade that helps the nation's economy flourish. Tankers bring oil, and passenger liners carry tourists to and from the great seaports of the world.

Israel's Main Ports

The ships of Zim, Israel's national shipping line, set sail from three major ports—Haifa, Ashdod, and Eilat—and from the small port of Yaffo. Haifa, Israel's largest port, handles over 80 percent of the nation's exports and imports. In 1965, the Israelis opened a second port at Ashdod. Located about twenty miles from Tel Aviv, the Ashdod port specializes in the export of citrus fruits, especially Israel's world-famous Jaffa orange. A lot of these are also shipped from the port at Yaffo. (By the way, *Yaffo* and *Jaffa* may look like different words but they are really different English spellings of the same Hebrew name. *Yaffo* represents the modern Sephardic pronunciation used in Israel.

The third major port, Eilat, is in the southern part of Israel on the Gulf of Aqaba. Eilat, now a modern, bustling place, is a seaport with an ancient history. From Eilat once sailed the ships of King Solomon himself, for this was the monarch's major sea outlet to Africa. Here, too, the marvelous royal barge of the Queen of Sheba once rode at anchor. It was in Eilat that the beautiful queen landed when she paid her visit to King Solomon's court.

Airplanes

El Al, meaning "up toward the sky" in Hebrew, is Israel's national airline. The airline began in 1948 with a

The Zim building in Tel Aviv.

104

few surplus World War II airplanes, manned by volunteers. Today, the airline has a staff of 2,800 and flies to four continents, serving all the major capitals and countries of the world. The company's headquarters are at the largest airport in Israel, the Ben-Gurion Airport, located ten miles from Tel Aviv.

Because El Al is the national airline of the Jewish state, all food served on El Al planes is kosher.

El Al also has a fleet of cargo planes. These flying trucks deliver perishable goods such as fruits, vegetables, and flowers to the four corners of the earth. Specially packed roses, picked early in the week on an Israeli kibbutz, can be flown by El Al planes in time to decorate the Shabbat table of an American home. You can enjoy a juicy Jaffa orange since El Al planes efficiently carry the fruits across the seas.

VOCABULARY AND CONCEPTS

Central bus station	תַּחֲנָה מֶרְכָּזִית
Railroad	רַכֶּבֶת יִשְׂרָאֵל
Sherut (taxi service on a fixed route)	שֵׁרוּת
Taxi	מוֹנִית
Zim (Israeli merchant marine)	צִי"ם
ElAl (Israel's national airline)	אֶל־עַל

El Al is the national airline of the State of Israel.

105

THE ISRAELI ECONOMY

A country's "economy" is the state of its wallet. Just like an individual person's wallet, a country's economy must have the money to cover all the country's needs, or else the economy will become troubled and shaky and finally collapse.

If a country is making money—if its farmlands are producing and selling successful crops, its businessmen are buying and selling goods, its factories are producing, and its natural resources have an international market—that country's economy will thrive. The country's currency will have a stable value. But if a country's earnings are few, and its small income is drained by many expenses, then the country's economy is under great stress.

Israel began as a Zionist settlement beset by incredible difficulties and funded by Jewish charities. Today, despite the many problems, the country is self-supporting. Its economy has grown rapidly in the areas of agriculture, industry, and tourism.

Agriculture

The first settlers came mostly from cities in Europe and knew little about farming. The land they found was swampy and malaria-infested, badly in need of drainage, or rocky, barren wasteland, or arid desert sand dunes. The settlers had to learn about agriculture fast, if they wanted to survive in Palestine.

The settlers put their Jewish resourcefulness and intelligence to work and became farmland experts. They

A Palestine newspaper ad (1890) advertises agricultural machinery for sale.

Out-of-season vegetables, fruits, and flowers are often grown under plastic covers. This method reduces water needs and speeds ripening.

Picking oranges.

became such masters of farming that today 90 percent of Israel's food is locally produced. Israel also produces crops of high-quality fruits and vegetables that are sold to European and American markets. Oranges, grapefruits, melons, avocadoes, lettuce, wine from Israel-grown grapes, and delicate, carefully packed fresh flowers are valuable Israeli exports. The success of Israel's agriculture helps strengthen Israel's economy.

Baron Rothschild helped found the wine-making industry in Israel. Through his generosity, the wine-growing settlements of Rishon-le-Zion and Zichron Yaakov were created. The world-famous wines produced in these two settlements have won many prizes.

Industry

Industry also helps strengthen Israel's economy. Skilled diamond cutters in Tel Aviv carve and polish tiny, gleaming facets into jewels; the finished stones are then internationally exported. Minerals used in industries the world over, like phosphate and potash, are exported from the Dead Sea. Cotton gins and weaving mills keep up

A wine cellar in Rishon-le-Zion.

Loading citrus fruits for export.

107

Cotton growing and picking have been mechanized. Israel's yields per acre are among the world's highest.

with Israel's cotton crop; in the next step of the garment-industry process, designers style raincoats, knitwear, and bathing suits that Israel exports. Israeli businessmen use their talent and expertise to keep their ventures going, from the boutique on a Jerusalem side street, to a cafe on Dizengoff Street in Tel Aviv, to a huge ironworks factory, in Haifa. Israelis also design and manufacture airplanes, and all sorts of planes are brought to the country for expert repairs.

Tourism

Tourism is another vital source of income for Israel. Throughout the centuries, travelers from every part of the globe have come to visit the holy places sacred to Jews, Christians, and Moslems. Archaeologists and scholars are fascinated by the historical sites that are everywhere in the Jewish homeland. Botanists travel to examine the land's unique forms of plant life. Many Jews who make their homes in different parts of the world come to Israel during the holiday seasons—Rosh

Assembling electrical components at an Israeli factory.

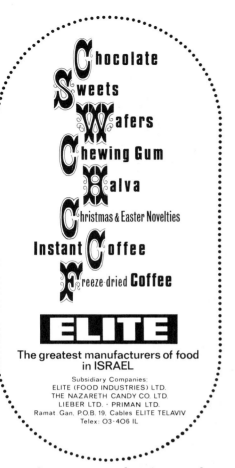

A newspaper advertisement from the Elite Company. The Elite Company exports its food products all over the world.

Communications and ·electronic equipment produced by Tadiran Industries.

Hashana, Yom Kippur, Sukkot, Pesach—to worship in the land of Zion. And pleasure-seeking vacationers enjoy the balmy climate of Israel's year-round seaside resorts, where scuba diving, sunbathing, and disco-dancing are lively ways to have fun. New hotels—inexpensive rooming houses as well as posh, deluxe establishments—are constantly being built.

"Tozeret Haaretz"

All products of Israel—from Jaffa oranges to jewelry, from Carmel wines to knitwear and electronics parts—are labeled with the proud stamp "Tozeret Haaretz"—"produce of the land."

The names of Israel's industries hint at the mix of past and present in the Jewish land. The Shemen factories produce soap, perfumes, and bath products. The Hebrew word *shemen* is used in the Bible to describe fine oil. The large Israeli glass factories are called Phoenicia after this ancient Palestinian glass-manufacturing region. And Shimson is the name of one of the cement factories because it refers to the strength of its product equaling the strength and endurance of the legendary biblical hero Samson.

Many Israeli products are exported in such quantity that Israeli manufacturers have offices in the United States. The Carmel Wine Company, Israel Aircraft International, Scientific Data Systems of Israel, Tadiran Israel Electronics, Intercontinental Auto Parts, Beged-Or (leather goods), Gottex of Israel (swimwear), Solel Boneh (construction), and Negev Ceramics are just a few such Israeli-based firms.

It is very important that the raw materials found in Israel be made available for industrial use and that the quality of Israeli manufactured goods remain high. The more manufactured products Israel makes and sells on the international market, the better chance the Jewish state has for maintaining a strong, healthy economy.

Israel's Modern Economy

In the last decade Israel has made great economic strides. The gross national produce, which ten years ago was 25-billion, is now approaching 70-billion. Israel's factories are producing high tech products, such as electronics, software, complex chemicals, pharmaceuticals and scientific instruments for international global countries.

Israel has also forged commercial and diplomatic ties with eastern Europe, former Soviet States, China and India. With these new markets, Israeli exports have risen 50% from 1992 to 1995.

More than 500-thousand Russian Jews have bostered domestic demand and provided a pool of skilled and educated workers for its high tech industries

Israel Currency—Past and Present

The shekel was the unit of currency in ancient times, first mentioned when Abraham paid 400 shekels for the Cave of Machpelah. The shekel unit of currency remained as the official coin during all periods of Jewish statehood in the land of Israel.

Israel's modern economy needs scientific research to sustain itself and to grow. This nuclear reactor near Nebi Reshon is dedicated to research.

Coins of one, five, ten, and twenty-five agorot. There are one hundred agorot to the shekel.

Emblem of the Israeli postal service.

Among the important archaeological finds in Israel are many coins, representing a priceless inheritance from the Jewish past. Archaeologists have found bronze and silver coins with ancient Hebrew inscriptions. The silver shekels and half-shekels are decorated with pomegranates and bear the words "Jerusalem the Holy." Archaeologists have also unearthed many coins minted during the second revolt against the Romans. The inscription on these coin reads, "Second Year of the Freedom of Israel." On these coins we see four pillars representing the Temple in Jerusalem. The symbols engraved on the coins also include the Lulav and the Etrog.

In modern Israel many of the ancient motifs and symbols have been minted on the current coins. The Knesset passed a law providing that the unit of Israeli currency would no longer be called the lira, but would be renamed the shekel.

Israel has also produced commemorative coins and medals marking important events in Jewish history, Jewish rituals, and contemporary life in the Jewish state. Among them are the liberation medal, the Massada medal, the Theodore Herzl coin, various Chanukah coins, the Ghetto Uprising medal, the Pidyon Haben coin, the Bar Mitzvah medal, the Bat Mitzvah medal, the wedding medal, the Shema Yisrael medal, and many more.

Inflation

Inflation rates in Israel zoom up and up, and the value of Israel's money sinks down further and further. In 1975, the Israeli pound, or lira, was equal to about 16¢. In 1982, it was worth less than a penny. The government had to introduce a new coin, the shekel, worth about 6¢ each.

As the American dollar fluctuates, and the Israeli economy changes from day to day too, the worth of the Israeli *shekel* is bound to change. Find out from your local bank how much Israeli money is worth today, in comparison with American money.

VOCABULARY AND CONCEPTS

Agora, Agorot   אֲגוֹרָה — אֲגוֹרוֹת

"Produce of the land"   תּוֹצֶרֶת הָאָרֶץ

Shekel(s) (Israeli unit of currency)

שֶׁקֶל — שְׁקָלִים

HOW ISRAELIS LIVE—CITY AND COUNTRY

The majority of Israeli's live in cities or suburban areas, and most of this density will be found along the coastline— from Haifa in the north to Ashkelon in the south—and around Jerusalem. Tel Aviv and its suburbs alone are home for about half a million people. These city dwellers are a sophisticated lot whose lives are similar to those of Parisians, Londoners, and New Yorkers. The style of life in Israel's cities would probably seem quite familiar to most of us, despite the fact that the language and culture are different.

While most Israelis live in or near the country's big cities, foreigners tend to think of the kibbutz as most distinctively Israeli. The kibbutz is a collective farming and industrial village. To understand the kibbutz, we must think for a moment about families.

THE KIBBUTZ: ALL ABOUT SHARING

Time out for music and fun on the lawn of a kibbutz.

Every family, if it is successful, learns how to share. Father, mother, sisters, brothers, and grandparents share their time, earnings, talents, and love with one another. Everyone shares, and the family as a whole benefits. Members of a family take turns washing dishes, buying groceries, and bathing the dog. Together the family decides about major purchases and vacation plans. One person in the family may make more money, another may be better at fixing things, a third may be the most efficient shopper, but each member does his or her part, and all share equally in the family's ability to provide necessities and luxuries.

How Kibbutz Members Help Each Other

A kibbutz (the word comes from a Hebrew root meaning "to group together") operates on the same basic principle. Kibbutzim are like large communal families. All the members own the kibbutz together and work together to help each other. The land of the kibbutz is leased from the Jewish National Fund. No one is richer or poorer than anyone else. The members as a group make decisions for the kibbutz. As individuals they do the work of the kibbutz—raising and selling crops, tending livestock, running the kibbutz factory or supermarket, building homes, cooking or caring for the children. All the members do their best, according to their individual talents and abilities.

When the farm manager and the field hand leave work, they find themselves eating the same sort of food in the communal dining hall, together with their families. All have an equal choice from the communal clothing and furniture stores, and have the same music, sports, and movie facilities at their disposal.

How Kibbutz Members Are Paid

The members of the kibbutz "family" are not paid money for their labors; whatever the kibbutz earns is combined into one account, and this sum is used to satisfy the needs of everyone on the kibbutz. In return for their work, kibbutzniks receive all kinds of services: a furnished apartment, meals in the kibbutz dining hall, clothes, complete medical and dental care.

If there is one privileged group in the kibbutz family, it would be the children. Many kibbutz communities are focused around the upbringing of sons and daughters. Most kibbutz money is spent on fine schools for their young people.

Kibbutz mothers need not stay home to watch their babies,

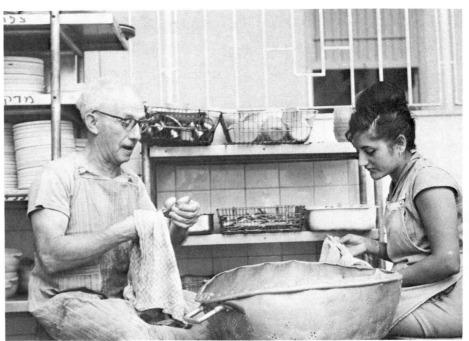

Men and women, young and old, share the kibbutz duties.

for the kibbutz children are lovingly and carefully tended by specially trained teachers. Children may even sleep in a separate children's dormitory.

Different kibbutzim, of course, provide different services. Some traditional kibbutzim have built their own synagogues and serve strictly kosher food; children are provided with formal religious instruction and receive Bar Mitzvah, Bat Mitzvah, and Orthodox wedding ceremonies from the kibbutz. Members of prosperous kibbutzim may receive choice theater and concert tickets, university tuition, spacious living quarters, wedding and honeymoon arrangements, air-conditioners, and excellent library facilities.

How Kibbutz Members Choose Their Leaders

All kibbutzniks elect their leaders once a year. These leaders, who still do their full share of work, become responsible for assigning jobs to other members. Some jobs are assigned on a more or less permanent basis; the kibbutznik who is a topnotch dentist, an accurate typist, or a beloved kindergarten teacher will probably be assigned to work at his or her specialty much of the time. But most jobs are shared equally. Everyone takes turns at nearly everything, since jobs are rotated by the week. Men and women alike pick oranges, drive tractors, feed chickens, scrub pots, mend socks, and sing songs with preschool children.

Once a week, all the kibbutzniks get together for a general meeting. All problems can be aired here, and everyone votes to resolve all difficulties. Dani may raise the possibility of the kibbutz investing in a new device that will make milking the cows much more efficient; the

After a hard day's work in the fields and factories, these kibbutz members relax by catching up on their reading.

115

proposal may be discussed at length but voted down as too expensive. The third-grade teacher, Gila, may describe her crowded classroom and ask for an assistant. Ari, in charge of the kitchen, may complain that those assigned to wash the breakfast dishes have not been arriving on time. And on and on, until everyone's grievance has been expressed.

The Advantages of Kibbutz Life

Life on a kibbutz can be happy and secure. Kibbutz-niks can relax after a day of work and enjoy a good book, listen to some music, or have fun with their families. Kibbutz members do not have to worry about ironing their shirts, cooking dinner, paying the telephone bill, or making the next mortgage payment. They need not concern themselves with vacation costs, the price of their children's new winter coats, or how to pay for expensive orthodonture or violin lessons. They do not have to fear that there will be no one to take care of their families if they get sick or when they are too old to work. The kibbutz provides for all the needs of the members of its large "family."

Since everyone shares equally in the kibbutz's ability to provide clothes and furniture, kibbutzniks usually feel less rivalry about these material possessions than other people. Nobody on the kibbutz has any more luxuries than anyone else, so there are no flashy outfits or appliances to envy.

A kibbutz dining room.

Another advantage of kibbutz life is the sense that each person truly has an important voice in the government of the community. All members can express themselves freely at the weekly assembly, run for office, and involve themselves actively in the discussions about community problems.

The Disadvantages of Kibbutz Life

But kibbutz life does have its disadvantages. What are they? Why do so few Israelis choose to live on kibbutzim?

The kibbutznik must accept a very basic but very difficult principle: the kibbutz as a whole comes before the kibbutznik as an individual. Kibbutz members must be satisfied, for instance, to receive from the kibbutz just the same as their neighbors receive, even if their neighbors are obviously far less talented and less competent at their work. Kibbutz members must be satisfied to do their assigned task of feeding chickens or typing letters, even if they feel themselves far better suited to the job of office manager or carpenter. They must learn to like the kibbutz food, which may be excellent but nevertheless cannot suit everyone's taste just so. They must realize that everyone in the kibbutz will know about every purchase they or their family make. They must know that even if they disagree with the opinions of the other members, the majority rules. Finally, they must remember that if they ever decide to leave the kibbutz, they will receive only a limited amount of money with which to start a new life.

Feeding the chickens.

The courtyard of Kibbutz Tel Chai in the Huleh Valley. Notice the surrounding walls and the watchtower. The defense of this outpost in 1920, during which Joseph Trumpeldor and seven of his comrades fell, led to the inclusion of this region in the territory of the British Mandate over Palestine.

The Kibbutz in Israeli History—Degania

The first kibbutz, Degania, was established near the Sea of Galilee in 1909, and kibbutzim have been growing up through the country ever since. In those early and difficult days, the commune was the ideal settlement plan for the isolated Jewish communities—which were struggling to survive in an alien and hostile environment. The kibbutz also expressed the political and social feelings of a pioneering generation which had fled the oppressions of Tsarist Russia.

The Jewish National Fund bought some swampy land from the Arab landowners in the Jordan Valley, and twenty kibbutz members formed Degania. They would work all day and discuss matters until late at night—how to divide up income, how to handle work. As time passed, the young men and women of Degania fell in love, married, and had children. Then they argued about how the kibbutz would bring up their children. More members

The early kibbutzim were protected against Arab marauders by the Shomrim. These brave fighters were really the first members of the modern Israeli army.

Degania Alef. The Sea of Galilee is to the left.

Kibbutz Degania-B in the Jordan Valley.

joined Degania, and the small, exciting little experiment grew bigger and bigger. From the intimate farm society of twenty members, the collective village grew over the years until today there are communities of between six hundred and fifteen hundred.

Today, the kibbutzim are drifting more and more toward light industry, and even tourism. These fields allow older kibbutzniks, no longer able to do strenuous farm work, to do their share for the kibbutz.

Would You Like to Live on a Kibbutz?

Often people "try out" kibbutz life for a brief period of time. They want to see if sharing with a large "family" is acceptable for them personally. The kibbutz members benefit from having guests, who bring new talents and personalities to the "family circle" and who help with the necessary work. The guests benefit from the chance to experience the unique kibbutz lifestyle and to decide for themselves if they wish to become permanent members.

Kibbutz Movements

There are many kibbutzim in Israel. Each has its own name, its own history, its own philosophy and goals. But some kibbutzim find that they have a great deal in common with other, similar groups. Such kibbutzim find that it is helpful to tackle similar problems together and to work as one toward resolving them. As a result, they have formed loosely organized kibbutz movements.

One such kibbutz movement is HaKibbutz HaDati, "The Religious Kibbutz," founded in 1934. Another movement, Kibbutz Artzi Shel HaShomer HaTzair, "The National Kibbutz of the Young Guard," includes kibbutzim that are associated with HaShomer HaTzair, a political party which practices a blend of practical Zionism and Marxist Socialism. Other kibbutz movements are HaKibbutz HaMeuchad, "The United Kibbutz," founded in 1927, and Ichud HaKvutzot ViHaKibbutzim. All of the kibbutzim together are represented to the government by the Union of Kibbutz Movements.

119

Just as the members of an individual kibbutz work together to achieve common goals, so the kibbutzim that belong to the same kibbutz movement work as one to resolve common problems and to realize shared aims.

While the kibbutzim have only 4 percent of Israel's population, they provide 12.1 percent of the Gross National Product, with 28 percent of all Israel's farm production and 5.8 percent of the country's industrial output.

Think over the advantages and disadvantages of kibbutz life. Can you add any? Who do you think would be happiest on a kibbutz? Who do you think should not become a member? Would you like to live on a kibbutz?

Kibbutz Maagan Michael manufactures plastic parts.

Kibbutz Ma'ale Hahamisha in the Judean Hills.

VOCABULARY AND CONCEPTS

Kibbutz (collective industrial and farming village)	קִבּוּץ
The Religious Kibbutz	קִבּוּץ דָּתִי
The United Kibbutz	קִבּוּץ הַמְיוּחָד
Degania	דְּגַנְיָה

120

THE MOSHAV

Many Israelis are inspired by the kibbutz idea but do not feel completely comfortable with a communal lifestyle. They believe that parents and children should live together in one home, and they prefer to make their main decisions as a family unit rather than as a community. Yet these Israelis know that a cooperative effort with their neighbors will make their farms more efficient and more productive.

The Moshav Combines Elements of Two Lifestyles

For these Israelis, the moshav is the answer. Moshavniks believe that their way of life combines the best of both worlds—the privately owned farm and the kibbutz. The moshav is a mixture of collective farming and private living. The first moshav, Nahalal, was established in 1921 at the foot of the Galilean mountains.

Moshavniks are fiercely protective of their private and family rights. Each moshav family owns its own home, where the parents and children live together and where the family cooks and eats. Each family owns its own plot of farmland and manages its own budget, making its own choices about what to buy and where. In these ways, a moshav family lives just like a family on a privately owned farm.

Today, Petach Tikvah is a densely settled city, with many large industries, including metals, rubber tires, textiles, and food.

Moshavniks Work Together Too

But like the members of a kibbutz, moshavniks work together as a group. Farmland is communally farmed and small industries are owned by the community. Moshavniks decide together when it comes to major purchases that affect all the farms on one settlement. David may need a tractor, Gideon may wish to invest in a machine that will milk the cows, and Tovah may have heard of a new crop which has been grown successfully in a neighboring village. One farmer alone could not afford the new machinery or the new materials—but together, if everyone pools their money, the group makes purchases that will benefit the entire moshav.

Together, all the farmers buy their seed and fodder. Often they get a better price from dealers because their purchases are made in such large quantities. The moshavniks also sell their products as a team, working together to produce the best crops at the best possible prices. Some moshavs can and pack their own fruits and vegetables in factories, and sort and box their own eggs.

Since the Six-Day War, many new moshavim have developed in areas that were empty and desolate while under Arab control. Gilgal and Argaman are two such settlements that have flourished on the West Bank since Israelis reclaimed the area in 1967.

Air view of moshav Nahalal.

VOCABULARY AND CONCEPTS

Farmer	אִכָּר
Pioneers	חַלוּצִים
Moshav (synthesis of collective farming and private living)	מוֹשָׁב

122

CULTURE IN ISRAEL

Israel spends a great deal to develop its defense, agriculture, and industry, but Israelis are not only fighters, farmers, and factory workers. Many Israelis are novelists, poets, jazz guitarists, classical violinists, Shakespearean actors, sculptors, and chemists. Israel is a land of pioneers—not just in the army and the border settlements, but in the area of culture—literature, art, music, and science.

חַיִּים נַחְמָן בִּיאָלִיק

CHAIM NACHMAN BIALIK
(1873–1934)
The greatest Hebrew poet of
modern times

Chaim Nachman Bialik was born in the village of Radi, near Zhitomir, into a very poor home. When he was six, his family moved to Zhitomir, where his father ran a saloon on the outskirts of town.

Bialik was seven when his father died. He was sent to live with his paternal grandfather. The stern, pious old man made sure his grandson received a traditional religious education in Bible and Talmud.

But the young man had many interests, such as Zionism and modern literature. He began to read the inspiring Zionist essays of Ahad Ha'Am, and to write poetry in the Hebrew language. Bialik's first poem was about his longing for *Shivat Zion*, the Return to Israel. Bialik supported himself as a businessman, teacher, and publisher, always continuing to write the great Hebrew poetry for whch he has become world-famous.

In 1903, in the Russian city of Kishinev, Christians killed innocent Jews in a savage pogrom. Bialik's poem *Al Ha'Shecheta*— "On the Slaughter"—cried out at the brutal, unjust act of violence.

In Israel today, Bialik is considered the national poet, just as Shakespeare is in English-speaking countries.

LITERATURE AND NEWSPAPERS

Books have always been one of the most vital forms of communication. Without books it would be very difficult to teach and share knowledge.

We Jews are known as *Am Ha-Sefer*, "the people of the book." This name refers to our love of learning and to our reverence for the greatest book ever written, the Torah.

In biblical days people wrote books on parchment, using an ink made from vegetables, or painstakingly scratched their information on clay tablets. Today in Israel, giant printing presses produce thousands of books and magazines in Hebrew.

Books and Bookstores

Israelis are avid readers. They read books in many languages and are very proud of their home libraries. A visitor entering an Israeli home for the first time is sure to be shown the books in the well-stocked family library.

Israel has more bookstores per capita than any country in the world. Nearly every street of an Israeli town or city seems to have a bookstore—at least one! Enthusiastic Bible students buy traditional books of Bible commentary, and nature-lovers buy the newest wildflower handbook. American best-sellers, translated into Hebrew, are eagerly bought up by Israelis who wish to keep pace with their neighbors across the seas.

שְׁמוּאֵל יוֹסֵף עַגְנוֹן

SHMUEL YOSEF AGNON
(1888–1970)
Nobel Prize winner

Shmuel Yosef Agnon was born in
the small Galician *shtetl* (town) of
Buczacz. His father, a fur merchant, was a follower of the Ha-
sidic rebbe of Chortkov, and
Shmuel Yosef grew up fully immersed in the rich traditions of
Jewish life in the Eastern European shtetl. Even as a boy, he
wrote stories and poems describing people and places he had come
to know. He continued writing and
became a great and famous novelist.

Agnon was an ardent Zionist as
well as a keen observer of the
shtetl. In 1907, at the age of nineteen, he moved to Israel (then
called Palestine). There he became
secretary of the Hoveve Zion
("Lovers of Zion") committee. He
continued to write stories about
Jewish life, now describing the
people and places of his new
home, modern Jerusalem.

Agnon received many awards,
including the Israel Prize in 1954
and 1958. The crowning honor
was the Nobel Prize for Literature
in 1966, the first granted to a Hebrew writer.

The Publishing Industry

More than two thousand books a year are published in
this tiny Jewish state. They include textbooks, books on
science, art, history, music, and sports, children's stories,
and even comic books, as well as Bibles and Hebrew
religious classics of all kinds.

In addition to books in Hebrew for the domestic
market, Israel's highly efficient publishing industry can
also produce books in many other languages. Foreign
firms often contract Israeli printers to produce books for
them, and the Jerusalem International Book Fair, held
every two years, is one of the major international trade
gatherings of publishers from all over the world.

Israeli Writers Are World-Famous

Many Israeli novelists and poets are internationally
known and admired. Their works, translated into English
and many other languages, are popular throughout the
world. In 1966, when the novelist S. Y. Agnon was the
honoree, Israel scored its first Nobel Prize for Literature.

Newspapers

Newspapers and magazines are available in many
different languages in Israel, since many new immigrants
are still unable to read the Hebrew dailies. A typical Tel
Aviv newsstand may sell publications in Hebrew, English, Yiddish, Ladino, Arabic, French, Russian, Greek,
Spanish, and Italian. Almost five hundred magazines are
sold in Israel, catering to special interests of all kinds—
medical science, zoology, photography, economics,
computers, archaeology, and theater, just to name a few.
Some Israeli magazines and professional journals are read
by scholars and scientists in many other countries.

Three of the leading newspapers of Israel are *Davar,
Maariv,* and *Ha'Aretz*. The *Jerusalem Post* is the English-
language newspaper of Israel. It is one of the world's
most respected English-language newspapers.

אַחַד הָעָם

AHAD HA'AM (1856–1927)
"One of the Nation"

"The pen is mightier than the sword." This saying is certainly illustrated by the great accomplishments of Ahad Ha'Am's pen. This great Zionist writer helped change the course of Jewish history with his essays and articles.

Ahad Ha'Am's works are collected in four volumes called *Al Parashat ha'Derakhim,* which means, "At the Crossroads." He felt that the Jewish people of his time stood at a crossroads, a turning point, in their history. He felt that the right turn would be settlement in the Jewish homeland, Israel, and he believed his own role was to inspire and educate Jews to settle in their land.

Ahad Ha'Am's real name was Asher Hirsch Ginsberg. His Hebrew pen name, which means "One of the Nation," shows how close he felt to the Jewish people and to the issue of the Jewish homeland.

Israeli newspapers do not appear on Saturday, the Jewish Sabbath. A large Friday edition has a special magazine section in the middle, with special articles, stories, poems, and translations of important articles from major newspapers in other countries.

Special Newspapers for Newcomers

New immigrants who have trouble with the Hebrew of the regular newspapers can buy a special daily paper, *Omer*—"Speak"—which encourages the oleh to speak Hebrew. The words in *Omer* have vowels to help the immigrant with pronunciation. On each page, the more difficult words are translated into six different languages, so the reader does not even have to use a dictionary! The popular weekly paper for new immigrants is called *Shaar La'Matchil*—"The Gate for the Beginner." This widely read paper is in easy Hebrew and also includes vowels.

A display of Israeli Hebrew and Yiddish newspapers.

VOCABULARY AND CONCEPTS

Israeli daily newspaper	הָאָרֶץ	Israeli daily newspaper for new immigrants	אֹמֶר
Israeli Labor Party daily newspaper	דָּבָר	Israeli weekly newspaper for new immigrants	שַׁעַר לַמַתְחִיל
Israeli evening newspaper	מַעֲרִיב		

126

MUSIC AND DANCE

Israelis listen to all sorts of music. Indeed, music is a big part of life in Israel, and all its forms are available and appreciated. Cantors make records of beautiful synagogue chants and melodies. Composers continually turn out popular new songs of love, peace, and war. Israeli rock groups are good enough to win international acclaim—in 1978, for instance, one of them finished first in the Eurovision Song Contest.

Classical Music

It's only fair to admit that classical music dominates the Israeli musical scene. Every town and village, however small, has its own classical music ensemble of some kind. Israelis of all educational backgrounds and income levels love classical music, and as a result the Israel Philharmonic Orchestra holds the world's per capita record for annual subscriptions.

The Israel Philharmonic was founded in 1936 by Bronislaw Huberman, and its first concert was conducted by Arturo Toscanini. Today its home is Tel Aviv's 2,700-seat Mann Auditorium, and more than half of its mem-

An outdoor concert in the ancient Roman amphitheater in Caesarea.

Members of Inbal, the National Dance Theater of Israel, in a scene from the Shepherd Dance, which dates from ancient times.

bers were born and trained in Israel. The Israel Philharmonic presents some 230 concerts a year, attended by an annual audience of about 60,000.

Music for the People

Most orchestras perform indoors, at concert halls or auditoriums. Israel's Philharmonic Orchestra has a beautiful concert hall in Tel Aviv—the Mann Auditorium—but this orchestra does not always stay indoors. The Israel Philharmonic performs in informal settings all over Israel—on quickly-set-up stages at army posts on the frontiers, outdoors for the pioneers of a new development town, and in cleared-off areas of kibbutz dining rooms. It travels through the land to bring music to the people no matter where they are. During Israel's War of Independence, the orchestra members piled onto trucks which bumped up to Jerusalem along the Burma Road, a rough path which had just been cut through the mountains.

Tel Aviv: Israel Philharmonic concert.

During Israel's five military campaigns, it played at army posts from Sinai to Quneitra, raising the morale of the troops.

Israel also has several other orchestras and chamber ensembles as well as an opera company, a national jazz festival, and many choral groups which compete in national contests. Many Israeli musical groups and musicians perform in major cities throughout the world.

Dance

When foreigners think about dance in Israel, they often imagine kibbutzniks cavorting across productive fields, singing and dancing the hora, a well-known Israeli folkdance. Israelis love folkdancing. Almost every town and settlement has a folkdance group, and several holidays inspire street-dancing, but other dance forms are also popular. While children study folkdancing in school, some have outside lessons in ballet, ethnic, or modern dance. Kibbutz dining halls often become dance halls on Saturday nights, about the same time that urbanites gather at popular discos or hotels with dance bands. The bands in these places usually have members from assorted backgrounds, and must be able to switch easily from pop or waltzes to polkas, rock, or Oriental rhythms to meet the dancers' demands. In addition to these forms

Israeli dance group performs on an en-air stage.

of the dance, Israel also has a ballet company as well as a unique Yemenite dance group, Inbal, which uses the special music and movements of the graceful Oriental tradition. Founded in 1949, Inbal collects rave reviews whenever it goes on one of its frequent world tours.

Theater

Israel's National Theater, Habimah ("The Stage"), is located in Tel Aviv. Next in prestige is Cameri, Tel Aviv's Municipal Theater, founded in 1944. Several younger companies—all government-funded—include the Haifa Theater and Jerusalem's Khan Company (most of whose members are under thirty-five). Ohel ("Tent") is the Labor Theater of Israel, which presents plays of social criticism and satire. Classic dramas by Shakespeare and Ibsen sell out to Israeli audiences. So do newly written plays about modern Israeli conflicts and relationships.

Film

Israelis enjoy movies, and over two hundred movie theaters show films from around the world as well as Israeli-made films. Because Israel's weather is famous for eight guaranteed-rain-free months a year, many foreign filmmakers shoot their pictures here, where they know they can work without weather interruptions. Israel's film industry, though small, has made some notable movies, and such Israeli performers as Chaim Topol have appeared in many films made in other countries.

Art in Israel

Many of the immigrants who reached Israel's shores during the early days of Zionist settlement were talented artists. Some of them were able to study at the Bezalel School, an art center established by Boris Schatz in 1906, which offered courses in painting, sculpture, calligraphy, and handicrafts.

Some Israeli artists, captivated by the beauty of their beloved land and its diverse population, strove in their artwork to capture the color and light of the Israeli

Yaacov Agam is one of Israel's most famous modern artists. He designed this stamp for the Israeli Philatelic Services. Can you find the Magen David hidden in the design?

130

בָּרִיס שַׁ״ץ

BORIS SCHATZ (1867–1932)
Artist and founder of the Bezalel School

Boris Schatz, at age twenty-two, left his hometown of Kovno, Lithuania, and went to Paris to study art. He then became court sculptor of Bulgaria, a prestigious position. In 1903, Schatz met Theodor Herzl. This meeting changed the course of his life and career, for Herzl inspired him to become an ardent Zionist and join his destiny with that of Israel. In 1906, Schatz went to Jerusalem to found the Bezalel School, now a world-famous art school where students learn painting, sculpture, calligraphy, and many forms of handicrafts. Schatz himself was a prolific artist who worked mostly in sculpture. Many of his works are on Jewish themes. He died in Denver, Colorado, while on a fundraising mission for the Bezalel School.

landscape and the character of the Israeli people. Others followed the most modern trends and did painting and sculpture that was abstract and modernistic. Still other artists, who came from the Oriental Jewish community, chose to create works in the tradition of their forefathers, in embroidery, silver and copper, handweaving, woodworking, and rugs.

In modern Israel, there are art exhibitions in the beautiful urban museums as well as in the kibbutzim and moshavim of rural regions. Israeli artists also participate in exhibitions abroad, and their works have been shown in Paris, London, and New York as well as at international shows in Venice and São Paulo.

Radio and Television

Israel's radio station, Kol Yisrael ("The Voice of Israel"), made its first broadcast on May 14, 1948, when Israel's Declaration of Independence was read on the air. Today, Kol Yisrael offers programming as diverse as Israel's population. Kol Yisrael has three stations, each with its own special emphasis. One plays mostly classical music. Another plays mostly folk songs and popular music. The third station schedules mostly talk shows and in-depth news coverage.

Boris Schatz and his students at the Bezalel School of Arts and Crafts in Jerusalem.

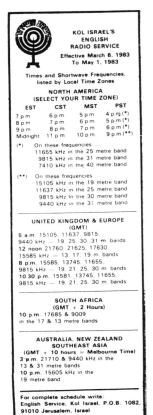

Every hour on the hour is news time on every station of Kol Yisrael. In this country so often ravaged by war and terrorism, many people carry transistors so that they can tune in to the news and keep up with the latest events. Many bus drivers carry radios and turn up the sound at news time so that all their passengers can hear. Tsahal has a special channel called Gallei Tsahal, which offers special programs for soldiers and their families.

The radio also offers Hebrew-language lessons, rabbinic advice, interviews with politicians and celebrities, symphony concerts, dramas, special holiday programs, and nightly Bible readings. A separate network presents broadcasts in Arabic, directed both to Arabs in Israel and to Arab listeners in other Middle Eastern countries.

TV in Israel

Just about everyone owns a television set, and most people have color TV, which was not available in Israel until recently. Daytime shows are mostly educational, teaching preschool children and offering homebound people courses in science, mathematics, and language. In the evenings, Israelis can watch television broadcasts of the news as well as all kinds of films and reruns of American shows are popular favorites   Israeli variety shows present music, dance, and humor. Live discussion shows often become heated debates among politicians and celebrities.

VOCABULARY AND CONCEPTS

Hora (Israeli folk dance)   הוֹרָה

Inbal (Yemenite dance group)   עִנְבַּל

Habimah (Israel's National Theater)   הַבִּימָה

Ohel (Labor theater in Israel)   אֹהֶל

The Voice of Israel (Israel's radio station)   קוֹל יִשְׂרָאֵל

Israel Defense Forces' radio station   גַּלֵּי-צַהַ״ל

SPORTS IN ISRAEL

Basketball is a popular sport in Israel.

Jews have traditionally been known as "the people of the book," since the Bible came to humanity through the Jews and since Jews have cherished their Torah and Talmud through centuries of strife. Devout European Jews spent their lives in scholarly contemplation, writing beautiful and imaginative biblical commentaries. In modern times, Jews have been famous mostly for their intellectual achievements—writing great books of literature and philosophy, making medical discoveries, working creatively in the fields of mathematics and scientific research. But Jews were never particularly famous for their ability in sports.

Modern Israelis, though, are enthusiastic sports lovers. They especially love soccer and basketball—maybe because neither of these games requires fancy or expensive equipment, and because both games are quick-paced and exciting. There are five soccer, four basketball, and three volleyball leagues, in which over one thousand teams compete.

An Israeli track meet.

Each year thousands of people participate in the noncompetitive "March to Jerusalem." On this march thousands of individuals and teams of all ages from many countries march through the hills of Judea to Jerusalem.

An Israeli basketball team, Maccabi Tel Aviv, is world-famous and was for several years the champion of all European teams.

A glance at the map will show you the long Israeli seashore along the Mediterranean, so it is no surprise that swimming is also a very popular sport. Israelis frequently take long hikes, called *tiyulim*, around the country, getting good exercise and an enhanced knowledge of their homeland at the same time. On Passover, thousands of Israelis hike all the way to Jerusalem, reviving the biblical custom of the pilgrimage to the Holy Temple on religious holidays.

At Chanukah time, there is a relay-race in which a torch is carried from the graves of the Maccabees at Modi'in to the Presidential Residence in Jerusalem.

At the Wingate Institute of Physical Education and Sports, training is provided for physiotherapists, phys-ed teachers and coaches, and athletes.

Bike riding is an up-and-coming competitive sport in Israel.

A javelin thrower highlights the stamp issued by the Israel Post Office on April 18, 1961, to mark the Seventh International Congress of Ha'Poel.

Israeli stamp issued in honor of the Ninth Maccabiah, in 1973.

The Maccabiah Games

Sports fans in Israel are always listening closely to the radio for news about the various amateur athletic leagues that compete throughout the country. But the most important sports event by far takes place only once in four years—the Maccabiah Games. These games, organized by the Maccabiah World Union, the international Israeli sports organization, are a Jewish Olympics for athletes who hail from all parts of the globe. Jewish athletes from all over the world meet and compete with one another in all kinds of athletic events. Many of the athletes who come to play eventually decide to come to Israel on aliyah, once they have caught the excitement and the love of country that they feel all around them.

The oldest sports association in Israel is Maccabi. Other sports groups are Ha'Poel ("The Worker"), whose members come from the Histadrut (Israel's labor union), and Elizur ("God is my Strength"), representing religious youth, and Betar.

The opening ceremony at the Ha'Poel Games in Tel Aviv.

VOCABULARY AND CONCEPTS

Maccabi (Israeli basketball team) מַכַּבִּי

Hike טִיּוּל

Ha'Poel (Israeli workers sports organization) הַפּוֹעֵל

Maccabiah (Jewish Olympics for athletes) מַכַּבִּיָה

135

FOOD IN ISRAEL

Americans and Israelis eat different kinds of meals. Americans usually eat light breakfasts and lunches and have their main meal of the day in the evening. The Israeli style is just the opposite! Israelis enjoy big, hearty breakfasts of vegetable salad, olives, a variety of cheeses, and plenty of citrus juice. For lunch, Israelis have the day's main meal. This meal often consists of soup, meat, salad, and dessert. In the evening Israelis eat lightly, usually dairy products, salads, and eggs. Many Israeli stores, businesses, and banks close down for several hours at midday, giving workers a chance to go home, eat lunch, and rest a while before returning to the afternoon's work.

A falafel stand in Haifa.

Shwarma is a favorite Israeli fast food. It is made of lamb's meat and is prepared on a rotisserie.

Foods from Every Land of the Diaspora

Just as Israel's people are a marvelously varied group of individuals, so too the foods of Israel are marvelously varied. Their aromas and spices are so distinct and fragrant. Rich, sweet Turkish coffee—a strong, black, and thick brew—is prepared in special urns called finjans, and a crisp strudel pastry called baklava often goes with the delicious drink. Street vendors everywhere sell falafel, a Yemenite delicacy—fried chickpea patties covered with tasty sauce, all sandwiched into a hard, flat roll called pita. A popular Arab proverb in the Middle East states that "a woman who doesn't know how to prepare eggplant 101 different ways is not yet prepared for marriage," and many immigrants to Israel from the Arab countries have brought along their many recipes for this popular vegetable. The Cochin Jews from India cook a highly spiced chicken curry, and Russian Jews have brought along recipes for hearty beet soup, borscht. The traditional specialties of Eastern European Jews are available throughout Israel—gefilte fish, lukschen kugel (noodle pudding), chicken soup with knaidlach (dumplings), and cholent, a long, slow-cooking stew of meat and beans.

Because so many of Israel's Jews follow the laws of Kashrut, many restaurants offer meals that are strictly kosher.

Shopping for groceries.

VOCABULARY AND CONCEPTS

falafel (Israel's national food—originally a Yemenite delicacy)	פָלָפֶל
pita	פִּיטָה
baklava	בַּקְלָוָואה
eggplant	חֲצִילִים

נפש בריאה בגוף בריא

The people of Israel have always been concerned with physical fitness. This ad for exercise equipment appeared in a newspaper in 1905.

The ad reads in translation, "A healthy soul in a healthy body."

Emblem of the Magen David Adom.

MEDICINE IN ISRAEL

Medicine in Israel

At the beginning of the nineteenth century, when Zionists began to resettle their beloved homeland, they found Israel ridden with disesases. The land had been under foreign rule and had not been tended properly; wide areas were swampy and infested with malaria, dysentery, trachoma, and tuberculosis. But the Zionist settlers were not daunted. They realized that they had to work hard to resettle the land of their dreams.

Two voluntary organizations helped. The Hadassah Women's Organization of America and Kupat Cholim, a medical-insurance fund of the Histadrut, aimed their efforts at improving health conditions in Israel. Money, time, effort, technical equipment, and medical professionals were all needed to help. Today, the land of Israel can boast of a life expectancy which matches that of Western countries, and of the latest in medical research and equipment. The doctors and nurses of Israel provide the best care for all the Jewish immigrants, who often come from lands with poor health care, and for the Druzes, the Bedouins, and the Arabs in administered lands, many of whom have never before received the benefit of good health care and modern medical equipment.

Most Israelis are covered by health insurance provided by the Kupat Cholim. These health-care plans, with low membership fees, provide free medical treatment, free hospitalization and convalescent care, and reduced rates for medicines and dental and optical care.

An ambulance of the Magen David Adom.

Magen David Adom

To Americans, the Red Cross is a well-known symbol of top-notch emergency care. Israelis have the Jewish version, the Magen David Adom, or "Red Star of David." This high-quality emergency ambulance service, funded largely by American supporters, saves lives in Israel every single day and night. Its ambulances rush the sick and wounded to hospitals and provide emergency medical aid.

VOCABULARY AND CONCEPTS

Kupat Cholim	קוּפַּת חוֹלִים
Magen David Adom	מָגֵן דָּוִד אָדוֹם

GEOGRAPHY OF ISRAEL

Why is it important for us to learn about geography? What does the physical terrain of a country have to do with its history and people?

Geography has a great deal to do with a nation's development. Israel's location at the crossroads of three continents—Asia, Africa, and Europe—has had a great impact on Israel's history and economy. The land's climate and soil affected decisions about the types of crops that could flourish on Israel's farms. The hot Mediterranean climate led Israelis to adopt working schedules different from those in our temperate climate. And the diversity of land areas in Israel allows the many different kinds of citizens to find the type of settlement that suits them most—whether they feel most at home in a hectic, exciting city or in the quieter, greener world of town and country.

ISRAEL AND THE WORLD

Modern Israel is surprisingly tiny. It isn't always easy to find the country on the map! Sometimes mapmakers have so much trouble fitting the word "Israel" onto the tiny strip of space representing the land that they give up altogether. The word "Israel" ends up printed onto the blue Mediterranean Sea, to Israel's west.

The Role of Geography in Israeli History

The unique location of tiny Israel gives the land a special geographic role. Look carefully at a map or globe and you will see that Israel occupies a central place in one of the world's most important regions—it forms a natural land bridge between Asia, to the east, and Africa, to the south, and is also very close to Europe, on the northwest.

Israel among the nations.

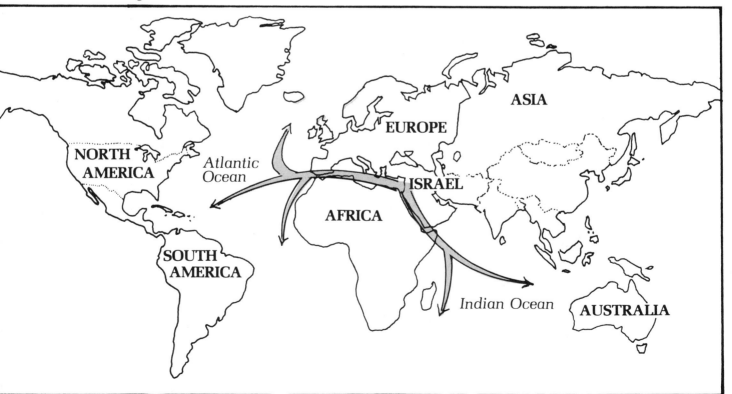

Israel's Strategic Location

In ancient times, the rulers of the surrounding countries realized that the special geographic location of Israel would be useful to them. Whoever controlled Israel—sometimes called Palestine—controlled the land route between Africa and Asia, as well as Europe's access to the East by way of the Mediterranean Sea. As a result, conquering armies strove constantly to win the Jewish homeland, and Israel fell into the hands of many foreign rulers.

Modern Israel, too, is affected by the country's unique location. At the main ports of Haifa, Eilat, and Ashdod, ships from the world over dock and unload exotic products from many distant lands.

VOCABULARY AND CONCEPTS

Mediterranean Sea	הַיָם הַתִּיכוֹן
Haifa	חֵיפָה
Eilat	אֵילַת
Ashdod	אַשְׁדוֹד

A glance at the map will show you how Israel is completely surrounded by Arab states.

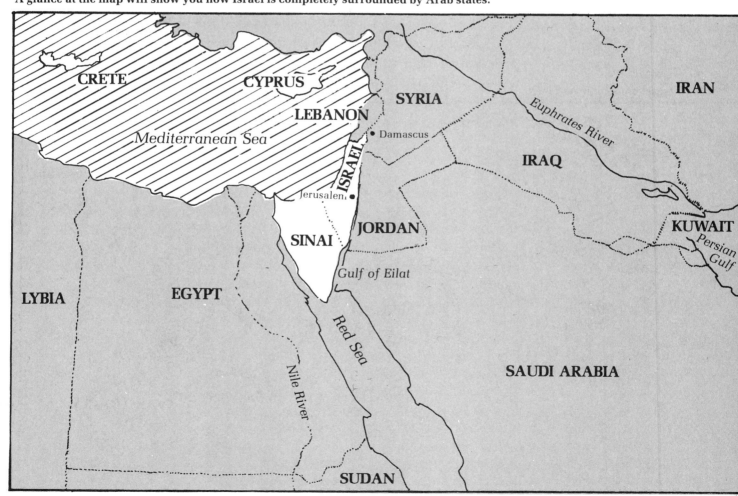

THE CLIMATE OF ISRAEL

There really isn't one climate in Israel. Rather, there are many different climates in this diverse land, which, like a miniature globe, has many different kinds of weather within its borders at the same time.

The wide variety of weathers results from the fact that the tiny land of Israel includes so many amazingly different types of terrain, ranging from snow-capped mountains to torrid deserts. In just a few hours, a visitor can drive from a wintry mountainside in the northern Galilee to a hot, sandy desert in the southern Negev. Then he can enjoy a dip in the cool, breezy beaches of the coastal plain. The snow-capped peaks of the Mountains of Galilee look like the Swiss Alps, while the Negev's weather resembles that of the Sahara Desert. The coast of the Mediterranean has warm summers and mild winters like those of Italy and Spain, while the Jordan Valley has a much hotter and more humid semi-tropical climate.

The Rainy Winter

The winter is more a rainy time than a cold time in most of the country. Between January and March, most of the year's rain pours down, sometimes in violent torrents that go on for hours and hours. Jews the world over include in their daily prayers a prayer for proper rainfall in Israel during the winter months. God is worshipfully addressed as "He who makes the wind blow and the rain to fall."

Winter sports on Mount Hermon.

143

The Hot Summer

Summer in Israel is very hot, and rain almost never falls during this season. A very hot, dust-laden wind sometimes blows over the country and lasts for a few unpleasantly hot days. This wind is called a *chamsin* in Arabic and a *sharav* in Hebrew; both words mean the same thing—"burning heat."

Partly because of the great heat on some summer days, Israel is a country that gets to work early in the morning, while the weather is still cool. By noontime, when the sun is at its hottest, everyone is ready for a break. Most Israelis go home for lunch and a short rest before returning for the afternoon's work. Visitors to Israel must remember that businesses, stores, banks, and offices are generally shut down for a couple of hours in the middle of the day.

The Tel Aviv beach on a hot summer day.

VOCABULARY AND CONCEPTS

Hot, dust-laden wind (Arabic)	חַמְסִין
Hot, dust-laden wind (Hebrew)	שָׁרָב
Summer	קַיִץ
Winter	חֹרֶף

144

THE REGIONS OF ISRAEL

Israel is a small country, yet an incredible variety of land types abound within her borders: snow-capped mountains and sandy deserts, tropical humidity and cool, crisp winds—all within the space of a three-hour drive! The country may be divided into five distinct parts: the Coastal Plain, the Central Mountains, the Jezreel Valley, the Jordan Rift, and the Negev.

1. The Coastal Plain

The Coastal Plain lies to the west, along the Mediterranean Sea. Here the lush Plain of Sharon, with its fertile, well-watered soil, links Israel's major cities, Tel Aviv and Haifa. Here most of Israel's industry thrives—steel and textile plants, oil refineries, chemical factories—as well as the country's rich vineyards and citrus plantations. Two-thirds of Israel's population lives in the Coastal Plain region.

2. The Central Mountains

The Central Mountains extend from the Galilean Mountains of northern Israel through the Samarian and Judean Mountains of central Israel. Farmers in the valleys of this region grow abundant crops of many varieties of fruits and vegetables, as well as wheat, and also raise large numbers of poultry and dairy cattle. Olive groves and newly planted forests cover the rocky slopes of the Galilee. Many Jewish and Arab farm villages coexist peacefully in the Central Mountain region.

145

Between Major Cities in Israel

		Miles
Jerusalem to	Haifa	94
	Tel Aviv	38
	Nablus	41
	Jericho	21
	Bethlehem	5
	Beersheba	54
Tel Aviv to	Haifa	59
	Beersheba	67
	Gaza	48
Beersheba to	Eilat	146

The barren Judean desert (where David hid from Saul) and its drop to the Dead Sea. There is now a thriving kibbutz on the desert sand.

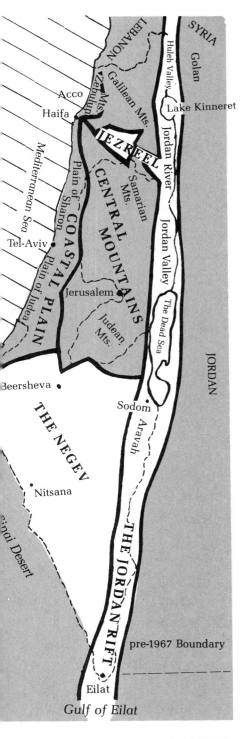

3. The Jezreel Valley

The Jezreel Valley, called the Emek ("Valley") in Hebrew, is a flat, fertile region separating the high peaks of the Mountains of Galilee from the lower Mountains of Samaria. The Emek is a region of rich soil, and the proud farmers of its many kibbutzim, moshavim, and privately owned farms raise highly profitable crops of all kinds—wheat, fruits, and vegetables—as well as the dairy cattle and poultry that provide such important elements of the Israeli diet.

4. The Jordan Rift

The Jordan Rift lies all the way along Israel's eastern border, from the northern to the southern tip of the country. Down from the Huleh Valley, a vast swamp which the early settlers drained, transforming it into rich farmland, the Jordan River flows into the Sea of Galilee (Lake Kinneret) and then down through the very hot Jordan Valley, finally ending in the Dead Sea. The Aravah Valley lies between the Dead Sea and the Gulf of Eilat to the south.

5. The Negev

The Negev, the biggest region of the five, has the smallest number of people. Until very recently, this large triangle on Israel's south was barren wilderness, a hot, dry desert where no one but roving Bedouin tribes chose to make their home. But the ingenuity and labors of Israel's scientists have paid off. The Negev has begun to bloom. Water is piped in from the Jordan River to irrigate the desert soil, and crops of fruits, vegetables, and flowers are flourishing. In addition, there are important copper mines, and the Dead Sea provides important minerals like bromine, phosphates, and potash.

VOCABULARY AND CONCEPTS

Valley of Jezreel	עֵמֶק יִזְרְעֶאל
Jordan Rift Valley	עֵמֶק הַיַּרְדֵּן
Huleh Valley	עֵמֶק הַחוּלָה
Aravah Valley	הָעֲרָבָה
Israel's southern region	נֶגֶב

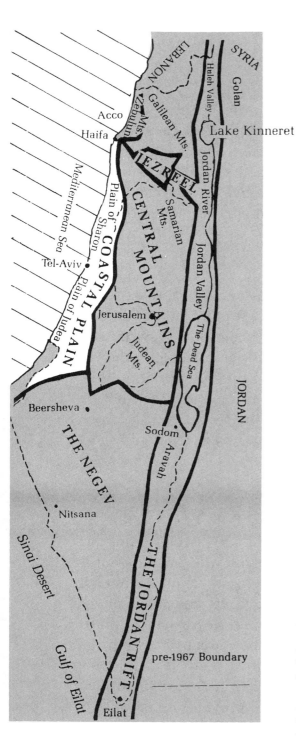

Acco
Haifa
LEBANON
SYRIA
Huleh Valley
Golan
Galilean Mts.
Mts. Zebulun
Lake Kinneret
JEZREEL
Jordan River
Samarian Mts.
Mediterranean Sea
Plain of Sharon
COASTAL PLAIN
CENTRAL MOUNTAINS
Tel-Aviv
Jerusalem
Plain of Judea
Judean Mts.
Jordan Valley
The Dead Sea
JORDAN
Beersheva
Sodom
Aravah
THE NEGEV
Nitsana
Sinai Desert
THE JORDAN RIFT
Gulf of Eilat
Eilat
pre-1967 Boundary

VOCABULARY AND CONCEPTS

Plain of Sharon (the coastal plain of the Mediterranean)
חוֹף הַשָּׁרוֹן

1. The Coastal Plain
THE PLAIN OF SHARON

In ancient times, the Plain of Sharon was known as the garden of Israel. Its rich soil offered up a wealth of grains, fruits, and flowers.

Today, as in the past, the Plain of Sharon is famous for its wonderful produce. Citrus groves dot the landscape, and their fruits—big, luscious oranges, grapefruits, and lemons—are exported all over the world, where they are prized for their quality. Numerous vegetable, poultry, and dairy farms also flourish throughout this region.

The Plain of Sharon is the most populated area in all of Israel. Yet a glance at the map will show how very close this area—home to so many Israelis—is to the surrounding Arab lands. Before the Six-Day War in 1967, which resulted in a change of borderlines, the Plain of Sharon was even more dangerously close to the reach of enemy fire. Israel's policy today is greatly affected by the closeness of "the heart of Israel" to the country's borders.

148

TEL AVIV–YAFFO

In the early 1900's, the place where Tel Aviv–Yaffo now stands was hardly more than sandy wasteland. Today this bustling city is one of the largest and most modern cities in Israel!

Actually, Tel Aviv–Yaffo is a combination of two cities. Yaffo (Jaffa) was one of Israel's oldest cities, and Tel Aviv was one of the very newest settlements. In 1929, the two cities merged.

In 1909 Tel Aviv was nothing more than a series of sand dunes. This rare old photo shows the allocation of plots of land to the first residents of Tel Aviv.

Life in Tel Aviv–Yaffo

Like most big cities, Tel Aviv–Yaffo is a study in contrasts. Some parts of the city are rundown slums, where people live in crowded apartments. Other parts are attractive, well-kept residential areas with beautiful parks and elegant houses. At the heart of Tel Aviv rises the Shalom Tower, the highest skyscraper in the Middle East.

Business and Industry

Most of Israel's big business firms and banks are here, and almost half her factories. Many of the foreign embassies of the world's nations are located in the city's central streets; as are most of Israel's book and newspaper publishers.

Tel Aviv has played an important role in Israeli history. The independence of the new State of Israel was proclaimed in this city, in the small municipal art museum, on May 14, 1948.

The Shalom Tower in Tel Aviv is the tallest building in Israel.

A modern thoroughfare in Israel.

Recreation and Culture

City Hall in Tel-Aviv.

Besides the business and industry, Tel Aviv–Yaffo has another element. This sparkling city is also known as Israel's playground. On the fashionable, lively streets lined with mod boutiques and shimmering discothèques, people sit for hours, slowly sipping iced drinks and spooning ice cream in outdoor cafes, shaded by colorful awnings. They watch the tourists, bohemians, and "beautiful people" of Tel Aviv go by, and are watched in turn themselves. The city has spacious parks and boulevards, theaters, operas, a splendid library, Israel's best zoo, and one of the world's finest orchestras, the Israel Philharmonic. Along the coast, a whole chain of hotels has been built, most with their own beaches and entertainment spots.

The main streets of Tel Aviv are Dizengoff Street, named for the city's first mayor, and Allenby Street, named for the British general who captured Israel (then

The shops on Dizengoff Street and Ben-Yehuda Street are filled with merchandise from all over the world.

The Yemenite quarter in Tel Aviv, Israel.

called Palestine) from the Turks in 1918. On these streets, one can immediately sense Tel Aviv's big-city rhythm. Tourists from all over the world visit the attractive shops, using their traveler's checks to buy Israeli-made clothing, artwork, silverwork, and handicrafts. In the business districts, powerful leaders of the country's industry negotiate important contracts. And in the evenings, Tel Aviv's busy cultural centers attract many Israelis and tourists who love the varied presentations of theater, opera, music, and cinema.

Population

Of Israel's nearly four million Jews, about one million live in Tel Aviv and the surrounding cities! Little wonder, then, that this lively city is a hectic urban center. It is the second-largest city in all of Israel, surpassed in size only by Jerusalem.

Along the shore connecting Tel Aviv and Haifa are several cities and towns which play a large role in Israel's economy: Natanya, Caesaria, Herzliya, Acco, Ashdod.

The Peace Process

The agreement between Israel and (Palestinian Authority) calls for Israel's army to pull back from 6 Palestinian towns. This retreat of Israel's armed forces will place the city of Tel Aviv ten miles from the Arab town Qalqilya.

The town of Kfar Sava with a population of 80,000 people, ten miles from Tel Aviv, will become a border town of one mile from Qalqilya.

The prospect of an army pull out and the entry of Palestinian forces has brought a sense of danger and unease to the residents of Kfar Sava. Although Israeli soldiers will remain outside Qalqilya some of the residents are fearful of continued attacks by Arab militants.

Prime Minister Yitzchak Rabin has assured the residents that every effort will be made to insure the security of the town.

VOCABULARY AND CONCEPTS

Tel-Aviv	תֵּל אָבִיב
Yaffo	יָפוֹ
Dizengoff Street	רְחוֹב דִּיזִינְגּוֹף
Allenby Street	רְחוֹב אֶלֶנְבִּי
Shalom Tower (the highest skyscraper in Israel)	מִגְדַּל שָׁלוֹם

HAIFA

There is a saying among Israelis that Jerusalem is the soul of their nation. Tel Aviv its heart, and Haifa its muscle. The visitor to Haifa can readily see why this city is so called, for this major industrial center pulses with energy.

Haifa is Israel's third-largest city (population about 220,000). The beginnings of this town are not known, but it dates back to ancient times. The name Haifa first appears in talmudic literature from the third century C.E. There are many and various suggestions about the origin of the name. Most popular is the one that the Hebrew words *hof yafeh*, "beautiful coast," were contracted at some time long ago to form one word: Haifa.

A view of Haifa from atop Mount Carmel.

Israeli stamp featuring the emblem and the port of Haifa.

The Port of Haifa

Occupying the slopes of beautiful Mount Carmel and the low-lying land at its base along the seafront, the city of Haifa is built on three levels. The first level is the old city in the port area. This is Israel's main port, and it displays the usual parade of sheds, cranes, and ships, the litter of cargo, and the masthead flags of many nations. In Haifa's port, you can see sleek gray warships, stubby, untidy little fishing boats, and merchant vessels from all over the world. Through its docks have poured most of Israel's million immigrants of the last twenty years, as well as a substantial portion of Israel's commerce. During the years of the British Mandate, however, ships carrying Jewish refugees were not allowed to dock in Haifa because the British officials refused them entry. The British sent boats full of Jewish people away from Israel to the island of Cyprus, or sometimes all the way to Nazi Europe. When the ship called the *Exodus* arrived in Haifa, the British officials refused to let its refugee passengers come ashore and forced them to return to Germany—back to the nightmarish world of the Nazi Holocaust.

The *Exodus.* A ship filled with immigrants seeking to enter Palestine "illegally."

Industry

Haifa is an important center of heavy industry. Its many industrial plants include such factories as Nesher Cement, Vulcan Foundry, Phoenicia Glass, the large steel mills on the road to Acco, and shipyards. The area is also served by an oil zone with refineries and oil storage tanks.

The Bahai Temple

Haifa is not just a factory town, however. It is also the home of important cultural and educational institutions. One of the city's most unusual religious sites is the magnificent Bahai Temple. Buried in the temple is Mirza Ali Mohammed, founder of the unique Bahai faith, which seeks to unite all religions into one belief under the One God, with Moses, Jesus, Mohammed, and Buddha as coequal prophets. The Haifa temple is the religion's world center; nearby, the faith's archives and museum are kept in a Parthenon-type building, surrounded by lush, well-tended gardens.

The Bahai shrine in Haifa.

A view of the Technion in Haifa.

A view of the Technion in Haifa.

The Technion

Haifa's prize place of learning, however, deals with advanced science—nuclear physics, electronics, various types of engineering, aerodynamics, and architecture. It is the Israel Institute of Technology, the "Technion" in popular language, and often known as Israel's M.I.T. The world-famous Technion is Israel's largest school for science.

Hadar HaCarmel

Halfway up the slope of Mount Carmel is Haifa's second level, the area called Hadar HaCarmel, "The Beauty of Carmel." Here the residential part of the city begins, with its own shopping and recreational areas. Rising from the wooded slopes of the mountain are hundreds of modern apartment buildings, their balconies facing the beautiful blue Mediterranean. The mountainside is also dotted with thousands of small homes whose flower and rock gardens make a patchwork of brilliant colors.

As the population of Haifa expands, the houses seem to "walk" higher and higher up the mountain.

Har HaCarmel

The third and highest level of Haifa is called Har HaCarmel, "The Mountain of Carmel."

The restful quiet, the groves of sweet-smelling pine trees, and the cool mountain breezes all add up to make Har HaCarmel a very popular vacation and health resort area. Winding mountain trails and bridle paths offer ample opportunities for hiking and horseback riding.

The Carmelit

Israel's only subway is in the city of Haifa. The subway, called the Carmelit, connects the harbor area with Hadar HaCarmel and goes all the way up to Har HaCarmel. It is tunneled through the solid rock of Mount Carmel. The mountain's slopes are so steep that cars and buses can only make their way up and down by slowly following a winding series of roads that encircle the mountain. By the Carmelit subway, it takes only nine minutes to get from the port to Har HaCarmel. The same trip by car takes forty minutes. Thus the Carmelit saves the people of Haifa many hours of travel.

The Carmelit subway of Haifa. The Hebrew sign reads *yitziah,* which means "exit."

2. *The Central Mountains*

THE GALILEE

Some Israelis prefer the greenness and the solitude of the Galilean forest to the glittering discothèques of the big city. Some Israelis find the satisfactions of farm life—tilling the soil, watching green buds grow into thriving plants—more rewarding than the glamour and prestige of banking or business careers. Some Israelis would rather "rough it" in a newly started settlement than live where thousands have already established homes and schools and shops. These pioneering citizens make their homes on the mountainous slopes of the Galilee.

Jews and Arabs Living Together in Peace

Jewish and Arab farm villages coexist here. Working with the same types of soil, facing the same kinds of day-to-day problems, Arab and Jewish neighbors in the Galilee communicate with one another about farm methods and supplies. Sometimes Arab and Jewish schoolchildren visit one another's schools, especially at holiday time, to learn about the customs and traditions of their neighbors.

The Galilee has the highest mountains in all of Israel. The very highest spot is Mount Meron's peak—at 3,692 feet! How much taller is Mount Meron than you? Than your teacher? Than all your classmates put together, each one standing on the shoulders of the others?

The Political Future of the Galilee

One sixth of Israel's population (910,000) are Arabs. Most of them live in the Galilee, and speak both Hebrew and Arabic. At this moment (1996) in time, the Palestinian Arab citizens are quiet, but highly politicized by the success of the new Palestinian Authority (PA) which will have control of the West Bank

Some Israeli officials believe that the Galilee will be the next area to demand a divorce and separation from the State of Israel.

The village of Peqi'in in central Upper Galilee, where Jews have lived uninterruptedly since the Second Temple.

VOCABULARY AND CONCEPTS

The Galilee	הַגָּלִיל
Mount Meron	הַר מֵירוֹן

KIRYAT SHEMONA

Kiryat Shemona is a development town—one of the new towns created since 1948 in order to provide a home for the influx of *olim* (new immigrants) to Israel. The town's name means "Town of the Eight." The name reminds us of the bravery shown by Joseph Trumpeldor and his seven heroic comrades, who gave their lives defending nearby Tel Chai in 1920.

New Immigrants Find a Home

Today, many of the children of Kiryat Shemona are sabras, for whom the Galilean town has always been home. But in the early years of the state, a typical classroom in Kiryat Shemona might have included children from India, Iran, Persia, Morocco, Tunisia, Poland, and Romania, for when the independent Jewish state was declared in 1948, Jews from all over the world streamed into the land.

Olim in new towns like Kiryat Shemona were given help in housing, job training, Hebrew classes, and living expenses. *Olim* worked on nearby kibbutzim or helped create new Galilean roads and forests.

Terrorist Attacks

A glance at the map will show you how very close Kiryat Shemona is to the Arab land of Lebanon. Until the Israel Defense Forces drove them out in mid-1982, terrorists called the PLO based themselves in Lebanese towns, where they got help and shelter. From these bases, the PLO fired artillery and rockets at towns and villages along Israeli's northern border—the Galilee. Kiryat Shemona was a favorite target. On April 26, 1974, PLO terrorists invaded Kiryat Shemona.

159

Life in Kiryat Shemona is not easy. It was hard for *olim* to adjust to a new home, to learn a new language and new job skills. It was hard when the harsh, wet winter months arrived and farm work had to stop. And it was terribly hard when cruel Arab terrorists destroyed the lives of innocent people.

Despite all this, the people of Kiryat Shemona did not give up. With the stubbornness and pride that has kept the Jewish people alive for centuries, the settlers of Kiryat Shemona stood their ground, determined not to abandon their town. Now that the Israel Defense Forces have destroyed the military might of the PLO, maybe life in Kiryat Shemona will be a bit easier.

Ruins of the Crusader fortress of Montfort in the Upper Galilee.

VOCABULARY AND CONCEPTS

Development town in the Galilee

קִרְיַת שְׁמוֹנָה

New Immigrants

עוֹלִים חֲדָשִׁים

LAKE KINNERET

Judaism teaches that we have the free will to choose the path of good or the path of evil. The history of Lake Kinneret (also known as the Sea of Galilee) illustrates this teaching. For the fate of this lake has depended upon the choice of the people who occupied the Kinneret region.

How the Lake Got Its Name

In ancient times, when the Jews ruled over their homeland, the area around Lake Kinneret was lush and well tended. Luscious grapes for wine grew in the fertile soil, as well as figs and olives. Great numbers of fish swam in the lake's clear waters. The mountains around the Kinneret seem to change their colors as the sky changes from red to yellow, blue to purple. The area was so beautiful that a Jewish legend explained its name in this way: "From all the seas which God created, He chose for Himself only the Sea of Kinneret. And why is it called Kinneret? Because the voice of its waves is as pleasant as the voice of the harp." (The Hebrew word for "harp" is *kinnor*.)

How the Pioneers Won the Fight Against Pollution

When foreign rulers took over Israel, the area was sadly neglected. Its fertile shores became dirty swamps. Fish suffocated in polluted waters. Lake Kinneret had lost its great historical beauty.

The Zionist pioneers who came to Israel in the early 1900's were eager to work hard at rebuilding their land. "It is our only home," they said, "and we must do our best to make it healthy and strong." They struggled to drain away the dirty waters and the pollution and to plant new crops. They worked hard, long, aching hours to recreate the Lake Kinneret area. And their work paid off. The lands of the Kinneret area once again became beautiful and fertile. A rich supply of fish swims in the lake's waters. Fishermen from lakeside settlements catch many varieties, which are sold all over Israel. And the waters of the Kinneret are specially channeled to the Negev, to make crops grow.

A bountiful catch from Lake Kinneret.

Fishermen on Lake Kinneret emptying their nets.

VOCABULARY AND CONCEPTS

Harp	כִּנּוֹר
Sea of Galilee	יַם כִּנֶּרֶת

162

רַבִּי מֹשֶׁה בֶּן מַיְמוֹן (רַמְבַּ"ם)

MAIMONIDES (1135–1204)
Torah scholar and physician
Born in Spain, Maimonides moved with his family to Eretz Yisrael in 1165 and settled in Acco. But when the Crusaders came, they brought tumult, violence, destruction, and danger. Maimonides left Israel and resettled with his family in Egypt. There he became a leader of the Jewish community. A renowned Torah scholar, Maimonides wrote great works of Jewish commentary and philosophy.

He was also a talented and expert doctor, so good at his profession that he became the court physician of the Arab ruler, Saladin.

Maimonides died in Egypt and, at his request, was buried in Israel, in Tiberias. The tomb of this great Jewish teacher and leader has been a center of Jewish pilgrimage throughout the centuries.

TIBERIAS

On the western shore of the Kinneret lies Tiberias. The climate here is always mild, even when the rest of Israel suffers a cold, windy winter. The town has become a popular winter vacation spot for Israelis seeking an escape from harsh winter weather.

The Hot Springs

Nearby, the natural hot springs and thermal baths—famous for their curative powers since Roman times—attract many visitors. Enterprising businessmen have set up modern, hotel-like facilities where tourists can enjoy the baths under medical supervision. People with all kinds of aches and ailments bathe in the waters that surge up through the earth's crust.

Tiberias is also famous for the shrines and landmarks of ancient Jewish communities. Visitors can see the tomb of Maimonides, the famous medieval Jewish philosopher.

The Tomb of Maimonides (Rambam) in Tiberias.

VOCABULARY AND CONCEPTS

erias   טְבֶרְיָה

SAFED

The Maron Bayit Joseph Synagogue in Safed. This was the synagogue of Rabbi Joseph Caro, the compiler of the *Shulchan Aruch*, the Code of Jewish Law.

The cobblestone streets of this ancient city are so old and narrow that cars cannot enter. Visitors must leave their cars outside and make their way by foot through the old city.

Safed's small, picturesque houses seem alive with all the history they have witnessed. The very air of Safed, cool and fragrant, seems mystically scented. You can almost hear the chants of the rabbis and scholars who prayed and studied, hundreds and hundreds of years ago, in this lovely Galilean forest town.

A Center of Torah Study

All through the Middle Ages, Safed was a center of Torah study. Great schools and synagogues were established here. Isaac Luria, a famous rabbi of the sixteenth century who lived in Safed, encouraged his followers to become closer to God by studying Jewish mysticism—the special Jewish books known as the Kabbala.

Safed was also the home of Rabbi Joseph Caro, another great rabbi, born in Spain in 1488. The Jews were expelled from Spain in 1492, and Rabbi Caro fled to Portugal, to Turkey, and finally to Safed. Here he compiled one of the most well-known and useful works of Jewish law—the Shulchan Aruch. This book, written in clear Hebrew, discusses the *halacha* (Jewish law), of every aspect of Jewish life. Many Jews consult the Shulchan Aruch daily to find out the proper law.

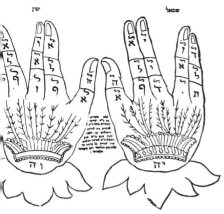

A Kabbalistic drawing with combinations of Hebrew letters. The Kabbalists regard the Hebrew alphabet and their combinations as having mystical meanings.

Modern Safed

Right under the towering Mountains of Galilee, Safed attracts many artists, who try to capture the magnificent scenery on their canvases. They set up their easels in all parts of the ancient town, attempting to recreate in their paintings the colors and the beauty of Safed's time-worn stone houses.

A new suburb has gone up just outside Safed. Thousands of *olim* have settled in this very modern part of town. Factories hum, children with their bookbags skip to school, and burly construction workers pour the cement foundations of new housing. What a contrast from the ancient Safed nearby—yet what a characteristically Israeli blending of the ancient and the modern!

Interior view of the Ari Synagogue in Safed.
The Ari (1534–1572) was Rabbi Isaac ben Solomon Luria, a famous Kabbalist. He lived in Safed and was famous for his saintly deeds and supernatural powers.

VOCABULARY AND CONCEPTS

...le of Jewish Law	שֻׁלְחָן עָרוּךְ
...ed	צְפַת
...bbala	קַבָּלָה
...bi Isaac Luria	רַבִּי יִצְחָק לוּרְיָא (הָאֲרִ"י)
...bi Joseph Caro	רַבִּי יוֹסֵף קַארוֹ

165

NAZARETH

Nazereth is filled with sites venerated by Christians of all denominations.

Nazareth, mostly populated by Arabs, stands in the hills of Upper Galilee. Each year, thousands of Christian pilgrims from all over the world travel here to see the places where Jesus lived as a boy. Arab guides lead tourists up a steep hill to visit the seven holy churches of the town.

The town of Nazareth is so closely connected with the beginnings of the Christian religion that in Hebrew the word *Nostri*, or "Nazarene," means "Christian."

VOCABULARY AND CONCEPTS

Nazareth	נַצֶּרֶת
Jesus	יֵשׁוּ
Christian	נוֹצְרִי

JERUSALEM

Israeli stamp with a quotation from the Psalms, "Pray for the peace of Jerusalem."

High in the Judean Mountains, in the heart of Israel, stands Jerusalem—the largest city in all of Israel. It has been called a sacred city of enchantment, the soul of Israel, the City of David, Zion, and the center of the universe. The rabbis believed that the air here is rarer and clearer than anywhere else on earth. The light seems to have a luminous, crystal-clear quality, and every building and every face seems more vivid in Jerusalem. The city is surrounded by the Judean Mountains, sometimes crowned at sunset with a misty radiance. The rosy brown stones of Jerusalem's houses come from these mountains. Softly colored earth tones suffuse this ancient, holy city with a wondrous light.

Jerusalem in Jewish History

The city's name, Jerusalem, means City of Wholeness, Perfection, Peace—the words are difficult to translate, and the mood of grace, beauty, and serenity is hard to express.

The city of Jerusalem has the deepest meaning for the Jewish people. Wherever Jews were scattered during the long, dark night of exile, they prayed for a return to Zion—the biblical name for Jerusalem. "If I forget thee, O Jerusalem, may my right hand forget its cunning," the exiles had wept. Every Passover, at the end of the Seder, Jews said the hopeful prayer, *LeShana HaBaa BiYerushalayim*, "Next Year in Jerusalem."

Emblem of Jerusalem.

The Holy Temple

When King David unified Israel in the tenth century B.C.E., he made Jerusalem the capital city. His son Solomon built the glorious Temple here and dedicated it to God's worship. The Bible records the labor and the genius combined in the creation of the magnificent Temple—the cedarwoods, metalwork, rare gems, and intricate embroideries. Jews from all over Israel came to Jerusalem at holiday times, proud to worship in this noble House of God.

The Prophets

The prophets knew these ancient streets well. Here they spoke their passionate, eloquent message of brotherhood and justice. Isaiah and Jeremiah fearlessly denounced the sinners and encouraged the Jewish people to leave corruption and cruelty and return to the God-given Torah laws. The Bible records the fiery, poetic words of Isaiah and Jeremiah in the books that bear their names. As we walk the streets of Jerusalem, if we try very hard, we can still hear the strong, sure voices of these divinely inspired prophets, ringing out with clarity and truth.

Christians and Moslems, too, regard Jerusalem as a holy place. Here Jesus last preached to his followers, and according to the Moslems, Mohammed went up to heaven from Jerusalem.

Love for Jerusalem Through the Ages

Without the unshakable bond that Jews through the ages felt for Jerusalem, there would be no Israel today. The scattered Jews would have combined with the surrounding nations if they had not held fast to their dream of the return to Zion. The special love of Jews for Jerusalem, their holy capital city, kept alive their faith in an eventual return. The love of Israel for Jerusalem has stayed unchanged from the time King David made Jerusalem the capital to the time David Ben-Gurion did the same, three thousand years later.

Even in the worst of times, Jews always lived in Israel. This photo (1870) shows Jews praying at the Western Wall.

168

Hechal Shlomo (Palace of Solomon) in Jerusalem. Hechel Shlomo is the seat of the Orthodox Rabbinate in Israel.

A street scene in Me'ah She'arim, the ultra-Orthodox section of Jerusalem. Notice the inscription on the entrance to the quarter.

Modern Jerusalem

The Knesset Building and the Prime Minister's office stand in the Kiryah, a center of government. Here, in buildings adorned with paintings, mosaics, and sculptures by Israeli artists, the leaders of the land make important decisions that affect all citizens. Presidents, Prime Ministers, and other important people from other countries who want to meet with Israel's leaders must come to Jerusalem's Kiryah.

At the Hebrew University of Jerusalem, students from all over Israel and from foreign countries attend lectures in law, medicine, Bible, botany, and literature. One of the world's greatest libraries stands at the campus center.

Sanhedriyah is one of the most beautiful areas of the city. Here, in delightful public gardens, are the tombs of the members of the Sanhedrin, the Supreme Court of Israel in biblical times.

Theodor Herzl, the founder of modern Zionism, is buried on a hill named for this great man: Mount Herzl. Nearby, a special memorial honors the six million Jews murdered by the Nazis in Europe.

The Old City of Jerusalem

People from all over the world stream through the gates into the Old City of Jerusalem. Tourists and Israelis mingle side by side in the narrow, cobblestoned streets. Most move toward the Temple Mount and the Kotel HaMaaravi—for Jews, the holiest places in the world.

The Temple area spreads over sacred Mount Moriah, where our forefather Abraham was ready to sacrifice his beloved son Isaac to the Almighty. On this same spot the glorious First and Second Temples of ancient Israel stood. All that remains of these wondrous temples is the Kotel HaMaaravi—the Western Wall. It is believed that the Divine Presence rests eternally upon these stones.

The gray stones of this great wall have been worn soft by the tears of the countless worshippers who have come here throughout the generations to pray and to weep for

The memorial to President John F. Kennedy of the United States, in Jerusalem. This monument was erected with contributions from the American citizens whose names are inscribed on the glass panels. In the middle burns a perpetual light in front of a portrait of the President.

The Kiryah in Jerusalem is the center of the Israeli government.

VOCABULARY AND CONCEPTS

Kennedy Memorial	יָד קֶנֶדִי
The center of government	הַקִּרְיָה
Mount Herzl (cemetery for Zionist and Israeli leaders)	הַר הֶרְצֵל
The Biblical Zoo	גַּן הַחַיּוֹת הַתַּנַ"כִ"י
Hadassah (hospital and medical school)	הֲדַסָה
Jerusalem	יְרוּשָׁלַיִם
The Western Wall	הָעִיר הָעַתִּיקָה
The Old City	הַכֹּתֶל הַמַּעֲרָבִי

the suffering and misery of their people. Many worshippers write their own special prayers on little slips of paper and place them in the cracks between the stones of the Western Wall. At night the stones are covered with drops of dew, which legend declares to be the tears the Wall sheds while reading the notes and weeping with all Israel.

The Rechov HaYehudim—Street of the Jews—in the Old City was the focus of Jewish life in Jerusalem from medieval times to 1948, when the Arabs completely destroyed it. In 1967, during the Six-Day War, the Old City, including this section, was liberated by Israel. Now Israel is restoring and redeveloping the Rechov HaYehudim. Many Israeli families now make their homes in the Old City of Jerusalem.

Hadassah Hospital

At Jerusalem's Hadassah Hospital, doctors and nurses work around the clock to save the lives of sick people, and researchers labor to find cures for diseases. In the hospital synagogue, twelve stained-glass windows present in glorious color the stories of the Twelve Tribes of Israel. The artist Marc Chagall created this magnificent display of color and light.

The Biblical Zoo

The children of Jerusalem are fortunate to live so near the Biblical Zoo! In this unique zoo, every animal, reptile, and bird mentioned in the Bible is represented. Each cage has a sign with the animal's name—as well as the biblical passage where the animal is mentioned.

Yom Yerushalayim

The date was the 28th day of the Hebrew month Iyar. Each year on this date Jews celebrate Yom Yerushalayim - Jerusalem Day. Israeli's rejoice at the reuniting of the Holy City and at the same time sadly morn the brave soldiers who fell in battle.

170

3. Emek Yizrael—The Jezreel Valley

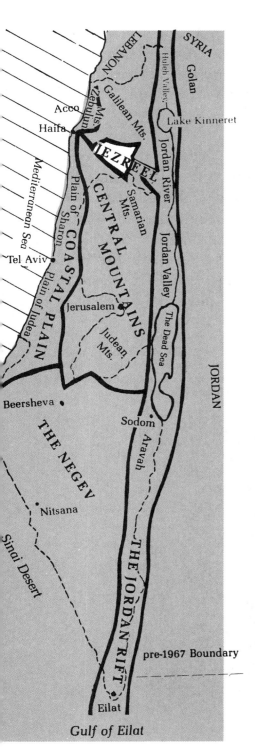

The fertile Jezreel Valley, with its patchwork of well-tended fields, lies between the peaks of the Galilean Mountains and the Samarian Mountains. But this thirty-mile sweep, stretching east to west between Haifa and the Jordan River, was not always so lovely. It used to be a slimy, mosquito-thick swamp, and the Arabs called it the Gates of Hell. The Zionist settlers of the early Yishuv drained the swamp and made the Emek (a short name for Emek Yizrael) a panorama of fields and trees.

Nahalal

The moshav of Nahalal stands at the foot of the Galilean Mountains. Tall, proud eucalyptus trees welcome the visitor to this farming village, established in 1921. An agricultural school here teaches men and women how to tend their farmlands and take care of animals and poultry.

Nahalal is shaped like a huge doughnut! In the central circle of the moshav stand all the public buildings—the dairy center, the school, the synagogue, and the community center. In the outer circle stand the privately owned farmhouses where each family of moshavniks lives.

The people of this moshav are hardworking, warm, and friendly. Many Nahalal families opened their homes to accept homeless refugee children who had fled Nazi Europe during and after the Second World War.

171

Kibbutz Beit Alpha

In Kibbutz Beit Alpha, diggers of an irrigation channel in 1928 came upon an unexpected find—the mosaic floor of an ancient synagogue! Archaeologists were called in, and they unearthed an exciting discovery—a beautifully inscribed mosaic floor with colored panels depicting a zodiac circle, animals and flowers, candelabras, scenes from the Bible, and religious emblems. Experts say the mosaic floor dates from the sixth century C.E.

Afula

In 1925, American Zionists who came to Israel on aliyah founded the city of Afula, twenty-four miles from Haifa. While builders were digging the foundations for homes, they discovered the remains of ancient tombs dating from biblical and medieval times.

Modern Afula is a factory center for the entire Emek. The rest of the valley consists primarily of farmland, but Afula buzzes and hums with the noise and bustle of modern industry.

The mosaic floor of the synagogue at Beit Alpha. The round panel shows the symbols of the zodiac. The names are in Hebrew. This mosaic is about 1,500 years old. A mosaic is a picture made by placing small pieces of colored glass or stone in cement.

VOCABULARY AND CONCEPTS

Nahalal	נַהֲלַל
Afula	עֲפוּלָה
Beit Alpha	בֵּית אַלְפָה
Jezreel Valley	עֵמֶק יִזְרְעֶאל

4. The Jordan Rift
THE JORDAN RIVER

The Jordan River is the major source of fresh water in Israel. According to the Talmud, the river's Hebrew name, Yarden, comes from the words *yored dan*—"descending from Dan." The ancient tribe of Dan settled near the river's starting point, and thus the river "descends from Dan," flowing southward from Mount Hermon in Lebanon.

Mount Hermon stands more than 9,000 feet tall. Melted snow from the top of this high mountain peak streams down the side of the mountain to form the headwaters of the Jordan River. Passing through the Hulah Valley, the Jordan then flows into Lake Kinneret, down through the Jordan Valley, and into the Dead Sea.

An aerial view of the Jordan River as it snakes its way across the land of Israel.

A short distance from the excavated mound of Jericho are found the ruins of a synagogue from the fifth or sixth century C.E.

The mosaic floor features a menorah with the Hebrew inscription, *Shalom al Yisrael,* "Peace be on Israel."

Crossing the Jordan River in the early 1900's.

The Jordan River in the Bible

The Jordan River is deeply important in Jewish history and is mentioned frequently in the Bible. In Jewish thought, the Jordan has become a traditional symbol of the gateway into the Promised Land, the doorway to freedom, rejoicing, and independence. This is because of a great miracle involving the Jordan that is recorded in the Bible. After the Exodus from Egypt and the forty years of wandering through the desert, when the ancient Israelites, led by Joshua, prepared to enter the Promised Land, the waters of the Jordan suddenly and miraculously stopped flowing. This miracle allowed the Jews to go over safely into the long-awaited homeland (Joshua, chaps. 3 and 4).

The Jordan River in Modern Israel

The Jordan River is modern Israel's main source of fresh water. By means of a giant pipeline, Jordan water is sent from the Kinneret through the hot Jordan Valley to the Negev. This marvelous irrigation system is called the Kinneret-Negev project. The Negev, which covers almost half of Israel, contains good farming land but has almost no water and receives very little rainfall. The pipeline carrying Jordan water to the desert has brought about a modern miracle. Where there were once empty sand dunes, farmers now grow cotton, sugar beets, wheat, vegetables, and corn, and new crops are introduced every year. The once-barren Negev is being transformed into a prosperous farming region.

The Jordan Valley

The Jordan Valley is a hot, almost tropical area. Temperatures here can zoom as high as 110 degrees. Israeli farmers in the Jordan Valley plant crops that thrive in hot, moist conditions—date palms, bananas, avocados, grapes, mangoes, pineapples, and papayas. Big, beautiful tomatoes, onions, cucumbers, cauliflowers, eggplants,

On the edge of the basin of the Jordan, palm trees flourish beside the spring of Ain es-Sultan.

cabbages, potatoes, artichokes, broccoli, and pumpkins grow here plentifully in the warm sunshine and lush soil.

Imagine a meal of fruits and vegetables from the Jordan Valley. What a remarkable variety of luscious foods! Which is your favorite?

Before the Six-Day War in 1967, the land in the Jordan Valley that had been held by the Arabs was barren. Only bleak military outposts manned by soldiers stood in the area. Now green fields, schools, and little farmhouses have been created here by Israeli settlers, and young families have moved into new moshavim.

VOCABULARY AND CONCEPTS

rdan River	הַיַּרְדֵּן
ount Hermon	הַר הֶרְמוֹן
leh Valley	עֵמֶק הַחוּלָה
rdan Valley	עֵמֶק הַיַּרְדֵּן

175

JERICHO—AN OASIS TOWN

Jericho is a sudden burst of color, fruits, and flowers in the midst of bleakness—down the mountains east of Jerusalem through the Wilderness of Judea, past a low plain. A gushing spring called the Spring of Elisha waters Jericho's soil. Here grow bananas, oranges, dates, papayas, poincianas, bougainvillea, and bright, green grass.

Jericho in the Bible

The history of Jericho goes back to ancient times. Jericho was the first of the powerful Canaanite cities that the Israelites had to conquer when they reached the Promised Land after the Exodus from Egypt and the forty years of wandering in the desert. The Bible tells us how Joshua, who became the Israelite leader after the death of Moses, sent two spies to get information about Jericho's defenses. The city was strongly fortified, surrounded by a mighty wall, but the Israelites were undaunted. Following God's instructions, they marched around the wall seven times; then, as the priests sounded the shofarot, the walls of Jericho miraculously came tumbling down, and the town was captured.

Near the Spring of Elisha is the beautiful mosaic floor of a fifth-century synagogue. It was found accidentally by an Arab digging the foundations of his house. In the middle of the floor is a menorah, and below it is written in Hebrew, *Shalom al Yisrael,* which means, "Peace be upon Israel."

Under the Arab Israeli peace treaty of 1993, Jericho and Gaza became the first two cities to come under Palestinian Authority.

The ruins of the palace of Hisham near Jericho.

The Arab Umayyad Caliph, Hisham, ruled at the beginning of the eighth century, and built himself a winter palace near Jericho in 724 C.E. Much of the palace is still standing.

VOCABULARY AND CONCEPTS

Jericho	יְרִיחוֹ
"Peace be upon Israel."	שָׁלוֹם עַל יִשְׂרָאֵל

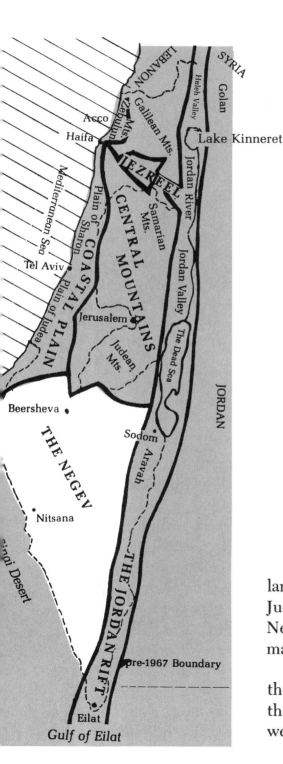

5. *The Negev*
THE LARGEST REGION OF ISRAEL

Looking at the map of Israel, you will note an area of land shaped like a triangle, with its base against the Judean Mountains. This is the hot, dry desert of the Negev, which means "south," the largest region of Israel, making up more than half of the country's land area.

From the hills, the Negev drops southward, down to the city of Eilat on the shores of the Red Sea. Hidden in the lonely, rocky hills of this barren desert lies untouched wealth in the form of valuable minerals.

The Negev in Bible Days

The Bible relates that the three patriarchs, Abraham, Isaac, and Jacob, pastured their flocks in the Negev in the vicinity of Beersheva, "the City of Seven Wells."

Until recently, scholars had been puzzled as to how large groups of people and animals could survive in such a desert. Then archaeologists discovered that in biblical times the Negev was a thriving area of farms and towns.

Until recently, scholars had been puzzled as to how large groups of people and animals could survive in such a desert. Then archaeologists discoverd the remains of ancient Negev settlements. Dams had been built, wells had been dug, crops grown and flocks grazed in the days of the patriarchs. Archaeologists even found evidence of some mining of metals.

Not too long after the era of the patriarchs, however, wandering bands of nomads invaded the Negev. These warlike people burned the settlements, destroyed the dams and wells, and forced the settlers to flee from the area.

Bird's-eye view of Avdat.

The Nabateans

For seventeen hundred years, the Negev lay idle and neglected, a playground for fierce desert winds and sun. Then the Nabateans arrived. A desert people, the Nabateans knew how to survive in the Negev desert. They knew how to trap and save water. They built dams during the rainy seasons that stored water for use in dry times. The Nabateans were excellent farmers and grew enough food for themselves as well as for the passing caravans.

The Nabateans, not content just to farm the desert land, also became very successful traders. They opened ports at Gaza and Eilat. From there they traded with India, Arabia, and Greece. Archaeologists have found traces of over three hundred Nabatean villages and believe that at one time there were more than 100,000 of these industrious desert farmers living in the Negev.

Drilling for oil near the Negev town of Heletz.

Two of these ancient Nabatean towns, Avdat and Shivta, have been restored by the Israeli government. By excavating the ancient houses, farms, dams, wells, and other water-saving devices, modern experts have been learning how the Nabateans became such successful farmers.

The Nabatean civilization ended with the rise of Islam. From that time until the rise of the State of Israel many centuries later, the Negev was again left to the mercy of the desert.

The Negev Today

Today, the Negev is once more being brought back to life. New towns and villages are being developed. Businesses are being built up and factories are being constructed. Giant pipelines now bring streams of water to the parched and thirsty land.

Once more, as in the days of the patriarchs, fields of golden grain ripple beneath the sunny desert skies and the cultivated land offers up rich crops of vegetables, sugar beets, corn, and cotton.

Now you can see natural gas, from Zohar and other places in the Negev, used in Israeli factories. Geologists continue to probe the Negev in search of oil, using sensitive, modern instruments. Someday, a giant oilfield may be discovered under the desert sands.

When Israel captured the Sinai desert in 1967, she had also captured several precious oilfields. But even more precious than oil was peace with Egypt. In 1982, Israel gave up the oilfields to secure a peace agreement with her Arab neighbor, Egypt.

VOCABULARY AND CONCEPTS

The Negev	נֶגֶב
Nabateans	נָבָּטִים
Heletz	חֵלֶץ

179

BEERSHEVA

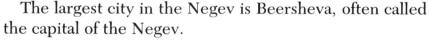

The largest city in the Negev is Beersheva, often called the capital of the Negev.

The origin of the name Beersheva is explained by the city's seven wells and by the seven ewes which, the Bible tells us, Abraham set aside as a sign of the agreement he made with Abimelech, the Philistine king. (In Hebrew, *be'er* means "well," and *sheva* means "oath" or "seven.")

After the Israelite conquest of the Promised Land, Beersheva became a city of the tribe of Simeon and later of the tribe of Judah. During the War of Independence in 1948, the invading Egyptian army made Beersheva its headquarters for the Negev. When the town was taken by Israeli forces in the same year, it was totally abandoned by its inhabitants, but early in 1949 Jewish settlers, mostly new immigrants, began to settle it once more. From 1951 large new suburbs were built, extending mainly to the north and northwest, while to the east a large industrial area sprang up.

A Bedouin encampment near Beersheva.

Why Modern Beersheva Is Important

Today Beersheva is a modern town that boasts a population of more than 120,000 Israelis. The city has several academic, scientific, and cultural institutions, among them the Soroka Medical Center Hospital, the Municipal Museum, and the Ben-Gurion University. At the Negev Institute for Arid Zone Research, scientists study ways to till dry desert land. In addition, Beersheva serves as a market center for the Negev Bedouins, a sight which delights tourists and brings back the flavor of the old nomadic town to a new and bustling city.

Like the spokes of a wheel, paved roads go out from Beersheva in all directions. These roads are the connecting links between the new towns, so that chemicals from the factories in Sodom and copper from the mines of Solomon in Timna can be transported to the port of Eilat and from there to cities around the world.

The roads also run past the oil fields at Heletz. At the present time, these oil fields only supply a small amount of the precious "black gold." But an intensive and determined search is going on constantly, with the hope that a greater supply of oil will one day be a reality.

Thursday is market day in Beersheva. On Thursday the Bedouin farmers and herdsmen converge on the city to sell and trade their produce and animals.

VOCABULARY AND CONCEPTS

southern part of Israel   נֶגֶב

he Negev   הַנֶּגֶב

eersheva (capital of the Negev)   בְּאֵר שֶׁבַע

THE DEAD SEA

The Dead Sea, the lowest spot on the surface of the earth, is a sort of treasure chest. It contains no sparkling rubies, sapphires, emeralds, or diamonds, no royal silks or gold coins; the treasure of the Dead Sea consists of salts, minerals, and chemicals that the world needs for the progress of science and industry.

The Origin of the Dead Sea's Mineral Wealth

Why does the Dead Sea have such a rich supply of such materials as potash, bromine, potassium, calcium, and table salt? The answer has to do with the sea's geographical location. The Dead Sea receives six million tons of water daily from the Jordan River and from five small streams in Jordan. However, there is no way for the water to leave the Dead Sea, so it just evaporates into the warm air. As the hot Negev sun evaporates the water, the salts and minerals suspended in the water remain in the sea. Year by year, as more water flows into the sea and then evaporates, the concentration of salts and minerals increases.

View of the Dead Sea and the Moab plateau.

Israeli stamp featuring one of Israel's most important chemical complexes, the Dead Sea Works.

A company called the Dead Sea Works, Ltd., processes these deposits for local use and for shipment abroad. The salts and minerals are dug out, and special little railway cars chug the valuable materials to a chemical plant. Scientists and engineers treat these materials so that they can be used for scientific experiments and industrial needs.

Some doctors believe that bathing in mineral-rich waters can cure certain ailments. For this reason, the Dead Sea in recent years has become a popular health resort. Under medical supervision, people with various complaints—especially skin conditions—take therapeutic treatments in the mineral-laden waters of the Dead Sea.

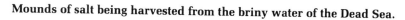

Mounds of salt being harvested from the briny water of the Dead Sea.

The water in the Dead Sea is so dense that it is impossible to drown. The high specific gravity of the water makes it so easy to float that bathers are able to read their favorite newspaper while taking a dip.

The Dead Sea Scrolls

Because of the hot, dry climate of the Dead Sea area, numerous ancient biblical scrolls have been preserved there. The famous Dead Sea Scrolls, found in 1947 in a cave near the sea, are now kept in a special Shrine of the Book at the Israel Museum in Jerusalem. These scrolls tell the story of a devout religious community of the Second Temple period, the Essenes. This group had separated itself from the rest of Jewish life and moved to this dry, desert place, seeking purity and peace in which to study and practice God's law.

The Dead Sea Scrolls are the oldest Hebrew manuscripts in existence. They are housed in the Shrine of the Book, in the Israel Museum, Jerusalem. The scroll of Isaiah is displayed fully opened around a drum.

VOCABULARY AND CONCEPTS

Eilat	אֵילַת
The Dead Sea	יָם הַמֶּלַח
The Dead Sea Scrolls	מְגִילוֹת יָם הַמֶּלַח
Jordan River	הַיַּרְדֵּן

184

EILAT

Eilat, situated on the Gulf of Eilat, Israel's outlet to the Red Sea, is mentioned in the Bible (I Kings 9:26) as a port city from which the ships of King Solomon's navy set sail for exotic lands. Modern Eilat, too, is a port city. It is Israel's gateway to the African continent and link to the Indian Ocean as well as to the Far East—China and Japan. All sorts of goods from faraway places are unloaded on Eilat's docks, and Israeli products leave this harbor for all parts of the globe.

A view of the modern city of Eilat.

Israeli stamp featuring the emblem of the port of Eilat.

How Eilat Was Settled

The early years of Eilat's settlement were fraught with problems. The hot, dry Negev climate and the seemingly barren ground discouraged people from moving here. They preferred to live near fertile farmland, green forests, pleasant beaches, and urban centers.

So few people wanted to move to Eilat in those early days that Israel's government made a special agreement with prisoners in the jails in Tel Aviv, Jerusalem, and Haifa. They were allowed to leave the jails if they promised to live in Eilat. In the newly settled town, the prisoners built homes and poured the concrete for roads and sidewalks. Eilat in those days was something like the frontier towns of the American "Wild West"—a place where only rugged individualists and pioneering spirits ventured.

Today Eilat is much more settled and civilized. Many people come to live in Eilat by choice, and the Israeli government no longer has to make deals with prisoners to populate this thriving Negev city. Many tourists come to visit the special display of beautiful glowing red corals in the Red Sea. A glass tunnel has been constructed, allowing visitors to stroll through the water and observe the rich reds, vibrant oranges, and crystal-clear aquamarine colors of the corals and the sea.

A skindiver prepares to explore the underwater wonders of the Red Sea.

VOCABULARY AND CONCEPTS

Eilat	אֵילַת
Gulf of Aqaba	עֲקָבָּה

186

HEBRON PRE-1967

The Cave of Machpelah

Abraham, the first Patriarch, purchased the Cave of Machpelah from Ephron the Hittite for 400 silver shekels. There he buried his beloved wife Sarah. Subsequently Isaac and Rebecca, and Jacob and Leah, were also interred there. The fourth couple, the Midrash tells us, was Adam and Eve.

As a reminder of the four holy couples buried in the Cave of Machpelah, Hebron is called Kiryat Arba ("City of Four").

Jews revere the Cave of Machpelah as the burial place of the Patriarchs and Matriarchs. Muslims venerate it as Al-Haram Al-Ibrahimi, the tomb of Abraham.

The Torah records a prophecy that Ishmael would become "the father of a great nation." Based on this prophecy, the Koran, Islam's sacred book, identifies Ishmael as the ancestor of the Arabs.

About 3,000 years ago, Hebron was King David's capital before he conquered Jerusalem. The city was destroyed by the Romans in the first century C.E., and the Byzantines built a Christian church on the site of the Cave of Machpelah.

The Crusaders captured the city in 1100 C.E. , and expelled all the Jews. They turned the mosque and the adjoining synagogue into a church.

After the Expulsion in 1492, Jews escaping from Spain settled in the city. Under Ottoman Turkish rule they made Hebron a center for the study of Kabbalah.

The Riot of 1929

In 1929 the peaceful Jews of Hebron were attacked by a Arab mob. In the ensuing riot, 69 Jewish men, women, and children were murdered. Their homes were looted, their businesses were vandalized, and the city's synagogues were burned. The Jewish community of Hebron was totally destroyed.

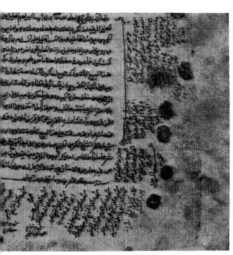

Over the centuries the Jews of Hebron have always legally purchased the land they occupied. In biblical times Abraham purchased the Cave of Machpelah from Ephron the Hittite for 400 silver shekels. In 1807, Chayim Ha-Mitzri purchased 4 dunams of land from an Arab. The illustration is a facsimile of the deed transferring the property.

THE JEWS IN HEBRON

The Arab rioters in 1929 demolished or burned all of Hebron's synagogues. This Jewish survivor managed to salvage a Torah scroll from the ruins of a synagogue.

As a result of the Six-Day War in 1967, Hebron came under Israeli rule as part of the territory of Judea and Samaria. The Israeli government restored the right to worship at Abraham's tomb but did not allow Jews to settle in the city. In 1972, as a compromise, it permitted a group of settlers to establish the community of Kiryat Arba about half a mile from the Cave of Machpelah.

By 1994 the Jewish community of Hebron numbered 400. Despite the hostility of the city's Arab inhabitants, the Jewish settlers lead secure and religiously meaningful lives under the protection of the IDF.

Dr. Baruch Goldstein

On February 24, 1994, Dr. Baruch Goldstein, a resident of Kiryat Arba, entered the Cave of Machpelah and opened fire on the Muslim worshippers. He killed 29 Arabs and was himself beaten to death. According to friends and relatives, Dr. Goldstein was deeply troubled by the Rabin-Arafat peace agreement.

The Hebron Massacre

In 1929 hundreds of highly organized Arab rioters attacked the Jewish community in Hebron and murdered 69 innocent men, women, and children. They did this even though there was no Israeli government or militant Jewish settlers to arouse their anger. The mere presence of a few Jews in Hebron was enough to provoke a massacre. When the riot was over, not even one Arab official bothered to express sympathy or to apologize.

In contrast, the 1994 massacre was the act of one deranged man, on his own, who felt abandoned by his government and was deeply troubled about the many Arab terrorist attacks on Jews that had taken place in the preceding months. In the aftermath, Israel's highest officials, starting with Prime Minister Yitzchak Rabin, apologized publicly for the murders and Israel is paying compensation to the families of the victims.

Pre-State

HISTORY OF ISRAEL

When we learn Jewish history, we discover the deep and ancient link between the Jewish people and the land of Israel. The modern state was declared in 1948, but when we study history, we know that King David ruled over a Jewish Israel in the glorious days of independence many years before. And we learn of our ultimate link to Israel—God's promise of the land to our forefathers, the very first Jews—Abraham, Isaac, and Jacob.

A knowledge of Jewish history strengthens our love of Israel, the Jewish homeland.

THE PROMISED LAND OF ABRAHAM, ISAAC, AND JACOB

Abraham grew up in Haran, where people worshiped the forces of nature and bowed down to idols. Even as a boy, Abraham questioned the religion of his family and community. Abraham understood that the idols of Haran were false gods, and that one true God alone is the Creator of our universe.

God's Promise to Abraham

God revealed Himself to Abraham and promised that Abraham's children would become a glorious nation, God's Chosen People—the Jews. God promised that the land of Canaan would become Abraham's new home and would forever be the homeland of the Jewish people.

The Origin of the Word "Hebrew"

In order to reach Canaan from Haran, Abraham and his wife, Sarah, had to cross the Euphrates River. In Canaan, therefore, Abraham was called the *Ivri*, which meant "from the other side." Abraham and his descendants were called Hebrews, a word derived from *Ivri*, and the language of Israel is called the Hebrew tongue.

Documents unearthed in Egypt speak of Habiru or Apiru people and describe Semitic tribes wandering through the hill country and the Negev.

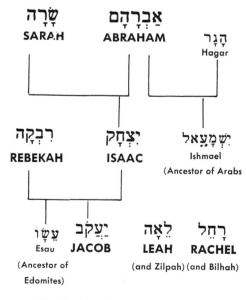

The Patriarchs and Matriarchs of Israel (Biblical lineage of the Patriarchal families.)

190

Isaac and Jacob

Abraham's son Isaac married Rebecca, who had grown up outside of Canaan. Like Abraham, Rebecca had to uproot herself from her home and its primitive religion. She too embraced the belief in the one true God. With Isaac and with Isaac's son Jacob, God renewed the promise of the land of Canaan.

Jacob left Canaan for a number of years, after a bitter quarrel with his twin brother Esau. Jacob married his cousins Leah and Rachel (in those days, marrying more than one wife was allowed).

Just before Jacob crossed the Jordan River on his return home to Canaan, God blessed him and gave him a new name, Israel. The name hints at the strange encounter Jacob had before he crossed the Jordan—a night-long wrestling match with a powerful stranger whom Jacob finally conquered. Jacob was now known as Israel, and his sons—eventually twelve in all—came to be known as the Children of Israel. The large families of these twelve brothers became the twelve tribes of Israel, also known as the Israelites. And the Jewish homeland of Canaan, which God had promised to Abraham, Isaac, and Jacob and to their descendants, became known as the land of Israel.

The Cave of Machpelah, where the patriarchs are buried, is behind the ancient walls of Hebron.

Hebron was David's capital until his conquest of Jerusalem. There was a Jewish community in Hebron during most of the Middle Ages and through the Turkish period. The modern Jewish community of Hebron was destroyed by the Arabs in 1929 and again in 1936. Hebron was incorporated into Jordan from 1948 to 1967. It came under Israeli control during the Six-Day War, when the West Bank territories were conquered. In 1968 a new Jewish settlement was established just outside of Hebron.

VOCABULARY AND CONCEPTS

braham's birthplace	אוּר
Hebrew	עִבְרִי
rael (Jacob's new name)	יִשְׂרָאֵל
he Cave of Machpeleh	מְעָרַת הַמַּכְפֵּלָה

191

SLAVERY IN EGYPT AND REDEMPTION

Jacob had twelve sons, but he loved young Joseph best. To Joseph he gave a special gift—a coat of many brilliant, beautiful colors. The other brothers became terribly jealous. Every time they saw that special, colorful coat, their hearts filled with envy and hatred for the favored boy. Finally, the brothers seized Joseph and sold him to some passing merchants, who resold him to an Egyptian officer. The brothers stained Joseph's coat with a goat's blood and lied to Jacob that a wild animal had attacked and killed his beloved child.

From Slave to Royal Officer

Joseph did not rot away in Egypt as a forgotten slave. His ability to interpret dreams brought him to Pharaoh's attention at court, where he soon became a powerful officer. Perceptive, handsome, ingenious, and personally charming, Joseph never forgot the religion of his parents and his ancestors all the time he was in Egypt. A skilled organizer, he directed the storage of Egyptian grain supplies so that if famine should come, Egypt would have enough food not only to survive but also to sell at great profit to neighboring peoples.

THE TWELVE TRIBES OF ISRAEL

לֵאָה	יַעֲקֹב	רָחֵל
LEAH	JACOB	RACHEL

רְאוּבֵן	Reuben	יוֹסֵף	אֶפְרַיִם Ephraim
שִׁמְעוֹן	Simeon	Joseph	מְנַשֶּׁה Manasseh
לֵוִי	Levi		
יְהוּדָה	Judah	בִּנְיָמִין	Benjamin
יִשָּׂשכָר	Issachar		
זְבֻלוּן	Zebulun		
	Dinah		

(Zilpah maidservant)		(Bilhah, maidservant)	
גָּד	Gad	דָּן	Dan
אָשֵׁר	Asher	נַפְתָּלִי	Naphtali

192

An ancient Egyptian wall-painting showing prisoners at work making bricks and building a wall.

Why the Israelites Went to Egypt

When famine struck the entire Middle East region, Egypt was well prepared with food supplies. But in Canaan, people suffered from hunger. Jacob's other sons, never dreaming that Joseph had become an important Egyptian official, journeyed to Egypt to buy some food for their starving families. Imagine the brothers' mixed feelings of pride, regret, fear, and wonder when Joseph made himself known to them in the Egyptian palace! But Joseph forgave his brothers for the past and invited them to move with their whole households to Egypt.

The Egyptians Enslave the Israelites

The Israelites lived peacefully in Egypt for a while, but then a new Pharaoh came to power. The cruel new king forced the Israelites to become his slaves and placed brutal taskmasters over them. Men, women, and children had to labor for unending hours under the fierce sun. They hauled the heavy bricks and mixed the mortar for the Pharaoh's deluxe palaces and pyramids, some of which still stand today in modern Egypt. Then the Pharaoh decided that he had enough Israelites. Fearing that the oppressed people might rebel if their numbers increased, he ordered all Israelite male babies killed.

Many scholars today believe that Rameses II was the Pharaoh in whose reign the Exodus from Egypt took place. Rameses II left many memorials, among them this massive rock temple at Abu Simbel in Lower Nubia. Four stone statues of Rameses II, each over sixty feet high, sit in front of the temple on the left bank of the Nile.

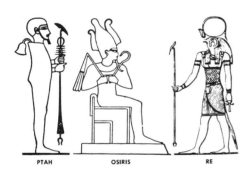

Some of the important Egyptian gods during the period of Israel's bondage and eventual exodus.

God Sends Moses to Liberate the Israelites

One baby boy, hidden by his mother among the bulrushes of the Nile River, was found by the Pharaoh's daughter. The princess loved the baby and had him raised in the royal palace. She called him Moses, which meant, "He that I drew forth from the water."

When Moses grew up, he yearned to ease the pain of his enslaved brothers. God revealed Himself to Moses and told him to ask Pharaoh to release the Israelites. "Let my people go," demanded Moses, but Pharaoh did not listen until God had smitten Egypt with ten plagues.

The Exodus

After the tenth plague, Pharaoh finally released the Children of Israel. Moses led the liberated slaves out of bondage, toward freedom, nationhood, and their promised homeland, Canaan (Israel). Every spring, Jews celebrate the joyful Passover holiday, which recalls the Israelites' liberation from slavery in Egypt. We thank God each Passover for the great miracle of this redemption.

An artist's rendering of the Tabernacle in the desert. The Tabernacle was the sanctu in which the Israelites worshipped God. It was constructed in such a way as to be ea portable.

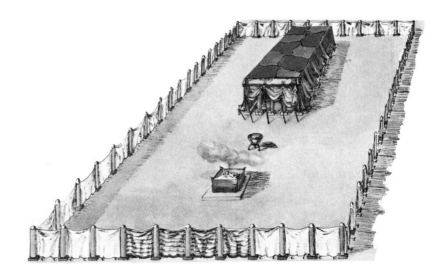

A photo of Mount Sinai. It was on top of this mountain that Moses received the Ten Commandments.

As they journeyed through the desert to Canaan, the Israelites lived in small, flimsy tents that could be moved easily. These tents were called *sukkot* in Hebrew. Jews today celebrate the holiday of Sukkot, remembering God's care and guidance over the Jews on their desert journey toward the Promised Land.

The Giving of the Torah

At Mount Sinai, the Israelites had an extraordinary experience that unified them as a people. Through Moses, God gave the Israelites the Ten Commandments and the Torah. These great works include the moral laws of honesty, faith, and brotherhood by which Jews guide their lives. These great teachings have influenced people of other religions too, all over the world. Each year, on the Shavuot holiday, Jews celebrate the receiving of the Torah and remember the experience at Mount Sinai.

VOCABULARY AND CONCEPTS

Israel	יִשְׂרָאֵל
Egypt	מִצְרַיִם
Pharaoh	פַּרְעֹה
Joseph	יוֹסֵף
Torah	תּוֹרָה
Moses	מֹשֶׁה
Mount Sinai	הַר סִינַי
Huts in which the Israelites lived during their desert journeys	סֻכּוֹת

195

IN THE PROMISED LAND

In 1896 the archaeologist Flinders Petrie discovered the stele (stone monument) of Pharaoh Merneptah. It is called the "Israel Stele" because it is the only ancient Egyptian artifact mentioning the name of the Israelite people.

| *un* | *I-sr-áa-l* | *feket* | *ben* |
| Is | Israel | laid waste, not [exists] | |

pert-f,	*Khar*	*kheperu em*	*khart*
his grain,	Syria	hath become as	a widow.
r progeny)			

Now the Israelites were ready to claim their homeland. Moses, the great liberator and teacher, died before they reached the Promised Land. Joshua led the people over the River Jordan. Under his leadership they battled the local Canaanite rulers and finally triumphed. The twelve tribes settled down after many years of wandering, each family making its home in a different part of Israel.

At first, each tribe ruled itself. When enemies attacked, leaders called judges (*shoftim* in Hebrew) arose who unified the tribes and combined their forces in times of crisis. One of these was the wise and brave prophetess Deborah. But many rivalries existed among the families. The Israelites decided to appoint one king over all twelve tribes, hoping that this leader would unify everyone.

The Monarchy (ca. 1020–1004 B.C.E.)

Saul became the first king of Israel. A great warrior, Saul won many battles against the Philistines and other enemies. Late in life, Saul grew jealous of David, a young shepherd who became popular after he had felled the giant Philistine Goliath in a famous duel. After Saul's death, David became king.

King Solomon's mines near Eilat. A modern copper mine has been opened on the same site.

The United Kingdom (ca. 1004–928 B.C.E.)

King David, greatly loved by the people, won many battles and widened Israel's boundaries. He chose Jerusalem, a city in the heart of the country, as the nation's capital.

King David was succeeded by his son, the wise King Solomon. Solomon made Israel a great trading nation and built the fortified cities of Hazor, Megiddo, Gezer, and Ezion Gever (Eilat) on the Red Sea. Israel's seafarers sailed to Africa and the Orient. They brought back exotic spices and gold from the mines of Ophir.

In the middle of Jerusalem, King Solomon built the Holy Temple, a glorious structure dedicated to the worship of God. Solomon spared no expense on beautiful products for the Temple. Exotic woods, sparkling gemstones, richly colored embroideries were imported from all over the world to Jerusalem. Jews came from all over Israel to pray at the spectacular Temple, especially on Passover, Sukkot, and Shavuot. The Jews prayed gratefully to God, who had redeemed them from Egypt and brought them to freedom in their beloved homeland.

Tomb of King David. The covering reads: "David, King of Israel, is alive and well."

The Division (ca. 928–586 B.C.E.)

After Solomon died, the government of Israel began to totter. The tribes disagreed so much among themselves that the country split up into two separate kingdoms. In the north, the Kingdom of Israel, consisting of the ten northern tribes, established its capital in the city of Samaria.

In the south, the Kingdom of Judah, consisting of the tribe of Judah and the tribe of Benjamin, kept its capital in army. Of course, neither of the separate kingdoms was as strong as the combined kingdom had been.

In 721 B.C.E., Assyrians stormed into the northern Kingdom of Israel and wiped it out. The Israelites who had lived there were scattered throughout the Middle East by the Assyrians and were never heard from again. History refers to these vanished Israelites as the "lost tribes."

The black obelisk was set up by Shalmanesser III in his palace at Nimrud. It is inscribed with the story of his battles.

The famous Moabite stone, discovered by archaeologists in 1868, records how Moab rebelled against the House of Omri.

In this panel Jehu, the king of Israel, is on his knees bowing before the victorious Shalmaneser.

It was the policy of the Babylonian kings to destroy the cities that they captured. The leaders were killed or deported and the city walls destroyed. This is a wall of stone blocks, some of the remains of the ancient walls of Jerusalem.

The Destruction of the First Temple

The southern Kingdom of Judah survived for about another century. But in 586 B.C.E., Babylonia invaded Judah, capturing Jerusalem and burning down the Temple on the ninth day of Av. A remnant of Judah's population continued to live as Jews in the Holy Land, but thousands of Judeans were taken as exiles to Babylonia. There they grieved for their lost freedom. As we are told in Psalm 137:

> If I forget thee, O Jerusalem,
> May my right hand forget its cunning.
> Let my tongue cleave to the roof of my mouth,
> If I remember thee not;
> If I set not Jerusalem
> Above my chiefest joy.

(Psalm 137: 1, 5, 6)

The idea of Zionism and Shivat Zion (Returning to Zion) originated with the Babylonian exiles. Ever since Babylonia, Jews no matter where they lived never stopped praying for Shivat Zion.

Detail from a Babylonian relief showing prisoners from Judah playing lyres and guarded by a soldier.

VOCABULARY AND CONCEPTS

e Kingdom of Israel	מַמְלֶכֶת יִשְׂרָאֵל
e Kingdom of Judah	מַמְלֶכֶת יְהוּדָה
lges	שׁוֹפְטִים
maria (capital of the northern ngdom of Israel)	שׁוֹמְרוֹן
usalem (capital of the kingdom Judah)	יְרוּשָׁלַיִם
n tribes	עֲשֶׂרֶת הַשְּׁבָטִים
e ninth day of the Hebrew onth of Av (the day the Temple in rusalem was destroyed)	תִּשְׁעָה בְּאָב

THE BABYLONIAN EXILE AND THE FIRST RETURN

Tomb of Cyrus the Great at his capital city, Pasargadae. The mausoleum is set above the level of the surrounding plain on several stepped courses.

Inscribed cylinder recording the capture of Babylon by Cyrus. It tells how "without battle and without fighting Marduk (god of Babylon) made him (Cyrus) enter into his city of Babylon; he spared Babylon tribulation, and Nabonidus the (Chaldean) king, who feared him not, he delivered into his hand." Nabonidus, the Chaldean king of Babylon, was not in favor with the priests, and they assisted in delivering the city to Cyrus.

In Babylonia the Jews continued their religious traditions. Great prophets and teachers like Isaiah and Ezekiel encouraged the exiles to study God's Torah and to observe God's commandments faithfully. Rabbinic scholars in Babylon began to put their traditional teachings into writing, creating the text of the Oral Law that became the Talmud. Since the Jews no longer had a Temple, they built synagogues where they prayed, studied, and hoped for an eventual return to Judea. They always faced toward Jerusalem when they worshipped.

The Return (ca. 522 B.C.E.)

Fifty years after the Babylonian conquest, the Persians won control over Babylonia. Now the fate of the Jews was in the hands of Cyrus, the Persian king. Cyrus was a kind and generous ruler; he announced that the Jewish exiles could return to Judea. He even encouraged them to rebuild the Temple in Jerusalem. The terms "First Return" and "Return to Zion" are applied to the joyous occasion when the Babylonian exiles went back to their Jewish national homeland.

Ezra and Nehemiah: The Second Temple

Two great leaders guided the Jews who returned to Judea: Ezra and Nehemiah. Ezra, a devoted teacher, tirelessly studied Torah with the people and brought back to Torah Jews who had neglected religious laws. Nehemiah organized the rebuilding of protective walls around Jerusalem so that the holy capital was made more secure. Together, Ezra and Nehemiah led the proud, happy Jews in the dedication of the Second Temple in Jerusalem.

Bust of Alexander the Great.

Alexander the Great being greeted by the High Priest Jaddua. From a fourteenth-century French picture.

VOCABULARY AND CONCEPTS

..riod of the Second ..mple	תְּקוּפַת בַּיִת שֵׁנִי
..bylon	בָּבֶל
..rus	כּוֹרֶשׁ
..ile	גָּלוּת
..e Return to Zion	שִׁיבַת צִיּוֹן
..ra	עֶזְרָא
..hemiah	נְחֶמְיָה
..e Hashmonaeem family	חַשְׁמוֹנָאִים
..accabee	מַכַּבִּי

The period of the Second Temple was a time of great creativity in Jewish literature and learning. Rabbinic scholars in Israel, as in Babylonia, compiled the Oral Law into the text of the Talmud.

The Hashmonaeem (166–37 B.C.E.)

When Alexander the Great and the Greeks conquered the Persians in the fourth century B.C.E., the Jews were not harmed. After Alexander's death, his generals divided up his empire. The Seleucid family ruled in Syria and eventually gained control over Judea. The Seleucid king of Syria, Antiochus, treated the Jews with harsh and maniacal cruelty. He tried to force them to bow down to pagan gods, but the Jews refused to violate the Torah and their belief in one true God. In 164 B.C.E., a small army of Jewish rebels led by Judah Maccabee drove the Syrians out of Jerusalem.

The Temple, which had been defiled by Antiochus' offerings to pagan gods, was rededicated and purified; the Menorah was relit. Miraculously, the Menorah burned eight days on a one-day supply of oil. Jews still celebrate this miracle on the eight-day festival of Chanukah ("Dedication," in Hebrew).

For years the Maccabee brothers and their descendants—the Hashmonaeem—ruled an independent Jewish state in the land of Israel. This period was called the Period of the Hashmonaeem.

THE ROMAN CONQUEST AND THE DESTRUCTION OF THE SECOND TEMPLE

Then came the Romans. When they conquered Judea, they allowed the Jews no political freedoms. Instead, the Romans appointed their own officials, called procurators, to rule over the land. These cruel procurators crucified many Jews for imagined crimes and stole the riches of the Holy Temple to line their own pockets. One procurator, Pontius Pilate, crucified the young Jewish preacher Jesus, who had been hailed by his followers as the Messiah. Jesus' followers began the Christian religion. The crucifixion took place in the year 30 C.E.

Several years after the crucifixion, a Greek Jew named Paul became a Christian. Paul traveled all over the Roman Empire preaching about Jesus. Paul told the pagans that they could be saved if they believed Jesus was the Messiah. He assured them that they could serve

The Romans were brilliant engineers and prolific builders. They left their imprint on the civilizations of the countries they conquered. Many Roman roads, monuments, aqueducts, and amphitheathers have survived the ravages of time and war.

This is one of the high-level aqueducts built by the Romans in Caesarea.

Earliest known manuscript of the letters of Paul, 200 C.E.

the one God of the Jews without having to follow the laws of Torah. Paul convinced many pagans, and many became followers of Jesus, or Christians. Eventually, as more and more pagans converted, Christianity became the religion of the whole Roman Empire.

The First Revolt (66–73 C.E.)

When Caligula, a Roman emperor, insisted madly that he be worshiped as a god throughout his empire, the Jews refused to bow down to his statue, no matter how powerful the legions who stood behind Caligula's demand. The Romans relented, but even so, the situation in Judea became intolerable for the Jews. In 66 B.C.E., in the time of another insane emperor, Nero, they revolted against the Romans and organized themselves to defend their beloved homeland against the inevitable military onslaught.

The Jewish soldiers fought valiantly, but their army was no match for the massive, powerful, and well-equipped Roman army. The Jews were pushed back to their main stronghold, Jerusalem, where they made a desperate last stand for Jewish freedom.

A copy of the carving of the Arch of Titus, showing the menorah and other furniture of the Temple being carried in triumph through the streets of Rome.

VOCABULARY AND CONCEPTS

ₑ First Revolt   הַמֶּרֶד הָרִאשׁוֹן

ₘans   רוֹמָאִים

A section of the relief on the Arch of Titus. The Jewish prisoners are carrying the Temple Menorah through the streets of Rome.

The Destruction of the Second Temple

For weeks, the small band of Jews defended themselves against legions of Romans. Jewish men, women, and children struggled to save the holy city. But the Roman general Titus and his legions, armed with the best weapons of those times, forced their way into Jerusalem. From within the Temple gates the Jews tried to defend themselves. But Titus had a stone wall built around the Temple, preventing the trapped Jewish fighters from getting food or water.

Famished with hunger, parched with thirst, overwhelmed by fatigue and by despair, the Jews felt completely drained of strength. In the year 70 C.E., on the bleak ninth day of Av—the same day of the year on which the First Temple had fallen—Titus and his troops set the Second Temple afire. The Romans massacred the Jews they found behind the Temple walls.

Jews today mark the ninth day of Av (Tisha Be'Av) as a day of fasting and mourning in memory of the martyrs who fought for Jerusalem in 70 C.E.—and in memory of all the heroes who struggled for Jewish freedom throughout our history.

Titus was so proud of his victory that he led a victory parade through Rome. Jewish prisoners were forced to carry the Menorah of their beloved Temple through the streets of the enemy. The government struck coins bearing the words *Judaea capta:* "Judea is taken." The Arch of Titus, built to celebrate the triumph, still stands in the ruins of the Roman forum.

A Roman coin with a bust of Vespasian, Titus' father, and the inscription *Judaea capta,* "Judaea is taken."

204

The Fall of Masada

The Romans had captured Jerusalem in 70 C.E., but some valiant Jewish soldiers refused to give up. This band of resistance fighters took refuge in the fortress at Masada, a flat-topped rock plateau in the desolate Judean desert, overlooking the Dead Sea. Although the Temple had been destroyed and Jerusalem had fallen, the Jewish fighters stood their ground. They refused to submit, no matter how powerful the Roman legions. For seven months, the Roman soldiers battled against the last Jewish stronghold, Masada.

It was the first day of Passover, 72 C.E. The Jewish leader, Eleazar ben Yair, called together all the soldiers. He advised his people to take their own lives rather than fall into the hands of the Romans:

> We know in advance that tomorrow we shall fall into the enemy's hands; but we still have the free choice of dying a noble death together with our loved ones. Let our wives die undisgraced, and our children free from the shackles of slavery! And after they have preceded us in death, let us perform a service of love for one another, and then the glory of having sustained freedom will take the place of an honorable burial.

Children whose parents were killed in the wars of liberation are taken to Masada for their Bar Mitzvah ceremony. Graduates of Zahal's paratroop school are also sworn in atop Masada.

The fortress of Masada, high on a rock near the Dead Sea, was the last Jewish stronghold to fall to the Roman conquerors following the destruction of the Temple.

205

Israeli postage stamps with views of the fortress of Masada

The Jewish soldiers at Masada agreed with Eleazar ben Yair, their leader. They chose ten men by lot to slay the others, and one of the ten to kill those remaining, and finally himself. The Romans entered Masada the next day—but their victory was empty. There were no Jews left to capture; all were already dead. The event became known through the historical writings of Josephus Flavius, who spoke to two Jewish women and five children who had escaped death by hiding away.

The Hebrew sign atop Masada reads, "Masada will not fall a second time."
Graduation exercises for members of Tsahal who have finished paratroop school are conducted on Masada. The paratroopers vow, "Masada will not fall a second time."

VOCABULARY AND CONCEPTS

Betar	בֵּיתָּר
The First Revolt	הַמֶּרֶד הָרִאשׁוֹן
Tisha Be'Av	תִּשְׁעָה בְּאָב
The Second Temple	הַבַּיִת הַשֵּׁנִי
Eleazar ben Yair	אֶלְעָזָר בֶּן יָאִיר
Masada	מְצָדָה

THE SECOND JEWISH REVOLT

The Second Jewish Revolt (131 C.E.)

The Romans had destroyed the Temple, and the Jews who remained in Israel lived greatly restricted lives, paying high taxes to the Roman conquerors. But the Jewish spirit was not dead. The yearning for national independence stayed alive and strong. Sixty-two years after the first revolt, the Jews again rebelled against the Romans, under the leadership of Simeon Bar Kochba and Rabbi Akiba.

Rabbi Akiba, the spiritual leader of the revolt, was a very old man when he met Bar Kochba, who became the Jewish military leader. The young man's real name was Shimon Bar Kozeba, but the wise rabbi renamed him Bar Kochba, which means "Son of a Star." Together, the old rabbi and the young warrior spoke to the Jews of Israel, gathering together fighters who would return the land of Israel to Jewish hands.

The letter in which Bar Kochba requests *etrogim, lulavim,* myrtles, and willows—the "four kinds" needed for Sukkot.

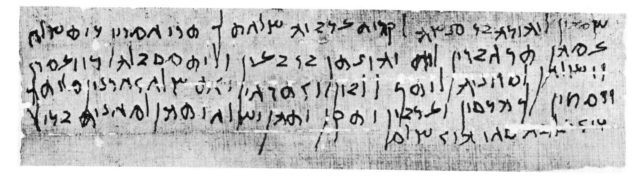

A silver coin issued by the revolutionary government of Bar Kochba. He and his followers set up a Jewish state (132–135 C.E.) which was soon crushed by the Romans.

Hadrian, the Roman emperor (117–138) who suppressed Bar Kochba's revolt against Roman tyranny.

When the Romans realized that a Jewish uprising had begun, they sent strong, well-armed legions out to fight the Jewish rebels. In the initial battles the Jews were triumphant. Bar Kochba and his fighters pursued the Roman army out of Israel, into Syria.

The Jewish army recaptured Jerusalem. Joyfully, led by General Bar Kochba, the people returned to the devastated site of their beloved Temple and offered up grateful prayers to God. At last Israel had once again become an independent Jewish state. Special coins were minted to celebrate the newly won independence of Israel. The coins showed the Temple gate with a star above it on one side, and the name of Bar Kochba and the date (131–132 C.E.) on the other.

But the independence of Israel under Bar Kochba lasted for only a short time. In the year 135, the Roman emperor sent in his most powerful troops. The Jews fought bravely, but after many brutal battles, the Romans ousted the Jewish forces.

Betar—Bar Kochba's Last Stand

Bar Kochba and his fighters made a final stand at Betar, a mountain fortress southwest of Jerusalem. The Romans outnumbered the Jews and surrounded them; no water or food reached the Jewish fighters, and many died of thirst and starvation. Bar Kochba and his fighters died in their last battle, defending Betar.

The Aftermath

According to Roman custom, Jerusalem was "plowed up with a yoke of oxen," renamed Colonia Aelia Capitolina, and barred to Jewish entry on pain of death. To blot out all ties with Israel, the Romans also renamed Judea "Syria Palestinia."

Many Jews were exiled by the Romans and scattered throughout the Roman Empire. Josephus records that of a probable Jewish population of three million before the First Revolt, more than a million died in the siege of Jerusalem alone.

Israeli stamp featuring a coin from the period of Bar Kochba.

There were countless victims in other parts of Judea, in Galilee, in Transjordan. Tens of thousands of Jews were sold into slavery.

Jewish sovereignty was interrupted until the proclamation of modern Israel—nineteen centuries later in 1948. But some Jews always remained in Israel, keeping alive the traditions of their ancestors. Jews in Israel and in every country of exile prayed that someday, God's promise that Israel would be the homeland of the Jewish people would once again be fulfilled.

VOCABULARY AND CONCEPTS

The Second Jewish Revolt	הַמֶּרֶד הַשֵּׁנִי
Palestine	פַּלֶשְׂתִּינָה
Bar Kochba	שִׁמְעוֹן בַּר־כּוֹכְבָא
Rabbi Akiba	רַבִּי עֲקִיבָא

THE MISHNAH AND THE TALMUD

Yavneh

After Jerusalem was destroyed by the Romans in 70 C.E., the Jewish people in Israel had to find a new center for Torah study and law. Yavneh, a town in the coastal plain, the southwestern part of the country, became the new spiritual capital of Israel. In Yavneh, great rabbis and judges came to live and teach the words of Torah; in the northern Galilean area, properous farms flourished in the fertile land. The ancients had a saying, "If you would acquire wisdom, go south. If it is wealth you seek, go north."

Rabbi Yohanan ben Zakkai re-established the Sanhedrin, (Israel's supreme judicial body,) which continued for several centuries as the center of Jewish communal life in Eretz Yisrael.

The title page of a tractate of the Jerusalem Talmud printed in Poland in 1866.

Bar-am, in the Upper Galilee, is the sight of one of the best preserved ancient synagogues in Israel. It dates to the end of the second or the beginning of the third century C.E.

Holy tombs in Tiberias, from a 1598 manuscript written in Italy. The large tomb, upper right, is that of Rabbi Akiba. The tomb, upper left, is that of Rabbi Akiba's wife. She is buried in the cave below the tomb. In between and below are the tombs of other rabbis.

A page of the Talmud: the central column is a section of the Mishnah and the Gemara; around the central column are commentaries and notes on the text.

The Mishnah

Traditionally, rabbis and scholars had interpreted the Torah orally. Directly explaining the biblical text to their students, the rabbis had applied the Torah laws and stories to Jewish life through the ages.

But in Roman times, many great rabbis, scholars, and teachers were killed by the Romans, who forbade the study of Torah. Rabbi Yehuda HaNassi, who headed the Jewish community in Israel, feared that the important oral teachings of our great rabbis might be lost. He decided that the oral teachings should be put into writing, lest they be forgotten in future generations. He labored long and hard to collect these teachings into a book called the *Mishnah*, a name which comes from a Hebrew root meaning "to study and to teach." Rabbi Yehuda HaNassi divided up the oral teachings into six books, each one dealing with Jewish laws about a different area of life.

The Making of the Talmud

In later generations, interpretations of the Mishnah developed. Rabbis and scholars in two major Jewish communities—Eretz Israel and Babylonia—compiled their commentaries on the Mishnah. These commentaries on the Mishnah are grouped together in the *Gemara*, or "Completion." The combination of the Mishnah and the Gemara is called the Talmud, or "Learning."

The rabbis and scholars in the land of Israel compiled the Jerusalem Talmud in 400 C.E. The teachers of the Babylonian community compiled the Babylonian Talmud in 500 C.E. The Babylonian Talmud became recognized as the most authoritative version of the Talmud.

But Roman persecution of Torah scholars began in Yavneh too. After the second revolt, led by Bar Kochba and Rabbi Akiba, the rabbis and sages again had to move the center of Jewish learning, this time to the north. Tiberias became the new center of Torah study.

Colophon of the Masoretic Codex of Moses ben Asher (897 C.E.).

In Galilee, Jewish communities began to flourish, and an academy in Tiberias became a center of study. Just as the scholars of Babylonia were especially noted for their knowledge of law, so the scholars in Palestine excelled in their talent for poetry. The land of their fathers filled them with inspiration and with a deep reverence for their history. Many of their beautiful hymns were preserved and later became part of the Jewish prayerbook.

The Masorah

An absorbing task that now occupied the scholars of Tiberias was the establishment of the Masorah. "Masorah" means "handing down," or more specifically, the establishment of the correct, standard text of the Holy Scriptures: the correct way of writing down the Torah scrolls and other biblical books for "handling down" to future generations. The scholars who performed this task are called the Masoretes, and the authentic text which they determined is known as the Masoretic text.

The Masoretes, concerned with preserving the true text and the true meaning of the Scriptures, laid down the text of the Bible word for word, letter for letter. Many non-Jews had translated the Bible during previous centuries; many of these translations had been inaccurate.

The Masoretes worked out a system of punctuation to provide the Hebrew script with clear marks for its vowels. In addition the Scriptures were provided with a system of accentuation that serves also as a system of musical notation for the cantillation of the public readings from the Torah and other parts of the Scriptures.

The Masoretes were active from the seventh through the tenth century (600-1000 C.E.). Their most outstanding scholars were Ben Asher and Ben Naphtali.

VOCABULARY AND CONCEPTS

Oral law created in Babylonia	תַּלְמוּד בַּבְלִי
Arch of Titus in Rome	שַׁעַר טִיטוּס
Jerusalem Talmud	תַּלְמוּד
Coastal town in Israel where a spiritual center was established	יַבְנֶה
Rabbi Yehudah Hanassi (compiler of the Mishnah)	רַבִּי יְהוּדָה הַנָשִׂיא
Six-volume work of the beginnings of the Oral Law	מִשְׁנָה
Masorah	מָסוֹרָה
Rabbi Ben Asher	רַבִּי בֶּן אָשֵׁר
Rabbi Ben Naphtali	רַבִּי בֶּן נַפְתָּלִי

THE BEGINNING OF ISLAM (570–632)

The Byzantines (313–636 C.E.)

With the Christianization of the Roman Empire after 312 C.E. under Constantine, the Christians settled in holy places such as Jerusalem and Bethlehem. Jews now became aliens in their own land. Jews were forbidden to enter the city of Jerusalem. Only on the Ninth of Av were they permitted to enter the Holy City.

In 614 the Persians invaded Palestine. Hoping to be permitted to worship freely once again, the Jews of the Galilee joined the Persian invaders and helped them capture Acre and Jerusalem.

The Persians handed over Jerusalem to the Jews for three years and then retracted the gift and gave it back to the Christians.

In 629 C.E. the Byzantines defeated the Persians and restored the cross to Jerusalem. They expelled the Jews. Jews were forbidden to live within a three-mile radius of the Holy City.

Byzantine warriors.

Mohammed: Prophet of God

The time was the beginning of the seventh century C.E. For hundreds of years, Jews had been scattered to many communities throughout Israel and the Middle East, celebrating their own holidays and traditions, worshipping God, and studying Torah.

There were even many Jews living in Arabia. Some Arab tribes converted to Judaism, including inhabitants of the city of Medina.

A poor, illiterate, young Arab camel-driver named Mohammed was hired by a caravan and began to travel around the lands of the Middle East. One of his journeys brought him to Palestine, or Israel. Here Mohammed met many Jews and became interested in their religion. He began studying its principles and holidays and ideas.

Mohammed also developed his own new religious ideas. Like the Jews, he believed in one God. But he called God "Allah," the Arabic word for the Supreme Being. And he declared that he himself, Mohammed, like Abraham and Moses, was a prophet of God.

Mohammed expected the Jews to accept his new religious ideas. But the Jews refused. They did not believe that Mohammed was truly God's prophet.

Mohammed and his followers persecuted and attacked the Jews who rejected Islam, the religion Mohammed founded. They forced the Jews to flee from the city of Medina, where Mohammed made his home. Many Jewish desert tribes in Arabia were attacked and some were destroyed. When Mohammed died in 632, Abu Bakr became the Caliph, or leader, of the Moslems. He in turn was succeeded as Caliph by Omar.

Palestine Under the Caliphate

Omar announced that he would spread the religion of Mohammed by force. He believed in waging a holy war, called in Arabic a *jihad*, against those people who did not accept Mohammed's teachings. Across the desert, Caliph Omar and his followers sped upon their swift Arabian horses. Full of fervent religious belief in Islam, these Moslem warriors had as their battle cries "Allah" and "for Mohammed."

Moslem warriors.

214

Omar conquered Egypt, Palestine, Syria, and Persia. Mohammedanism spread throughout these lands.

Because the Moslems believed that Mohammed had been taken to heaven from Jerusalem, they considered Jerusalem a holy city. Thus, in the year 650, they built the Mosque of Omar in the middle of Jerusalem, on the same area where Solomon's Temple had once stood. The golden-domed mosque (Moslem religious center) still gleams today, clearly visible from many parts of Jerusalem.

After Omar's conquest of Palestine, conditions there improved. The Arabs established a Moslem sanctuary in Jerusalem, which had now become the holy city of three religions. Once again the Jews were permitted to enter the city and pray before the ruined western wall of the Temple. Soon a little Jewish community was formed in Jerusalem.

Around the year 1000 C.E., there were about 1,000,000 Jews in the world. Most of them lived in lands under Moslem rule: Palestine, Persia, Babylonia, Spain, North Africa. Some Jews lived in Christian lands: France, Germany, Italy, Byzantium.

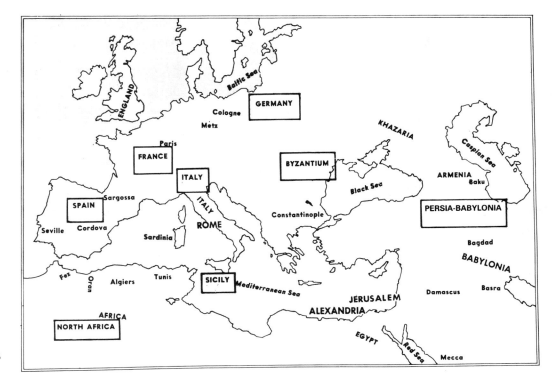

VOCABULARY AND CONCEPTS

ntines	בִּיזָנְטִים
os	עַרְבִים
ammed	מוּחַמַד
h	אָלָאה (אָלֹהַ)
ca	מֶכָּה
d	גִי׳הָאד

215

THE CRUSADES (1095–1291)

The Christian world strove, for four centuries, to wrest the land of Israel from Moslem control. This series of bloody wars to regain the Holy Land is called the Crusades.

The First Crusade was begun in 1095. A Church Council met in the South of France and declared a holy war against the Moslem "unbelievers." Knights, monks, as well as assorted adventurers, criminals, and misfits joined the ranks of the Crusades. All went forth to march eastward to the Holy Land and capture it from the Moslems.

To arouse the Christians to join the Crusades, priests made passionate, inflammatory sermons about "nonbelievers" in the churches of Europe. All "nonbelievers"—Jews as well as Moslems—were regarded as enemies. As a result, the Jews of Europe suffered greatly from vicious persecution during this period.

The Crusaders, wishing to spread Christianity, called themselves the Bearers of the Cross. But in the name of religion, they spilled much innocent Jewish blood. As they marched through the countryside, the Crusaders were brutal, harsh, and violent in their attacks upon defenseless Jewish communities. Jews in France, and the centers along the Rhine suffered from the Crusaders' cruelty.

The memory of the Jewish martyrs who perished in these brutal attacks is immortalized in special prayers written during this period—the *piyyutim* and the *Av HaRachamim* service. These prayers ask God to avenge the deaths of the many Jewish martyrs.

The Crusaders in Israel

As the Crusaders traveled eastward, from Europe toward Israel, they picked up large groups of followers who joined their ranks. After a long march through Asia

A Crusader knight.

216

Seal of Baldwin, first Crusader king of Jerusalem. In 1099, the Crusaders succeeded in capturing Jerusalem.

Battle between Crusaders and Moslems near Ashkelon, 1250. From a stained-glass window in a church in Paris.

Minor and Syria-Lebanon, they stormed Israel from the north. Other Crusaders arrived by sea. After bitter fighting, the Crusaders penetrated the massive fortifications surrounding Jerusalem. In a terrible bloodbath, the Christians entered the holy city and slaughtered most of Jerusalem's Jews.

For a while, it seemed as though the Crusaders had been successful. They had gained control of Jerusalem, Israel's capital city, and ruled over most of the land. But the Crusaders' Moslem foes had not been silenced for long. Eighty-eight years after Jerusalem was taken by the Crusaders, the Moslem leader Saladin recaptured it. Now Crusader rule was limited to the coastal plain and Galilee. The Moslems battled the Christians constantly in these parts of Israel. In 1291, the Moslems conquered Acco, putting an end to Christian rule in Israel.

The Mamaluks Conquer Israel (1291–1516)

In 1250, the followers of Saladin were themselves conquered by the Mamaluks, who took control of Egypt. Syria and Israel. The Mamaluks, originally slave-soldiers in Egypt who had rebelled against their masters, brought an era of relative peace to the region.

However, Jews under the Mamaluks did not fare well. The Jewish minority was subject to pogroms, the closure

A page from a French history book written in 1337. The painting shows the Crusader attack on Jerusalem.

Jerusalem Jews and Moslems at a celebration.

The Egyptian Jews formed one of the oldest communities, but declined under Mamaluk rule in the fifteenth century.

This woodcut pictures an Egyptian Jew on the right.

VOCABULARY AND CONCEPTS

Piyyutim	פִּיּוּטִים
Av HaRachamim	אַב הָרַחֲמִים
Crusades	מַסְעוֹת הַצְּלָב
Crusaders	צַלְבָנִים
Muslim	מֻסְלָמִי

of synagogues, and heavy taxes. Like Christians and Samaritans, they were forced to wear distinctive dress, in their case a yellow turban. Jews were forbidden to ride horses and in some periods were not allowed to drink wine. The Mamaluk government especially harassed the Jews in Jerusalem, and in about 1440 it imposed a heavy tax on them to be paid yearly. Most Jews were craftsmen or small merchants who could not afford to pay the tax. Many of them left Jerusalem. The Mamaluks did not, however, interfere with Jewish judicial autonomy in civil law.

Rabbi Ovadiah of Bertinoro

With the coming of Rabbi Ovadiah of Bertinoro, in 1488, the state of the Jewish community was changed. Rabbi Ovadiah, a famous Mishnah commentator, became the spiritual leader of Jerusalem Jewry, and during the period of his rabbinate he succeeded in uniting the community. He found in Jerusalem no more than seventy Jewish families and many widows. Soon afterwards, the government abolished the heavy tax, and at this time the immigration of the Spanish exiles began.

A Christian pilgrim from Bohemia (visiting in 1491–1492), Martin Kabtanik, wrote in his book *Journey to Jerusalem:*

> Christians and Jews alike in Jerusalem lived in great poverty and in conditions of great deprivation, there are not many Christians but there are many Jews, and these the Moslems persecute in various ways. Christians and Jews go about in Jerusalem in clothes considered fit only for wandering beggars. The Moslems know that the Jews think and even say that this is the Holy Land which has been promised to them and that those Jews who dwell there are regarded as holy by Jews elsewhere, because, in spite of all the troubles and sorrows inflicted on them by the Moslems, they refuse to leave the land.

All through these years, Jewish communities remained in Israel. All through these years, despite the bloody slaughter and the many battles in the name of religion, Jews worshiped God, celebrated their holidays and traditions as best they could, and studied their beloved Torah. Always they dreamed that one day, with God's help, the Jewish nation would once again be free and independent.

218

THE OTTOMANS RULE ISRAEL (1517–1917)

The Ottaman Turks Conquer Israel.

In 1517, Israel was once again conquered by a foreign power. This time, the Ottoman Turks occupied the Jewish homeland. But the four centers of Jewish life—Jerusalem, Tiberias, Hebron, and Safed—continued to thrive. The largest of the four was Safed, with about 10,000 Jews, most of whom were refugees from Spain, from which they had been expelled in 1492.

Various travelers of this period have provided us with information about Jews living in the country. George Sandys, son of the Archbishop of York, visited Israel in 1611 and wrote movingly of Jewish fortitude despite alien conquest:

> And in their land, they [the Jews] live as strangers, hated by those amongst whom they dwell, open to all oppression and deprivation, which they bear with patience beyond all belief, despised and beaten. In spite of all this, I never saw a Jew with an angry face.

For three centuries, under the rule of the Ottoman Empire, Palestine rotted in neglect. But Napoleon, a highly ambitious man had strategic designs on the Middle East. Military upheavals had weakened the Turkish Empire. Napoleon seized the opportunity to attack.

The Napoleonic Era

Napoleon (1769–1821) was a French emperor who strove throughout his reign to conquer more lands and gain greater power. As French ruler, he gave the Jews many economic and civil rights that they had formerly

_1._

This book called *Seder Hayom* ("daily order"), was written in Safed by Rabbi Moshe ben Machir, in 1575. It is a commentary on the daily prayers.

This book provides evidence of the cultural renaissance which occurred in and around Safed.

been denied, and under his rule, Jews began to leave the restricted ghetto life. But Napoleon could also be intolerant. He later issued the "Infamous Decree," which denied to Jews many of the same rights that he had previously granted.

In 1798, Napoleon began a military campaign in the Middle East. He hoped to conquer Palestine from the Turks, then Syria and Asia Minor, seizing Constantinople and gaining control over the whole Ottoman Empire. Napoleon wanted to control the lucrative trade routes of the Mediterranean.

Napoleon's army storming the walls of Acco. Napoleon abandoned the siege (and his plans to conquer Palestine) on May 26, 1789, and withdrew his army to Egypt: three months later he set sail secretly for France.

Before Napoleon started on this campaign, he announced his plan to restore a Jewish kingdom in Palestine, but we will never know whether he really meant to carry out this promise. The Turks resisted Napoleon's invasion. In February 1799, the French army captured the coastal towns of El Arish, Ramleh, Jaffa, and Haifa. They met heavy resistance at Acco, however, and Napoleon's troops were brought to a standstill. Finally, Napoleon abandoned the siege and his plan of conquering Palestine. In June 1799, his decimated army retreated to Egypt.

Israel Is Desolate

In 1858, Felix Bovet, a Protestant minister, visited Israel and wrote a summary of the past centuries of the land. He describes the loyalty of the Jewish settlements in Israel and the desolation brought by the foreign powers who had destroyed many regions:

> The Christians who conquered the land of Israel did not know how to hold it and it was never anything more to them than a battleground and a graveyard. The Saracens who took it from them also left and it was then taken by the Turks and the Ottomans who are still there. They have made a desert of it where it is scarcely possible to walk without fear. Even the Arabs who dwell there do so as temporary sojourners. They set their tents wherever there is pasture and seek refuge in the ruins of the towns. They did not create anything as they were in truth strangers, not masters of the land. The spirit of the desert, which had brought them thither, could in the same fashion take them away again and leave nothing behind. God who has given Palestine to so many nations has not permitted any one to establish itself or to take root in it. No doubt it is reserved for his people Israel.

The Jews of Eretz Israel remained in the Jewish homeland continuously, no matter what difficulties had to be endured. Their loyal communities helped keep strong the bond between the Jewish people and the Jewish homeland. Without their steadfastness, the Zionist of the nineteenth century would have found it even harder to return to the land.

VOCABULARY AND CONCEPTS

Napoleon	נָפּוֹלִיוֹן
Acco	עַכּוֹ
Egypt	מִצְרַיִם

221

THE RISE OF MODERN ZIONISM

צְבִי הִירְשׁ קַלִישֶׁר

**ZVI HIRSCH KALISCHER
(1795–1874)**
"Quest of Zion"

For many years, Jews had expressed their religious devotion through study, prayer, and observance of the Torah. In the late nineteenth century, young Zionist settlers began expressing their love of Judaism in a new way—by starting farm settlements in the Jewish homeland, Israel, then called Palestine.

Many people in Europe were afraid to go to Palestine. It was very far away, and its once-rich farmland, long neglected by Arabs and Turks and ravaged by many wars, was now barren desert, harsh rock, disease-infested swamp.

But Zvi Hirsch Kalischer, an Orthodox rabbi, took a strong stand for the Zionist settlers.
He raised money to open a school in Israel so that the new settlers could learn how to farm the difficult soil. He wrote an eloquent book called *Derishat Zion* ("Quest of Zion") explaining to Jews everywhere the importance of *aliyah*.

Rabbi Kalischer explained that praying to God and studying Torah were not enough. "There is no greater service for the religious Jew to perform than to rebuild the ruins of the Holy Land."

The Rise of Modern Zionism—Pogroms

In the 1800's, after centuries of suffering, the Jews of some European countries began to receive more equal treatment. Talented Jews were encouraged to enter all fields. Jews became poets, statesmen, scientists, and artists in the same lands that had once locked Jews up in dingy ghettos.

But anti-Jewish feeling had not vanished. In 1881, a series of brutal, murderous assaults against Jews went on throughout Russia. These terrible attacks were called "pogroms," a Russian word meaning "riot" or "disturbance." None of the attackers was punished, for the leaders of the Russian government were themselves instigating the pogroms. In May 1882, Czar Alexander III enacted a program of anti-Jewish laws. Persecution of Russian Jews increased, and pogroms continued to go unpunished, destroying the lives and property of innocent victims. In 1903, an organized massacre took place in the town of Kishinev, with savage, terrible destruction of lives and property. This tragedy horrified Jews all over the world.

Jews had begun to feel more comfortable and successful in the lands of exile. But now they realized that they could be truly safe only in their homeland. The dream of the return to Zion became a real goal for many determined Jewish pioneers.

THEODOR HERZL בִּנְיָמִין זְאֵב הֶרְצֵל
(1860–1904)
The father of modern Zionism

In his short life, Theodor Herzl became the great founder and leader of the modern Zionist movement. After being admitted to the bar he entered the Austrian government service. His interests were in his literary and journalistic work. He left his legal work and became a well-known playwright and journalist. In 1892 he was the Paris correspondent of a Viennese paper and witnessed the famous Dreyfus trial. He was deeply affected by this exhibition of injustice and anti-Semitism, and from this time on he devoted his life to the fate of the Jewish people. He wrote several books expressing his ideas on a Jewish national home, the best-known of which is *The Jewish State*. Herzl approached many important men in behalf of his Zionist aims; among them were Baron de Hirsch, the philanthropist, the German Kaiser, and the Turkish Sultan, whose empire included Palestine. Herzl called the First Zionist Congress in Basle, Switzerland, in 1897. He also traveled a great deal in the service of his ideas. He died in 1904 of a heart ailment. In his will he asked that his body rest next to that of his father in Vienna until "the Jewish people will carry my remains to Palestine." In 1949 the new State of Israel brought the body of the beloved leader of early Zionism to it final resting place on Mount Herzl in Jerusalem.

The idealistic young Jewish pioneers who left Europe and went to Eretz Yisrael soon learned that ideals were not enough—they needed sound agricultural training and enough money to build secure homes. They turned to Jews around the world for help.

Binyamin Zeev (Theodor) Herzl, who was born in Budapest in 1860 and became a Jewish writer in Vienna, caught a spark from the Zionist flame and became fiercely dedicated to the cause. In 1896, Herzl published a book—*The Jewish State*—declaring that the Jewish people should be allowed to set up their own state in the land of Israel. This idea shocked many people, because the Jews had not had their own state for nearly two thousand years. Soon after, Herzl founded the World Zionist Organization to make this dream come true.

Members of a Zionist group preparing to go to Palestine. In the center is young David Ben-Gurion.

223

The degradation of Captain Dreyfus.

The Dreyfus Case

How Herzl became one of the great leaders of the Jewish people is an interesting story. He was waiting in a crowd outside a military courtroom in Paris, France. The crowd and he were there to find out if a French Jew, Alfred Dreyfus, was going to be found guilty or innocent of spying. Suddenly, Herzl heard the crowd shout "Death to the Jews" over and over. How could the people of so highly civilized a country as France act so hatefully, he wondered. Right then the idea of a Jewish state came to Herzl.

Herzl immediately set to work to bring about a Jewish state. He gave speeches and wrote articles to spread his idea. Above all, he wanted to make it clear that a Jewish nation could be built, that it was not just a dream. "If you will it, it is no dream," said Herzl.

The Trial of Captain Dreyfus.

Bronze medal struck in honor of the Second Zionist Congress at Basle. The quotation, from the Book of Ezekiel, tells of God's promise to bring the Children of Israel from among the nations to their own land.

ARBEITS-PROGRAMM

UND

GESCHÄFTS-ORDNUNG

DES

ZIONISTEN-CONGRESSES

IN

BASEL

29., 30. und 31. AUGUST 1897.

VERLAG „DER WELT"

The program of the First Zionist Congress.

The First Zionist Conference

Many Jews throughout the world were attracted by Herzl's idea. These Jews called themselves Zionists because their goal was to return to Zion—to the land of Israel—and to establish there a state for the Jewish people. In 1897, at the First Zionist Congress, Herzl and these others gathered together to decide how to build the new nation. They formed an international body, the World Zionist Organization, and agreed to try to persuade the powerful nations of the world to give their approval to a Jewish state in the land of Israel. In order to make it possible for Jews to settle in Eretz Yisrael even before a state was born, they also decided to set up a Zionist bank to buy land there.

The Zionist Organization Continues Herzl's Work

Until his sudden death in 1904 at the age of forty-four, Herzl worked nearly without stop for a Jewish state. He went to the powerful nations to obtain their approval of a Jewish state, but he never got it. The Zionist Organization continued his efforts, however, providing spiritual and financial support for the Jewish settlers. With its help, thousands of Jews from many European countries moved to the land of Israel and set up homes, farms, and schools. In 1948, the work that Herzl and his followers had begun paid off—the State of Israel was born. By that time, nearly one million Jews were living in the land of Israel and building a nation.

VOCABULARY AND CONCEPTS

Zionist (a person who strongly supports Israel) צִיוֹנִי

Pioneer חָלוּץ

Quest of Zion (book explaining the importance of Aliyah) דְּרִישַׁת צִיוֹן

The Dreyfus case מִשְׁפַּט דְּרֵייפוּס

ALIYAH—"GOING UP"

Bilu pioneer plowing the soil.

Title-page of the original Statutes of the "Bilu" Organization. The Hebrew motto means: "The little one shall become a thousand, and the small one a strong nation" (Isaiah 60:22), and the Latin one: "Little things grow big by union."

Aliyah

The Hebrew word *aliyah* means "going up," which can be understood quite literally. We do a kind of aliyah when we climb up a mountain or a steep staircase. But the term can take on a much deeper, richer meaning, too.

Aliyah refers to the "going up" to the reader's desk in the synagogue to participate in the Torah reading. Every Jew feels proud to be honored with this kind of aliyah.

Aliyah also describes a symbolic kind of "going up." Aliyah refers to the return of Jews to the land of Israel—their ascent from Diaspora existence to the free, proud, independent life of Jews in a modern Jewish state.

Each Jew who settles in Israel receives the honorary title of *oleh* (for a man or boy) or *olah* (for a woman or girl)—which means, "one who goes up," or "makes aliyah."

The Bilu Movement

Seventeen young Russian Jewish students settled in Palestine after the pogroms of 1881 in Russia. These young people, known as Bilu'im, were deeply committed to the Zionist ideal. They labored long, hard hours in the fields under the glazing sun—and they suffered nights of cold, fear, and danger in the new farm settlements.

The Bilu'im took their name from the initials of the four-word Hebrew passage, *Beit Yaakov lechu Venelcha*—"House of Jacob, let us arise and go." The Bilu'im interpreted the passage as encouragement for Jews to rise up from their Diaspora homes and go to Israel to rebuilt the Jewish land.

Land for farming was purchased in Motza and Petach Tikvah, and the first agricultural school was founded in Mikveh Israel in 1870.

לִיאוֹן פִּינְסְקֶר

LEON PINSKER (1821–1891)
The author of
"Auto-Emancipation"

Leon Pinsker was born in Russia, where he became a doctor. He began a successful practice in Odessa, and in 1856 he served as a medical officer in the Crimean War. When the Russian pogroms spread in 1881, Pinsker became convinced that the Jewish people must return to national independence in the Jewish homeland.

He published an important booklet, *Auto-Emancipation*, which convinced many Jews to become ardent Zionists and work for the resettlement of Eretz Yisrael.

Victims of a Russian pogrom.

The "Lovers of Zion"

The group known as "Lovers of Zion" formed in response to a pamphlet written in 1882 by the physician Leon Pinsker. Dr. Pinsker wrote a powerful Zionist message to his fellow Jews. He explained that for Jews to become truly free and self-respecting, they must reclaim their national homeland, Israel.

New villages were established, and by 1880 Jerusalem became the largest city in Israel with a Jewish majority.

Israel's rebirth as a traditional crossroad of the world was speeded by the opening of the Suez Canal in 1869. Steamships now traveled regularly between Israel and Europe.

The stage was being set for the beginning of modern Zionist development.

The First Aliyah

Many European Jews felt shocked and frightened by the Russian pogroms, when mobs of peasants hurt and killed innocent Jewish people. In the 1890's, Jews heard the passionate speeches of Theodor Herzl, who called on them to settle in the Jewish state. The Jews were inspired by the Bilu and the Lovers of Zion movement, which encouraged many Zionist pioneers to reclaim the land. Between 1882 and 1904, 25,000 olim moved to Israel. They joined the 25,000 Jews already living in the four "holy cities"—Jerusalem, Hebron, Tiberias, Safed.

The first farm settlements in Israel were formed during the time of the First Aliyah—Petach Tikvah ("Gate of Hope"), Rishon-le-Zion ("First in Zion"), Rosh Pinah, and Zichron Yaakov. The names given the villages reflected the ideals and the hopes of the olim.

Hebrew was revived under the leadership of Eliezer Ben Yehuda. Within ten years Hebrew was to become the principal language of the Yishuv.

Alexander Zeid (1886–1938) was a pioneer of the Second Aliyah and one of the founders of Hashomer. He was killed by Arabs while on guard duty in 1938. A statue of Zeid on horseback was erected in the settlement of Givat Zeid, named in his honor.

The Second Aliyah

From 1904 to 1914, 30,000 more olim settled in Israel. These olim had new ideas about how the Jewish settlements should operate. They believed that by living together cooperatively as one large family, the group could work the land more efficiently and produce more and better crops. These olim did not believe in hiring Arab labor to do fieldwork.

The first kibbutz, Degania, was established in 1909, on the shore of Lake Kinneret, on land purchased by the Keren Kayemet. The settlers also founded the city of Tel Aviv.

These new olim began settlements where land and work were shared. They formed an armed and mounted guard force, Hashomer—"The Watchman," which eventually became the modern Israeli army.

The rulers of the Ottoman Empire tried to discourage Jewish immigration and settlement by restricting land sales and construction. They succeeded in temporarily slowing the flow of olim.

Women were an important force in rebuilding the land of Israel. These brave settlers helped reclaim the barren land.

All over the world, generous Jews continued to give money so the Zionist settlements in Israel could thrive.

The Second Aliyah settlers made up a lively song about their purpose in the land of Israel:

> We have come to the land,
> To build and to be rebuilt in it!
> To redeem it and to be redeemed in it!

The Hashomer Society

Hashomer means "the guard," "the watchman." The Hashomer society was formed to protect the Jewish settlements from Arab attacks. The brave fighters who were the members of Hashomer were really the first members of the modern Israeli army.

Hashomer had about 100 members, who had to live up to strict requirements—show great personal courage, be expert horsemen, and have strict self-discipline. The brave fighters of this group proved to the Arabs—and to the world—that Jews are strong and proud and ever-ready to protect their homeland.

Mounted and armed shomrim protected the settlements against Arab raiders.

אֶדְמוֹנְד רוֹטְשִׁילְד

BARON EDMOND DE ROTHSCHILD (1845–1934)
"Father of the Yishuv"

Baron Edmond de Rothschild came from a family of rich Jewish bankers and philanthropists. The Rothschilds were known for their great wealth and for their great generosity to Jewish causes.

In the family tradition, Baron Edmond de Rothschild gave much money and technical advice to the new Zionist settlements in Israel, Rishon le Zion, Rosh Pinah, and Petach Tikvah. The Zionist settlers were so thankful for Rothschild's crucial assistance that they called him the "Father of the Yishuv."

Rothschild helped develop the wine industry in Israel and started a glass factory to supply bottles for the wine. He provided money to enable the settlers on Israel's coastal plain to drain the swamps and plant large eucalyptus groves. This generous Jewish banker also helped establish the Hebrew University of Jerusalem.

The Rothschild family has continued its generous support of the State of Israel. The Rothschild family name comes from the red shield (in German: *roth schild*) which stood before the home of its founding father, Isaac Elhanan.

World Jewry Gives Aid

Jews all over the world followed with keen interest and concern the progress of the chalutzim and the rebuilding of Israel. Many gave money to help the courageous Zionist settlers.

Zionism, the Jewish national-liberation movement, became the modern response to centuries of oppression and persecution. The aims of Zionism were twofold: bringing the Jews home to the land of Israel, and creating a recognized country and nation for Jews in their historic homeland.

VOCABULARY AND CONCEPTS

"Lovers of Zion" (movement to realize the Zionist dream of Aliyah in the 1880's)   חוֹבְבֵי צִיּוֹן

"Going up" to the land of Israel   עֲלִיָּה

Bilu (movement of "lovers of Zion" from Eastern Europe who made Aliyah in the 1880's)   בִּיל"וּ

Hashomer ("The watchman," an armed and mounted Jewish force in Israel)   הַשׁוֹמֵר

Alexander Zeid (a leader of Hashomer)   אַלֶכְּסַנְדֶּר זַיְיד

PROMISED LAND

יוֹסֵף טְרוּמְפֶּלְדוֹר

JOSEPH TRUMPELDOR
(1880–1920)
The hero of Jewish resettlement
Joseph Trumpeldor grew up in Russia in a small town in the northern Caucasus. He became an ardent Zionist and dreamed of starting a farm settlement in Israel. But it was not easy for Trumpeldor to realize his dreams. Drafted into the Russian army, he lost an arm while fighting in the Russo-Japanese War.

In 1912, Trumpeldor went to Eretz Yisrael, where he worked in Degania (the first kibbutz) and fought to defend Jewish settlements in Galilee. During World War I, he helped Vladimir Jabotinsky form the Zion Mule Corps and later belonged to the Jewish Legion, the volunteer Jewish army which defended the Zionist settlements in Palestine.

After World War I fierce Arab terrorist attacks plagued the Jewish settlements in Galilee. Trumpeldor, now an experienced soldier, led the defense of Tel Chai in 1920. He was mortally wounded in the battle. The dying words of this Jewish hero reveal his intense idealism and love of Israel: *Ein davar; tov lamut be'ad arzeinu* ("Never mind; it is good to die for our country").

A large, successful youth group was named in his honor: Betar, short for B'rit Trumpeldor, "The Vow of Trumpeldor."

The Zion Mule Corps

During World War I, a group of Jews who had been expelled from Palestine by the Turks joined the British Army. These Jews formed their own company, the Zion Mule Corps. The unit of Jewish volunteers was organized by Vladimir Jabotinsky, a Russian Jew and an ardent Zionist. He was assisted by another great Jewish soldier, Joseph Trumpeldor.

The British authorities had specified that the unit would only be permitted to bring supplies and ammunition to the battlefront. But soon the Zion Mule Corps was in the thick of the action at Gallipoli, Turkey. The Jewish fighters became famous for their bravery and ingenuity in action.

The Jewish Legion

When the Zion Mule Corps was disbanded, Jabotinsky hurried to England to press for the formation of a larger-scale Jewish army. The result was the Jewish Legion, an army of volunteers from countries all over the world. The soldiers of the Legion were Jews with deeply held Zionist convictions. They fought to win Palestine away from the Turks in the hope that it could then become a Jewish homeland under British rule.

The soldiers of the Jewish Legion wore the Magen David on their uniforms, spoke Hebrew, and saluted both the blue-and-white Zionist flag and the British flag. The Legion's three battalions included 2,700 volunteers from the United States as well as men from South Africa, Russia, Argentina, and Mexico.

British field commanders praised the zeal and the courage of the Jewish Legion.

Lord Arthur James Balfour.

The Balfour Declaration in full.

Among the recruits to the Jewish Legion was a young Jewish immigrant from Russia, David Green—who was to become known to the world as David Ben-Gurion and who was to be the first Prime Minister of the State of Israel.

The Balfour Declaration

Lord Arthur James Balfour was a leader of England's Conservative party. During his tenure as foreign minister, he wrote to Baron Lionel Walter Rothschild, on November 2, 1917, that "His Majesty's Government view with favour the establishment in Palestine of a national home for the Jewish people, and will use their best endeavours to facilitate the achievement of this object." He promised that Britain would exert every effort to gain that end, under the condition that nothing be done to injure the rights of non-Jews in Palestine or of Jews in other lands. The Balfour Declaration was endorsed by France, Italy, Japan, and the United States. It later became part of the document that gave Great Britain its Mandate over Palestine. Although some British opposition to the intent of the Declaration developed later, it is considered a great stepping-stone to the establishment of the independent State of Israel.

Meeting in the Desert

In 1918 a British army led by General Allenby defeated the Turks and conquered Palestine. That same year World War I ended with victory for the Allies, who had been greatly assisted by America's entrance into the war in 1917.

As the British commander in the area, Allenby suggested that Dr. Chaim Weizmann, a prominent Zionist leader, meet with Emir (or Prince) Feisal, whose word carried great weight in the Arab world. In June 1918, Weizmann made a long, difficult journey by train, boat, car, and camel to the Emir's desert tent.

חַיִּים וַיִּצְמָן

CHAIM WEIZMANN (1874–1952)
Scientist and Zionist leader

The third of fifteen children, Chaim Weizmann was born in the Russian village of Motol. Because Russian universities at that time made it hard for Jews to be admitted, Weizmann left in 1892 to study biochemistry at a Germany university. There he joined a group of Zionist intellectuals. In 1896, he heard Theodor Herzl speak and was deeply inspired. Weizmann, a talented scientist, began to get actively involved in the leadership of the worldwide Zionist movement.

In 1903, the British proposed that instead of Palestine, Uganda (an East African country) become the homeland for the Jews. The British could not understand why the Jews would not accept the proposal. The British Prime Minister, Arthur James Balfour, asked Weizmann to explain. Weizmann then asked Balfour whether he would abandon London if he were offered Paris. Balfour answered, "No, London is the capital of my country." Weizmann replied, "Jerusalem was the capital of our country when London was a marsh." Weizmann, as well as most other Jews, would not agree to Zionism without Zion.

Weizmann worked for many years as an active Zionist leader, raising funds to save Jewish refugees and Holocaust survivors and to establish a scientific institute in Israel. When the State of Israel was established in 1948, Chaim Weizmann was elected its first President.

When Weizmann died, the scientific institute he began became known as the Weizmann Institute of Science. Today, this institute is the foremost place of scientific research in Israel, with 400 full-time scientists and 500 students.

Weizmann, as did Lawrence of Arabia, the British soldier-adventurer. In the Emir's tent, the Jewish leader and the Arab prince had a two-hour conversation which began a lifelong friendship. Weizmann explained the goals of the Zionists in Palestine, and the Emir listened with sympathy and understanding.

In London, on January 1919, the two men signed a peace agreement. The treaty said that the Arabs fully accepted the large-scale immigration of Jews into Palestine, and that the Jews agreed to fully protect the rights of Arab citizens within the Jewish homeland.

But rival Arab leaders would not let the Emir and his pro-Zionist beliefs gain control. The Emir had dreamed of uniting the Arab world under his leadership. But he was finally forced to yield to other Arab chiefs, who sought to destroy the Jewish settlement in Israel.

The rise of the Grand Mufti of Jerusalem to dominance on the Palestinian Arab scene in the early 1920's was a turning point in the course of Jewish-Arab relations in Palestine. It marked the end of any hope of implementing the Feisal-Weizmann Agreement of 1919, and it set the Arab world on a course of hostility to the idea of Jewish statehood.

Dr. Weizmann and Emir Feisal in Aquaba, June 1918.

233

Joseph Trumpeldor was buried near Tel Hai, and in 1934 a memorial was erected at his gravesite. Shortly after his death, a new settlement at the foot of Mount Gilboa was named Tel Yosef in his honor, and songs, poems, and stories were written about him as a hero of the Jewish resettlement of Eretz Yisrael. His lifestory served as an inspirational model to both the pioneering socialist youth movements and the right-wing youth groups. One of the largest and most successful of the latter was named in his honor: Betar, an abbreviation of B'rit Trumpeldor.

Arab Terrorism

But many Arabs in Palestine were opposed to the Balfour Declaration and to Jewish immigration in general. The wealthy Arab landowners were afraid that Jews coming from Europe would bring with them a standard of living much higher than that of the poor Arab peasants, who tilled the soil of Palestine with the same primitive tools as their ancestors had used for centuries, and that the peasants would become discontented with their lot. Arabs were incited to raid Jewish settlements in an attempt to force the Jews to leave the land. But the Jews fought back. They worked their land by day and guarded it at night with their guns.

Arabs attacked Jewish homes and ambushed cars and buses on the highways. These terrorists murdered many young Jewish pioneers.

VOCABULARY AND CONCEPTS

The Balfour Declaration   הַכְרָזַת בַּלְפוּר

Zev Jabotinsky (Zionist leader, one of the founders of the Jewish Legion during World War I, and also the founder of the Hagana and the Irgun)   זְאֵב ז'בּוֹטִינְסְקִי

ALIYAH INCREASES

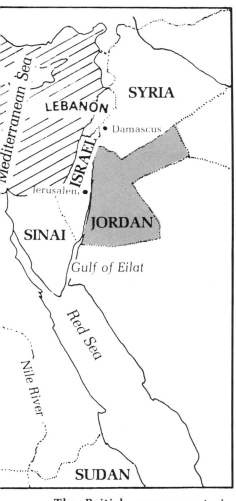

The British government, in 1922, divided the promised Jewish homeland by cutting off three quarters the land area of Palestine. A new Arab state was created, called Transjordan. In 1946, Transjordan became independent.

The British Mandate (1922–1948)

In July 1922, the League of Nations entrusted Britain with a Mandate which included the Balfour Declaration and recognized the historical connection between the Jewish people and the land of Israel. The League of Nations called upon Britain to smooth the way for the creation of a Jewish National Home. It was a Mandate extending over both banks of the Jordan.

The League also provided for the Zionist Organization to set up a "Jewish Agency" to advise and cooperate with the British in matters affecting the establishment of the Jewish National Home.

Within a few months, defying the League of Nations, Britain partitioned the area of the Mandate, establishing an autonomous Arab state in eastern Palestine called Transjordan. The Jewish National Home was now a third of its original size.

February 1948. The scene following the blast which devastated Ben Yehuda Street in Tel Aviv. Hundreds of residents were wounded and killed.

Graduation of the first training course for officers of the newly formed Hagana, Tel Aviv, 1920.

Riots in Palestine

From the early days of the Mandate, the leaders of the Jewish community tried to reach an understanding with their Arab neighbors, who refused to recognize the men and women and children in Hebron and destroyed the synagogues. This attack brought an end to a Jewish community which had dwelled in the city of the patriarchs for two thousand years.

Because of this riot and other disturbances, the British caved in to Arab pressure and recommended that aliyah and land purchases by Jews be limited.

The Third Aliyah

The Third Aliyah (1919–1923) was spearheaded by young members of the Hechalutz (pioneer movement) in Russia and Poland who joined hands with the pioneers of the Second Aliyah.

Forty thousand more olim reached Israel in the years between 1919 and 1924. These settlers, too, devoted themselves to rebuilding the Jewish homeland.

These olim believed in the same goals as the previous Zionist settlers—working and sharing, social justice, self-defense, and speaking Hebrew.

These pioneers endured great hardships, but they persisted in their work to rebuild Israel. They made up a song which expressed their energy and endurance:

> A chalutz, chalutz is what I am,
>   a chalutz, do or die!
> Without a coat or pair of shoes,
>   or even a necktie!

צַ׳רְלְס אוֹרְד וִינְגֵּייט

CHARLES ORDE WINGATE
(1903–1944)
British official, Jewish supporter
A British army officer who served
in Palestine from 1936 to 1939,
Orde Wingate became a strong
supporter of the Jewish cause. He
trained Jewish soldiers, many of
whom became military leaders in
the State of Israel.

Born in India into a family of
Christian missionaries, Wingate
was a deeply religious man. He
always carried his Bible with him,
so that he could read it whenever
he had a spare moment.

In Palestine, he organized
groups of Jewish volunteers,
known as Night Squads, to detect
and defeat Arab terrorist activities. The Jews called him *Ha-
Yedid*—"The Good Friend." But
the British disapproved of Wingate's Zionist sympathies and sent
him to the Far East. He was killed
in Burma during World War II in a
plane crash at the age of forty-one.

Wingate remained devoted to
the Jewish people and Eretz Yisrael
until his tragic death. Israel, in
turn, has not forgotten Wingate,
and has named a forest, a college
of physical education, and a children's village, Yemin Orde, after
him.

During Israel's War of Independence, Wingate's widow arranged
for his beloved Bible, together with
supplies, to be dropped into Yemin
Orde, then besieged by Syrian
troops. In it she wrote a dedication
to the defenders of Yemin Orde:

Since Orde Wingate is with you
in spirit, though he cannot lead
you in the flesh, I send you the
Bible he carried in all his campaigns. . . . May it be a covenant
between you and him, in triumph or defeat, now and always.

Hebrew literature, journalism, and theater came into
being. The Hebrew University of Jerusalem and the
Haifa Technion opened their doors.

Despite the restrictions and the difficult living conditions, there were more than 650,000 Jews in the Land.

The Haganah

The Haganah began in 1920, after the first defense
organization of Israel, Hashomer, disbanded. Haganah
members actively defended Jewish settlements against
attacks by Arab marauders. Haganah members protected
major cities in Israel as well as moshavim and kibbutzim.

Since modern weapons were hard to come by, the
Haganah members had to protect themselves and their
vulnerable settlements with revolvers and homemade
hand grenades. Special Night Squads, led by Charles
Orde Wingate, a British military officer who was a friend
of the Jewish cause, raided Arab terrorist bases and
defended Jewish settlements on the remote borders of
the country.

Night squad on patrol.

237

Stockade-and-tower settlement established during the 1930's

June 7, 1936 edition of the *Palestine Post* detailing the beginning of the widespread terror and destruction which Arab uprisings were to inflict upon Jewish settlements during the next three years.

During World War II, the Haganah continued its defense of the Jewish settlements in Israel and expanded its defense of Jews to include those in Nazi-occupied territories. The Haganah developed the Palmach strike force, which parachuted members into areas under the Nazi rule. Here the courageous envoys of the Haganah would train Jewish youth in resistance and aid Nazi victims. One brave girl who parachuted into Hungary for this purpose was captured and killed. Her name was Hannah Senesh, and she became a symbol of the martyrdom and bravery of the Haganah members.

The Fourth Aliyah

The Fourth Aliyah (1924–1928) was of a different social background: It brought shopkeepers and artisans, mostly from Poland, where economic restrictions were being applied. The majority of the new arrivals settled in the cities of Tel Aviv, Haifa, and Jerusalem.

During the years 1924 to 1929, some 50,000 Jews came on aliyah to Israel. At the end of this period, the Jewish population of Israel was about 170,000.

The Fifth Aliyah

During the Fifth Aliyah (1929–1936), the largest number of olim flocked to the land. More than 165,000 Jews entered legally, and thousands of refugees from Nazi Germany entered illegally. By the spring of 1936 the Yishuv numbered more than 400,000.

Members of HaShomer, "The Watchman," the mounted armed force founded in the early days of Zionist settlement.

The land of Israel was no longer barren wasteland; settlers now were en route to a thriving, developing land, and thus more and more people felt encouraged to link their destinies with Israel's.

Another reason, too, explains the upsurge in *aliyah* during the early 1930's. Already, the European horizon was darkened by threats of war and by Jewish persecution. Some Jews, fearing Hitler's rise to power in Nazi Germany, left Europe for Israel, escaping the terrible Nazi Holocaust that decimated the Jewish population of Europe.

In 1931, a national command for the Haganah was organized. The Haganah was now a nationwide but still undergrown defense force.

The Land Blooms

The enthusiastic *chalutzim*—the Bilu'im and the Lovers of Zion and the pioneers inspired by them—found themselves in a land that seemed without promise. The soil was barren, rocky, full of malaria-infested swamps. The new settlers, who came mostly from towns and cities, knew little about farming. They had to learn—fast.

The *chalutzim* had to irrigate the dry places and dry up the swamps. They had to plant new fruit orchards and fields of vegetables to replace the barrenness they had found. They had to learn to speak Hebrew, the language of the Torah and of Jewish freedom. And they had to protect their new settlements from hostile Arabs, who tried to terrorize the *chalutzim*.

During the day the settlers tilled the soil of their beloved homeland. At night, they took turns standing guard, defending their settlements from attacks by Arab terrorists. Eventually, the swamps were dried and the dry lands watered. In places that had been barren, orange groves bloomed and olive trees gave forth rich crops.

The Zionist settlers struggled and survived—against all odds. Their work ultimately became the land of Israel, blooming and flourishing, as it is today.

VOCABULARY AND CONCEPTS

Mandatory Regime	שִׁלְטוֹן הַמַּנְדָט
Aliyah	עֲלִיָה
Haganah	הַגָּנָה

AMERICAN JEWRY
TAKES THE LEAD

The Master Race

In 1933, Adolph Hitler became the leader of Germany. Hitler promised the German people, defeated in World War I, a powerful Germany that would conquer the world and become an empire again, as it had been under the Kaiser; indeed, he promised that he would make Germany even greater than she had ever been under any previous leader.

Hitler and his followers, the Nazis, developed the theory that the German people were a "master race," superior to all other nations. They and other "Nordic" peoples, they declared, were the master race of mankind, which would rule and dominate the world and wipe out all inferior peoples.

Hitler announced that the Jews would be the first to be eliminated, since they were the lowest on the scale among the inferior races.

Where Did the German Jews Flee?

Many Jews fled from Nazi Germany to other European countries. Among the refugees were prominent bankers and merchants, renowned artists, writers, and scientists.

Many others went to the United States, where the first German Jews had settled in the middle of the nineteenth century. Many German Jews who had formerly ignored or opposed Zionism now contemplated emigration to Palestine. The Fourth Aliyah was composed primarily of Jews from Central Europe.

German community leaders and rabbis expounded the ideas of Zionism and the timeless values of the Jewish

Hitler and his generals.

240

לוֹאָס דֶמְבִּיץ בְּרַנְדֵיס

LOUIS DEMBITZ BRANDEIS
(1856–1941)
Zionist leader, first Jewish
Supreme Court Justice

In 1916 the first Jew was appointed to the United States Supreme Court. He was Louis Brandeis, born in Louisville, Kentucky, son of immigrants from Prague.
As a boy Brandeis developed a deep concern for his fellow man. He graduated from Harvard Law School in 1877 and became an outstanding lawyer. Always ready to fight for the rights of the poor, simple worker, Brandeis was called the "People's Advocate" ("advocate" means "friend").

In 1910, a strike broke out in the New York garment industry, and Brandeis was asked to help resolve the differences between the bosses and the workers. Most of the people involved were Jewish. As Brandeis worked to end the strike, he learned more and more about the Jewish people, their hopes, their religion, their special lifestyle. He became proud of his Jewish roots. He began to be an active leader of the Zionist movement in the United States.

Brandeis loved Israel and worked hard to raise funds and build settlements there. He himself donated large sums of money, and he involved many talented American Jews in the Zionist effort. When Brandeis was the leader of the American Zionist movement, its membership grew from 12,000 in 1914 to 176,000 in 1919, and its budget grew from $15,000 to $3,000,000.

A colony in Israel was named after Brandeis—Ein Ha'Shofet, "Spring of the Judge." The name reminds everyone of the Zionist leadership performed by this great judge, the "People's Advocate."

tradition. Many young German Jews joined the Zionist organizations and prepared themselves for settlement in the land of their forefathers. Many of them were high school students who had been expelled from school by the Nazis. The Fourth Aliyah also included many of Germany's young Jewish academicians, doctors of philosophy, science, and medicine. Today many of them still live in Israel's villages and kibbutzim, contented and productive farmers.

There were many Jews, however, who hesitated to leave their homeland, the land where their families had lived for hundreds of years. Like many other Germans, they still believed that Hitler's power would soon come to an end.

American Jews Help

Palestine was still under the British mandate, but as the Nazis gained in strength and occupied one European country after another, Jewish settlers were arriving there in increasing numbers. Despite considerable Arab opposition, the settlers built strong communities, joining in the efforts of the earlier pioneers. Nothing could stop this new Aliyah. If there was not enough land for planting, the settlers made new land by reclaiming dry areas and swamps. They fought drought and malaria. No hardship or political problem could stop them.

Dr. Chaim Weizmann, who had guided the Zionist organization for many years, was now at its head. He had able helpers in many countries. In America: Louis D. Brandeis, Justice of the United States Supreme Court; Julian Mack, a collaborator of Judge Brandeis; Louis Lipsky, one of the most active leaders of the Zionist Organization of America; Rabbi Stephen S. Wise, one of the most dynamic figures in American Jewish life; Felix Frankfurter, who was later to become a Justice of the United States Supreme Court; Rabbi Abba Hillel Silver, eloquent preacher and author, who was to play a decisive role in the subsequent establishment of the State of Israel. All these leaders and many others worked to help finance and increase the growth of the communities in Palestine.

America's Zionist women, led by Henrietta Szold (1860–1941), had founded Hadassah in 1912. Under the leadership of Ms. Szold and her successors, Hadassah founded hospitals and health and welfare services in Palestine. These services were open to all the people of the country, Jews and Arabs, Moslems and Christians alike.

Also under the leadership of Miss Szold, Youth Aliyah was organized to rescue as many children and teenagers as possible from Nazi Europe.

An aerial view of the Hadassah Hospital in Jerusalem.

VOCABULARY AND CONCEPTS

The Second World War.	מִלְחֶמֶת עוֹלָם הַשְּׁנִיָּה
Adolf Hitler	אֲדוֹלְף הִיטְלֶר
Nazi	נַאצִי
Germany	אַשְׁכְּנַז
Concentration Camp	מַחֲנֵה רִכּוּז

THE HOLOCAUST

Aliyah Bet

In these dark days a desperate new kind of Aliyah began. Operating illegally and in secret, it was called Aliyah Bet—Immigration Wave B. In Palestine and in Hitler's lands, desperate men and women of the Haganah secretly began to buy boats. These were usually old, dilapidated vessels—no other kind could be had under the circumstances. An "underground railroad" was organized so that Jews could reach these boats and sail for the Land of Israel. Many such groups were organized—but only a few ships succeeded in reaching Palestine and landing there. Landings had to be made under cover of the fog of night. In spite of all the precautions, many boats were intercepted by the British guards, and the passengers were forced to turn back to Europe. Some of these ships never completed their journeys, but foundered and sank, and their passengers went down with them into the Mediterranean Sea.

The Outbreak of War

Then came September 1, 1939—and the Second World War.

The gates closed on Nazi-occupied lands, trapping millions of Jews. The darkest days for the Jews of Europe—and the blackest hours in Jewish history—had come. Before the war ended, the Nazis stooped to unthinkable acts. Scorning human dignity and decency, they sank to depths of cruelty and depravity that shocked and sickened all mankind. Their concentration camps became crematories for millions of innocent victims of their mad desire for world dominion.

A secret message from a British spy warning of the activities of two "underground" ships—The *Colorado* and the *Atratti*. In 1939, these two so-called illegal ships, crammed with desperate Polish-Jewish refugees escaping Hitler's Holocaust, were intercepted by British warships and turned back.

Nazis capturing Jewish fighters in the Warsaw Ghetto. Even the children fought the Nazis.

Hitler followed this policy of destruction in Germany and in all the countries conquered by Germany during World War II. Six million Jews were murdered by Hitler and the Nazis. This was the greatest tragedy that has ever happened to mankind. In many ways the world still has not recovered from the shock and horror. The events of this period are known as the Holocaust.

Each year on the twenty-seventh day of Nissan we observe Yom Hashoah, Holocaust Memorial Day. We remember the six million men, women, and children who were murdered by the Nazis.

A Nazi death camp. Millions of Jews were gassed, shot and burned to death in the camps.

VOCABULARY AND CONCEPTS

Adolf Hitler	אֲדוֹלְף הִטְלֶר
Nazi	נַאצִי
Germany	אַשְׁכְּנַז
Internment Camps	מַחֲנֵה רִכּוּז
Aliyah Bet	עֲלִיָה בֵּית
Holocaust Memorial Day	יוֹם הַשׁוֹאָה

244

BATTLE FOR SURVIVAL

Emblem of the Second Jewish Battalion, which fought in Italy in World War II.

Private Yaakov Butniky of the Second Jewish Regiment was killed in action in Italy on March 19, 1945.

Palestine Fights

During World War II the men and women of the Yishuv gave valiant aid to Britain in the fight against Nazi tyranny. At the outset, David Ben-Gurion had spoken for all the Jews of Palestine: "We will fight the war as if there were no White Paper," he said, "and we will fight the White Paper as if there were no war."

Very few Palestinian Arabs fought in the war, but many Jewish settlers volunteered for active service in the British Army. The Nazis, anxious for a foothold in the Middle East, flooded the area with agents and propaganda. They found many sympathizers among extreme Arab nationalists who hated the British and who were also opposed to Jewish immigration to Palestine.

Eventually, the British permitted the Jewish soldiers of Palestine to organize their own Jewish Brigade and to fight under their own blue-and-white flag, the Star of David.

The Haganah Fights

The men and women of the Haganah found another heroic way to fight in order to help the Jews who were trapped in Nazi-dominated lands. They accepted dangerous assignments which were to be carried out behind enemy lines. These self-sacrificing men and women were the unsung heroes of the Second World War. They volunteered for special intelligence work and were dropped by parachute into Nazi-occupied territory. Their task was to establish contact with the men and women of the local resistance movements, the fighters who sabotaged the Nazis in factories, fought them in guerilla bands in the mountains and villages, on country roads and city streets. Even though all Europe seemed powerless in the Nazi stranglehold, there were small, fearless groups who

חַנָּה סֶנֶשׁ

HANNAH SENESH (1921–1944)
*Poetess, martyred Jewish
freedom-fighter*

Tragically, Hannah Senesh lived for only twenty-three years. This talented young woman, an ardent Zionist, was tortured and killed by the Hungarian police. Hannah Senesh had parachuted into Nazi-occupied Europe to help organize Jewish resistance.

She had grown up in Hungary, where many Christians openly showed their hatred of Jews. While still a young girl, Hannah decided to move to Palestine and help rebuild the Jewish homeland. In September 1939, against the wishes of her widowed mother, she settled in Eretz Yisr'ael at the age of eighteen. Hannah became a student of farming at Nahalal, Israel's first moshav. She also began to write beautiful poetry.

In 1943, the Nazi terror was raging in Europe, and Hannah was desperately concerned about the survival of the Jewish community in Hungary. She decided she must go back to Hungary to help organize an aliyah of young people and to rescue her mother. She was parachuted into Italy, made her way to Yugoslavia, and then tried to enter Hungary. At the Hungarian border she was captured by police and taken to their Budapest headquarters.

The girl was cruelly tortured and beaten in the Nazi effort to force her to reveal information about Jewish underground activities. The Nazis even brought in Hannah's mother, who tearfully begged Hannah to reveal anything which might save her life. But the brave girl remained silent. The Hungarian police shot her dead in November 1944.

In 1950, Hannah Senesh's remains were brought to Israel and buried on Mount Herzl. In Israel and among Jews everywhere, her name became a symbol of devotion and self-sacrifice.

fought constantly, secretly using the radio and other means to keep in contact with the Allies. These courageous underground fighters, who faced torture and death if they were caught, prepared the way for the Nazi defeat.

The Jewish fighters from Palestine who were parachuted behind the enemy lines were part of the British intelligence service. They performed many missions for the Allies, as well as special missions for the Jewish people. They returned to their native lands and, under false names and with false passports, tried to organize "underground railways" to help Jews escape from the Nazi death camps. Many of these heroic fighters lost their lives. Many more were imprisoned and executed as spies.

Among the best-remembered of the Jewish heroes who operated in secret against the Nazis was Hannah Senesh. She had left a comfortable home and her parents to live the life of a pioneer in Palestine.

The Displaced Persons

In the lands which Hitler's armies had occupied during the war, entire populations had been uprooted. Thousands of people had been transported by the Nazis, as prisoners or slave laborers, to places distant from their homes. In the liberated concentration camps there were hundreds of thousands who had no homes, families, or source of livelihood to which to return. These people were called displaced persons or, for short, DP's.

The problem of the Jewish displaced persons was particularly acute. Not many Jews had survived the Nazi death camps. Those who had managed to stay alive no longer had homes or relatives. Many of the survivors wanted to go to Palestine.

Illegal Immigration to Palestine

But the British were still a pitiless barrier to further Jewish immigration.

The Haganah, the organization which had aided illegal immigration during the war, again went into action. "Underground railroads" were again organized. The

The ma'apilim were imprisoned behind barbed-wire fences and guarded by British soldiers with dogs.

survivors of Hitler's death camps, waiting in detention centers until their problems could be solved, had cause for new hope.

Once again ships were bought and people smuggled across the seas to Palestine. Again, Haganah assumed the perilous task of landing illegal immigrants in secret, under cover of night. Often the passengers, young and old, many of them scarred by years of prison life, had to wade through a stormy surf or row in small boats to elude the British guards.

The Irgun Zvai Leumi, Hebrew for "National Military Organization," a Palestinian underground movement founded in 1937 by members of the Betar youth organization, and the Zionist-Revisionist movement, was also very active in the organization and success of the "illegal" immigration of Jewish displaced persons.

The British showed little sympathy for the plight of the Jews. Their concern was for good relations with the Arab nations and no trouble in the Middle East. Because of the heavy British guard, very few of the Haganah ships succeeded in bringing their illegal passengers to Palestine. Most of the ships were intercepted by the British

Refugees at a detention camp strain at the barbed wire that keeps them from freedom and their homeland.

שְׁמוֹר בְּלִבְּךָ כֹּל הַיָּדוּעַ לְךָ לְרֶגֶל תַּפְקִידְךָ

A Haganah appeal to the people of Israel: "Keep in your hearts all you know as a result of your mission."

Thousands of Jews in overloaded boats risked the British blockade to reach Israel. After Israel gained independence, the gates were opened and hundreds of thousands arrived by air or by sea.

VOCABULARY AND CONCEPTS

Illegal immigrants	מַעְפִּילִים
The *Exodus*	יְצִיאַת אֵרוֹפָּה
Exodus	יְצִיאָה
Displaced Person	עֲקוּר
"Underground Railroad"	מַחְתֶּרֶת הַשִּׁחְרוּר
Internment camps	מַחֲנֵה מַעְפִּילִים

authorities. The passengers were arrested and sent to internment camps especially set up for them on the island of Cyprus. This was done despite the fact that these Jewish immigrants would never have been a burden to the British in Palestine. As always, the Jewish community itself was ready to take care of them. With funds collected by the Zionist Organization all over the world, these homeless Jews could have been settled on the land. They were turned back, but their spirits were not broken. Now they waited in Cyprus, sure that the moment would come when they would be able to ascend to the homeland.

The S.S. "Exodus"

In 1947 the British policy toward the Jews in Palestine became even more harsh. In order to set an example, they sent back to Germany the S.S. *Exodus*, a Haganah boat which had set sail for Palestine with a cargo of illegal immigrants—men, women, and children who had survived the Nazi death camps. These refugees had risked their lives to come to Palestine. Now they were sent back to Germany, where there was no room for them except in the displaced-persons camps, where for all they knew, they might live on for years without hope, waiting for a solution to the problem of their homelessness.

The fate of the *Exodus* stirred the Jews of Palestine to open rebellion. New groups formed and resorted to acts of sabotage against the British, who seemed willing to appease the hostile Arabs at the expense of the Jews.

The protest against the British closed-door policy now became a matter of open discussion. Since Britain was unable to find a solution for the "Palestine problem," the United Nations took up the question. In 1947 a new Committee of Inquiry went to Palestine, under the auspices of the United Nations. The committee returned with a proposal to partition Palestine into two separate states—one Arab and one Jewish. In this way, the committee believed, peace would be established, and the new Jewish state would deal with the problem of Jewish immigration as it saw fit.

248

HISTORY OF ISRAEL

The Birth of the State of Israel

After two thousand years of Jewish life in the Diaspora, we have finally returned home. On May 14, 1948, the State of Israel was declared an independent Jewish nation. Proudly and joyfully, Jews everywhere celebrated the wonderful event.

When we study the history of the modern State of Israel, we realize constantly the miracle of the Jewish return.

THE BIRTH OF THE STATE OF ISRAEL

After much bloodshed, the British formally announced to the United Nations that they were giving up their Mandate over Palestine. The United Nations suggested a plan for peace—a "partition" (division) which separated the land of Israel into two states, Arab and Jewish. Jerusalem was to be an international city. The plan had faults, but the Jews accepted it as a chance for peace. The Arabs furiously turned it down, and the violence against the Jewish settlements went on.

A banner headline announces the birth of the new State. Although the State of Israel was proclaimed on Friday afternoon, May 14, 1948, the paper is dated Sunday, May 16 because no papers in Israel are printed on the Sabbath.

If you can't come to town, please telephone 4607

Lighting, Heating, Cooking, Refrigeration

CARL MARX
2 PRINCESS MARY AVE., JERUSALEM

JERUSALEM
SUNDAY, MAY 16, 1948

THE PALESTINE POST

PRICE: 25 MILS
VOL. XXIII. No. 6714

THE PALESTINE POST
THE SUBSCRIPTION DEPARTMENT has returned to The Palestine Post offices, Hasolel Street, Jerusalem, Tel. 4233.

STATE OF ISRAEL IS BORN

The first independent Jewish State in 19 centuries was born in Tel Aviv as the British Mandate over Palestine came to an end at midnight on Friday, and it was immediately subjected to the test of fire. As "Medinat Yisrael" (State of Israel) was proclaimed, the battle for Jerusalem raged, with most of the city falling to the Jews. At the same time, President Truman announced that the United States would accord recognition to the new State. A few hours later, Palestine was invaded by Moslem armies from the south, east and north, and Tel Aviv was raided from the air. On Friday the United Nations Special Assembly adjourned after adopting a resolution to appoint a mediator but without taking any action on the Partition Resolution of November 29.

Yesterday the battle for the Jerusalem-Tel Aviv road was still under way, and two Arab villages were taken. In the north, Acre town was captured, and the Jewish Army consolidated its positions in Western Galilee.

Most Crowded Hours in Palestine's History

Between Thursday night and this morning Palestine went through what by all standards must be among the most crowded hours in its history.

For the Jewish population there was the anguish over the fate of the few hundred Haganah men and women in the Kfar Etzion bloc of settlements near Hebron. Their surrender to a fully equipped superior foreign force desperately in need of a victory was no foregone conclusion since Thursday morning, was whether and to what extent the Red Cross and the Trans Consuls would secure civilized

JEWS TAKE OVER SECURITY ZONES

The Battle for Jerusalem, which began when the British forces withdrew on Friday morning, continued all day Friday and yesterday. The crackle of small-arms fire and explosions of mortar shells were still being heard in the early hours of this morning as the battle entered its third day.

Repeated efforts on Friday morning and again on Satur-

Egyptian Air Force Spitfires Bomb Tel Aviv; One Shot Down

Kol Israel, the Tel Aviv broadcasting station, reported at 2 o'clock yesterday afternoon that Tel Aviv had been bombed three times in the previous evening and morning, and that one plane had been shot down and its Egyptian pilot taken prisoner.

In the first raid, four planes attacked from a height of 300 feet. Two dropped bombs, while the others strafed the

U.S. RECOGNIZES JEWISH STATE

WASHINGTON, Saturday. —Ten minutes after the termination of the British Mandate on Friday, the White House released a formal statement by President Truman that the U.S. Government intended to recognize the Provisional Jewish Government as the *de facto* authority representing the Jewish State.

A country-wide blackout was ordered by Air Raid Precaution Headquarters in Tel Aviv.

Mr. David Ben Gurion, the Prime Minister, broadcast from Tel Aviv yesterday to the people of America yesterday morning. As he spoke, Egyptian planes were bombing the city.

In the north, the settlements of Ein Gev and Shaar Hago-

Proclamation by Head Of Government

The creation of "Medinat Yisrael", the State of Israel, was proclaimed at midnight on Friday by Mr. David Ben Gurion, until then Chairman of the Jewish Agency Executive and now head of the State's Provisional Council of Government.

The first act of the Council of Government, as announced by its head, was to abolish all legislation of the 1939 White Paper of the late Mandatory Power, particularly the Ordinances and Orders relating

דָּוִד בֶּן גּוּרְיוֹן

DAVID BEN-GURION
(1886—1973)
Pioneer and statesman

David Ben-Gurion was born in Poland in 1886, studied law at the University of Constantinople, and moved to Palestine in 1906.

At this moment in history the Turks ruled Palestine, and they were strongly opposed to Jewish settlement. In 1915, the Turks arrested David Ben-Gurion and Yitzchak Ben-Zvi and exiled them to Egypt.

Palestine at this time was now under the rule of the British, who had defeated Turkey in World War I. In 1939, the British too restricted Jewish settlement and severely restricted Jewish immigration into the national homeland.

Ben-Gurion headed Israel's army in the War of Independence. On May 14, 1948, the proud leader proclaimed the birth of Israel, once again an independent Jewish state. He was named Prime Minister and Minister of Defense. In December 1949, David Ben-Gurion declared Jerusalem the capital of Israel

Ben-Gurion condemned the British policy and called for active Jewish resistance. By night secret shiploads of Jews were brought into their beloved Eretz Yisrael. In 1946, speaking to Holocaust survivors in Germany, Ben-Gurion said, "We shall not rest until every one of you who so desires joins us in the land of Israel in building a Jewish state."

In December 1953, Ben-Gurion resigned from the government after many years of strenuous service. But he did not retire to some luxurious estate to take a well-deserved rest. Instead, he moved to a pioneering kibbutz in the heart of the Negev—Kibbutz Sde Boker, "Fields of Morning."

Today, the Ben-Gurion University stands in the Negev, memorializing the great Zionist leader who was the land's first Prime Minister.

VOCABULARY AND CONCEPTS

United Nations	אֻמּוֹת מְאֻחָדוֹת (אוּ"ם)
Israel	יִשְׂרָאֵל

The Jewish State Gains Its Independence

Once the British Mandate was over, all the British officials and troops left the country. On the fifth day of Iyyar, 5708, on the Hebrew calendar (May 14, 1948), after the last British officer had gone, Jewish representatives from all over Palestine met in the Tel Aviv Museum. There David Ben-Gurion read the Declaration of Independence that proclaimed Israel an independent state and the homeland of the Jewish people.

The dream of the return to Zion—a dream that Jews had kept alive for centuries of exile—had become a miraculous reality. All over Israel, Jews danced joyously in the streets. Throughout the world, Jews felt a surge of pride in their hearts at the return of the determined Jewish people to their God-given homeland, Israel. At long, long last, we had come home and we were free.

Beneath the portrait of Binyamin Zeev Herzl, David Ben-Gurion, the first Prime Minister of Israel, reads the Declaration of Independence.

251

ISRAEL FIGHTS FOR HER LIFE

The War of Independence—1948

On May 14, 1948, Israel declared her independence. The very next morning, the new state was invaded by massive, powerful armies from the Arab nations: Egypt, Jordan, Syria, Lebanon, Iraq, Saudi Arabia. The Arabs are usually bitter rivals amongst themselves, but they joined in one united assault on the Jewish homeland. Israel was besieged on all sides and threatened with a terrible destruction.

Egypt borders Israel to the south. Egyptian armies advanced northward toward the sacred Jewish capital, Jerusalem, while Jordanians moved in on Jerusalem from the east. Two strong columns of Syrian troops descended from the north, aiming for the Jordan Valley and the Galilee.

The fighting of the War of Independence was long and hard. The suffering went on for more than a year. Thousands of Israelis were killed for the sake of the newborn state. But Israel's fighters stood their ground. Two thousand years of life in the exile had taught them resourcefulness, determination, and unyielding courage. Few in numbers and poorly armed, the Jews were rich in faith and bravery and ingenuity. They resisted the armed might of the Arab invaders. Unrelenting, the Jews were able to stop the Arab advance and finally drove the invaders out of Israel.

Arab Hostility and Terrorism Continue

The War of Independence ended when both sides signed an Armistice Agreement which promised that

Religious kibbutzniks take time out from guard duty during the tense times of 1948 to study the holy books.

252

דָּוִד מַרְקוֹס

DAVID MARCUS (1902–1948)
American army officer

Born and raised in Brooklyn, David Marcus studied at City College, the United States Military Academy at West Point, and Brooklyn Law School.

During World War II, Marcus fought bravely and advanced to the rank of colonel. After the war ended, he was stationed in Germany.

Marcus returned to New York and opened a law office in January 1948. That same month, an Israeli Haganah member, Shlomo Shamir, came to the United States and approached Marcus for help: "You have studied military tactics at West Point, and you can help us build our strength in Palestine. Please help us train our settlers to protect our Jewish land!" Shamir was successful in his mission. Marcus left for Palestine the same month. Smuggled into Tel Aviv as Michael Stone, Marcus dictated military manuals, led Haganah raids, and helped plan Israel's future defense.

Two weeks after Israel was proclaimed a state, Prime Minister Ben-Gurion appointed David Marcus the commander of the Jerusalem front. Thanks to Marcus's efforts, the Jewish forces successfully opened the road to their beloved, sacred capital, which had been cut off by Arab forces, thus saving Jerusalem's New City from the enemy. But David Marcus was killed in the fighting.

Buried in the cemetery of the U.S. Military Academy, Marcus was posthumously awarded the Israeli Medal of Independence.

there would be no more battles. But the Arabs did not live up to their promise of peace. Egypt started training bands of terrorists, who crept across Israel's borders at night under cover of darkness and murdered innocent people. These terrorists—called *fedayeen* in Arabic—blew up homes, burned down settlements, and shot at people in their homes. They wanted to scare the Jews away from Israel. The Jordanians and Syrians, too, sent murderous gangs of terrorists into Israel. The Syrian gang called itself El Fatah, which means "The Conquest."

The Jews, especially those who lived near the borders, suffered terribly from these sneak attacks. Many innocent people were wounded and killed. Homes, schools, and synagogues were bombed and burned.

Then Egypt refused to let ships enter or leave the Israeli port of Eilat. This act choked the Jewish state economically by halting its important trade with Africa and Asia by way of the Red Sea. Egyptian armies moved into northern Sinai and the Gaza Strip, directly threatening Israel and closing the Suez Canal to Israeli ships and to ships of other nations bound for Israel.

The hostility of the encircling Arab nations compelled the Jews of Palestine to fight for their security and independence. Haganah troops march to relieve the siege of Jerusalem in April 1948.

Israeli soldiers under attack.

The Sinai Campaign—1956

Israel struck back on October 29, 1956. The Israeli forces moved into Sinai and the Gaza Strip and defeated the Egyptian armies there. By November 4, the Egyptians had been driven out of the Sinai and Israeli forces had reached the Suez Canal.

Now the Arab nations went to the United Nations and begged for help. They called Israel an "aggressor," conveniently ignoring the fact that the Arabs had forced Israel to defend herself. The United Nations pressured Israel into leaving the positions taken by the army in the Sinai and the Gaza Strip. Because Egypt promised peace, Israel withdrew, and troops from the United Nations took over. For the next decade, there was relative peace on the Israel/Egypt border.

Israel had regained her freedom to use the port of Eilat without fear of an Egyptian blockade. The victorious Sinai Campaign enabled Israel to begin an era of growth and expansion, trade and communication.

Arab Terrorism Resumes After the War

The Arabs never fulfilled their promise of peace. Bands of terrorists renewed their sneak attacks on Israel in the dead of night, maiming, killing, and destroying. Arab leaders provoked their people into hatred of Israel, calling for a "holy war" to destroy the Jewish nation and "drive the Jews into the sea." Russia supplied the Arabs with billions of dollars worth of arms.

Israel went to the United Nations and asked for help, urging it to protect the Jewish state from its enemies. But Russia and the Arabs insisted loudly that Israel's charges were false, and the United Nations did nothing.

But the United Nations did come out in protest when Israel retaliated against her enemies by attacking a Jordanian village used by terrorists. The United Nations criticized Israel, but ignored the Arab murders and invasions that had triggered Israel's move.

אֵלִי כֹּהֵן

ELI COHEN (1924–1965)
Patriot and master spy

Born in Egypt, Cohen learned the language and customs of the Arabs while he was growing up. Later he moved to Israel and trained to become a spy. He was sent to Syria, where he pretended to be a rich Syrian citizen, using an Arabic name and identity. Because he spoke the language so well and knew exactly how to behave, no one guessed that he was really an Israeli.

Cohen was very successful in his daring work for Israeli intelligence. He became friendly with top government officers, who told him important secrets. He was taken on tours of hidden Syrian army bases. He was able to help the Israeli government and army with this crucial information.

Cohen fit so well into Arab society that he began his own show on Syrian radio and became well-known throughout the entire nation (with an Arabic name, of course)! He was discovered by Russian intelligence and sentenced by the Syrians to be hanged.

In 1965 thousands of people viewed Eli Cohen's public hanging on television. Those in Arab nations cheered, while those in Israel mourned the loss of a brave man who had given his life for his country.

Espionage

Espionage, or spying, is the secret gathering of information about one nation for the benefit or defense of another. The United States espionage bureau is called the CIA, short for Central Intelligence Agency. Britain has the MI5 and the Russians have the KGB. The espionage bureau of Israel is called the Shin Bet, the Hebrew initials for its full name, Sherut HaBitachon, which means "Security Service."

Israel is surrounded by enemy nations which openly declare their opposition to her very existence. In addition to the Arab nations plotting Israel's downfall, the Russians support the Arabs with arms, training, and supplies. Israel needs the espionage of the Shin Bet to secure the vital information needed for the Jewish nation's survival and safety.

One of the most famous Shin Bet officers was Eli Cohen. He became friendly with high-ranking officials in the Syrian government and helped Israel get much-needed data from within Syria. Cohen's activities were discovered by the Syrians and he was publicly hanged in Damascus in 1965.

Wolfgang Lotz, another Shin Bet officer, spied for Israel in Egypt during the 1960's. Lotz provided Israel with important information that led to Israel's victory in the 1967 Six-Day War.

The Six-Day War—1967

In May 1967, Egypt demanded that the United Nations withdraw its forces from the Sinai. The United Nations gave in. Once there were no longer any peace-keeping troops on the scene to protect Israel from a full-scale attack, the Arab nations massed together against the Jewish state. Egypt once again blockaded Israel's port at Eilat. Arab armies from all the countries surrounding Israel converged on the borders of the small Jewish homeland.

Israel appealed to the United Nations, asking for international action to stop these threats to her life. But

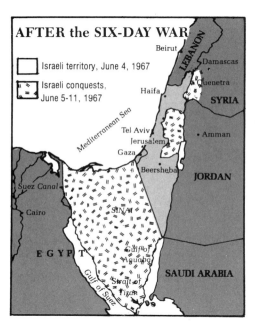

AFTER the SIX-DAY WAR

☐ Israeli territory, June 4, 1967

▨ Israeli conquests, June 5-11, 1967

Beirut · Damascas · LEBANON · Haifa · Quenetra · **SYRIA** · Tel Aviv · Jerusalem · Amman · Gaza · Beersheba · **JORDAN** · Mediterranean Sea · Suez Canal · Cairo · SINAI · Gulf of Aqaba · **EGYPT** · Strait of Tiran · Gulf of Suez · **SAUDI ARABIA**

During the Six-Day War in 1967, Israel captured the Sinai, the Gaza Strip, the Golan Heights, and Judea and Samaria (West Bank).

VOCABULARY AND CONCEPTS

Suez Canal	תַּעֲלַת סוּאֵץ
United Nations	אוּמוֹת מְאֻחָדוֹת (אוּ״ם)
The Six-Day War	מִלְחֶמֶת שֵׁשֶׁת הַיָּמִים
David (Mickey) Marcus	דָּוִד מַרְקוּס
Arab terrorists	פְדָאִין

no one seemed to be on Israel's side. Russia and France openly sided with the Arabs. The United States and other Western countries urged Israel to "hold back," "wait," "show restraint."

No one offered any real aid. Meanwhile, the Arab armies grew stronger and advanced closer to Israel's vulnerable border settlements. Over the Arab radio, their leaders shouted to the people to prepare for the "holy war" against the Jews. The Israelis saw that the United Nations was not helping. Threatened on all sides, disappointed by the silence of the United Nations, the Israelis decided they had only themselves to count on and went into action. On Monday, June 5, 1967, the war broke out.

What followed astounded the world. With unbelievable speed, flying in below Arab radar detection, Israel wiped out the air forces of Egypt, Jordan, and Syria in a surprise raid: 451 Arab planes were destroyed, compared with Israel's loss of 9. The Egyptian invasion troops in the Sinai were smashed by the Israel Defense Forces. The Jordanian and Syrian armies were demolished.

The whole war took an incredible six days—hence its name, the Six-Day War. Israel broke Egypt's blockade of Eilat and took over large areas that the Arabs had used to threaten the security of the Jewish state. The Golan Heights, the Gaza Strip, the Sinai, and the West Bank were won from Syria, Egypt, and Jordan. And the Old City of Jerusalem was reclaimed by joyous Israeli soldiers.

Two Israeli soldiers plant the flag of Israel atop the Western Wall, June 7, 1967.

Entering the Old City of Jerusalem; *from right to left:* Chief of Staff Gen. Yitzhak Rabin; Defense Minister Moshe Dayan; Gen. Uzi Narkiss, Commander of the Central Sector.

JERUSALEM REUNITED

What is a city?

A city is a group of buildings where people live and work. Stores sell many different products, businesses thrive, and everywhere in a city there seems to be a flurry of activity.

But a city is also a history, a place with a special mood, a unique atmosphere, a feeling. London is not Paris, New York is not Rome, though there are buildings and people in all of these places. A nation's capital city, especially, stands for a country's independence and the heart of her history and traditions.

The Special Meaning of Jerusalem for Jews

The city of Jerusalem is the most special city in the world for Jews, for it is the capital city of their homeland. In this holy city, the prophets and kings of ancient Israel taught and ruled. It is the site of the Temple of King Solomon. There the Israelites of distant days brought baskets of colorful fruits on the holidays of the Jewish year; there they offered solemn prayers and offered up their sacrifices.

When the Jews returned from the exile in Babylonia, they rebuilt their beloved Temple in Jerusalem, on the same spot where the magnificent First Temple had stood in all its glory. But the Second Temple, too, was destroyed. The Romans conquered Jerusalem in 70 C.E., and they burned the Temple to the ground. All that remained was the fire-charred Western Wall, which became a sacred place where Jews worshipped and wept and yearned that God would restore their city of Jerusalem to proud Jewish independence.

257

מֹשֶׁה דַּיָּן

MOSHE DAYAN (1915–1982)
Israeli general and statesman
Moshe Dayan was born in Kibbutz
Degania and at an early age was
taken to live in Nahalal, the first
moshav. He studied farm techniques at Nahalal's agricultural
school and as a teenager joined the
Haganah, the Jewish underground
defense force. Later, during the
Arab terrorist attacks in 1936,
Dayan served with Orde Wingate's
Special Night Squads. The British
arrested him in 1939 for possess-
ing illegal arms, but he was released in 1941 to serve in the British invasion of Syria. During this
battle, Dayan lost his left eye when
a bullet drove his telescope into
his eye socket.

During Israel's War of Independence, Dayan held the rank of lieutenant colonel and commanded
various fronts. He became a major
general in 1953 and led the Israeli
army during the Sinai Campaign
in 1956.

In 1957 Dayan left the the army
to enter politics. He studied law,
economics, and political science
and became Minister of Agriculture in David Ben-Gurion's cabinet. Just before the Six-Day War in
June 1967, Dayan was appointed
Minister of Defense. After the great
Israeli victory, Dayan administered the areas occupied by the
Israel army on the West Bank of
the Jordan River. His firmness,
fairness, and humanity in dealing
with the people living in these areas earned him the respect of the
Arab population.

Jews came to worship at the Western Wall all through
the centuries of exile, wailing so much in their pain at
their people's exile that the wall became known as the
Wailing Wall. The wall itself was considered so holy that
it became a custom for Jews to write down their prayers
on scraps of paper that they would wedge in between the
soft, rosy stones.

Jerusalem Under Jordanian Rule

In 1948, Jordanian troops captured the ancient part of
Jerusalem where the Western Wall stood. The Jordanians
refused to return this part of Jerusalem, called the Old
City. The United Nations split up the city of Jerusalem
into two parts, and it remained divided for nineteen
years; the Old City, with all the most sacred places for
Jews, was under Arab control, and the New City was
under Jewish control.

The Arabs signed an agreement allowing Jews into the
Old City to worship at their holy places. But the Jordanians did not live up to their promise. They refused to let
in any Jews.

Not only that, the Jordanians looted and vandalized
many buildings sacred to Jews in the Old City. They
bulldozed ancient graves in the Jewish cemetery on the
Mount of Olives and built a road through it.

The Israeli Liberation of Jerusalem

When the 1967 war broke out, Israel promised King
Hussein of Jordan that no harm would come to his coun-
try if he kept out of the fight. But Hussein did not listen
to Israel's warning. Jordan began bombing the New City
of Jerusalem, the Jewish part of the city. To save herself,
Israel counterattacked. When the fighting was over,
Israel had won back the Old City, and the capital city of
Jerusalem was once more reunited.

Steel-helmeted soldiers leaned on the ancient stones of
the Western Wall and wept. Even those who did not see
themselves as "religious" felt the need to say a prayer.
General Moshe Dayan, following the old tradition, wrote
out a prayer that he set between the time-worn stones:

258

Rabbi Shlomo Goren, Chief Chaplain of the Israel Defense Forces, blowing the shofar during the first prayer service at the liberated Western Wall, Jerusalem. June 1967.

American Jews *(foreground)* and American Arabs holding counter-demonstrations in front of the White House in Washington, June 8, 1967, the third day of the Six-Day War. The Jewish demonstrators had come to the White House to call for full U.S. support of Israel, and when it was announced that Egypt had accepted a cease-fire, the demonstration turned into a victory celebration.

"May peace come to Israel." Then he pronounced the vow: "We have returned to the holiest of our holy places, never to depart again." The date was the twenty-eighth day of the Hebrew month of Iyyar. Each year on this date, Jews celebrate Yom Yerushalayim—Jerusalem Day. We rejoice at the reuniting of our holy capital city, and we mourn the brave soldiers who fell in the battle.

On Shavuot, a week after the war ended, 200,000 Jews worshiped at the Wall. Their tearful joy at the return of the Jewish people to their sacred Old City expressed itself in prayer and in song.

The liberators of the Old City at the Western Wall.

VOCABULARY AND CONCEPTS

Mount of Olives (ancient Jewish cemetery in Jerusalem)

הַר הַזֵּיתִים

The 28th day of Iyyar (day on which Old and New Cities of Jerusalem were reunited)

יוֹם יְרוּשָׁלַיִם

259

THE YOM KIPPUR WAR—1973

Israeli soldiers erecting a Chanu-kah menorah on the west bank of the Suez Canal, following the Yom Kippur War, December 1973.

Almost daily between 1968 and 1970, marauding Arab terrorists sneaked across Israel's borders to attack innocent people. Tel Aviv was shelled. A school bus was blown up in Eilat, injuring twenty-eight children. The Arab leaders ignored their promises of peace and encouraged their people to hate the Jewish state, resent the 1967 defeat, and prepare for renewed battle. Russia sent the Arabs billions of dollars worth of arms.

PLO Terrorism

Having failed at war, the Arabs started a new kind of battle against Israel—a propaganda battle. They made up lies about Israel, ignoring the facts of history and claiming that Israel had no right to exist. They said the land

The Israeli participants in the 1972 Summer Olympics in Munich, Germany, prepare to board an El Al flight home, taking with them the bodies of eleven comrades who were brutally massacred by Arab terrorists.

When troops of the Israel Defense Forces took the Old City of Jerusalem on June 7, 1967, they made these startling discoveries: Of the thirty-five ancient Jewish houses of worship that had stood in the Old City until its tragic division in 1948, some of them for hundreds of years, only one still survived whole and unmolested. The rest had been plundered, Interior of Nissan Bek Synagogue: a hollow shell

Israeli border police inspect the site where two Israeli watchmen were murdered by Arab *fedayim*.

rightfully belonged to the "Palestinians," as the Arabs now began to call themselves. The brutal terrorists of the Palestine Liberation Organization received money, arms, and training from Russia.

At the 1972 Olympics, Arabs murdered eleven Israeli athletes. In reprisal, Israel hit terrorist bases in Syria and Lebanon. Tension in the area was beginning to rise ominously.

A Sneak Attack on Yom Kippur

On the holiest day of the Jewish year, Yom Kippur, October 6, 1973, the Arabs attacked Israel on two fronts at once—Syria attacking on Israel's northern Golan front and Egypt attacking across the Suez Canal into the Sinai.

Since Yom Kippur is the most sacred day of the Jewish year, most soldiers were in the synagogues with their families; the veteran soldiers were with their families on this solemn day of prayer and fasting, and the borders of Israel were guarded by new recruits. The country's television and radio systems were shut down. The Arab sneak attack found Israel off guard.

By the time the orders went out and the Jewish troops could assemble to defend their land, the invading Arab armies had broken through the Israeli lines to both the north and the south. Massive Egyptian and Syrian armies penetrated the Israeli defenses, the Egyptians pushing into Sinai and the Syrians moving into the Golan Heights.

Israel Fights Back

Israel recovered fast and started to fight back, with all her might. Jews—sometimes with prayerbooks still in their hands—left the synagogues and rushed to the battlefield. They left off praying, and started fighting and praying together. In nine days, the Israeli army pushed back all the invaders. The Egyptian army was surrounded in the Sinai and Israeli troops threatened Cairo, Egypt's capital. The Syrian troops, too, had been forced back. Israel was poised to attack Damascus, Syria's capital.

Now that Israel was winning, the Arabs and the Russians went to the United Nations and screamed for help.

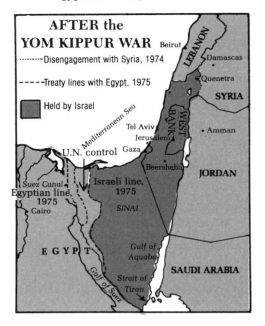

AFTER the
YOM KIPPUR WAR Beirut
········· Disengagement with Syria, 1974
------ Treaty lines with Egypt, 1975
Held by Israel

Now that Israel was in a position to demolish Cairo and Damascus, the Arabs "forgot" that they had started the fighting. Now they called for a cease-fire and demanded help from the international authorities.

Israel's Desire for Peace

The Jewish nation wanted peace, not bloodshed. And so Israel agreed to a cease-fire, despite her position of strength at this point in the war. She could have destroyed the Arab capitals. But she listened to the Arabs' promises of peace and withdrew her troops. The war, begun by the Arabs on the Jewish fast-day, became known as the Yom Kippur War.

After the cease-fire, all of Israel mourned the nation's loss of 2,523 people. Golda Meir, the Prime Minister of Israel, said, "For the people of Israel, each human life is precious. Our dead soldiers are the sons of all of us. The pain we feel is felt by all of us."

But the Arabs did not speak of peace, even after signing the cease-fire agreement. Egypt and Syria pretended they had won the war, even though they had been soundly beaten by Israel's forces. The two Arab nations claimed a victory because they had been successful for the first two days of war, after the Yom Kippur surprise attack. After the cease-fire, President Anwar Sadat of Egypt did not speak of future peace. He said, "I am prepared to sacrifice one million lives each year in order to recover Sinai."

VOCABULARY AND CONCEPTS

War of Independence	מִלְחֶמֶת הַשִׁחְרוּר
Yom Kippur	יוֹם כִּפּוּר
Olympics	אוֹלִימְפְּיָאדָה
PLO	אַשַׁ"ף

DURING WARTIME, ISRAEL BECOMES ONE FAMILY

Israeli warplanes being loaded with bombs ·

In 1973, the war lasted for seventeen days before the fighting was over. As in 1967, all of Israel worked together so the country could survive the war.

The workers of the nation had all gone off to war. Who would bring medicines and meals to sick people in hospitals? Who would sort and deliver mail, teach children to read, harvest the fall crops, collect garbage, unload milk at the grocery, and keep the factory assembly lines going? The children, teenagers, and older people of Israel volunteered! Those too young and too old to fight worked together wherever help was needed so that Israel could remain strong. Children picked fruits and teenagers became volunteer drivers. A retired general who had fought in the War of Independence drove a garbage truck.

All over Israel, at the sides of the roads leading to Egypt and Syria, little booths went up. At these stands women and children brought foods and drinks, which they offered to the soldiers marching to the battlefields. Many of these soldiers had no home telephones and were anxious to let their families know that they were safe. The women took down the soldiers' names and addresses and promised to send messages to their families.

Israel's Arabs During the War

Generally, Israel's Arab citizens supported Israel. Arabs stood on the long waiting lines at hospitals to give blood for the wounded, and Arab women helped Jewish women at the little booths along the roads. Many Bedouins came in from their desert homes to volunteer their services.

The Jews of Other Countries Help

Jews all over the world responded with generosity and love during Israel's time of crisis. Millions of dollars were needed—for arms, ammunition, medical equipment. Jews and non-Jews who felt that Israel's survival was vital sent in money to the United Jewish Appeal's Israel Emergency Fund. Children brought in boxfuls of dimes, nickels, and quarters that they had collected in their apartment buildings, from their relatives and classmates and teachers. Television stars appealed to their fans on the air in Aid-Israel telethons. Many people not only gave money but volunteered to go to Israel themselves to help out in any way possible.

War orphans who have reached Bar Mitzvah age are taught how to put on tefillin at communal Bar Mitzvah celebration at Kfar Chabad.

VOCABULARY AND CONCEPTS

United Jewish Appeal (Jewish fund to help Israel and Jews in other countries)   מַגְבִּית מְאֻחֶדֶת

264

THE ISRAEL/EGYPT PEACE TREATY

In May 1977, a new government was elected in Israel. The Likkud party, headed by Menachem Begin, became the largest party in the Knesset.

Sadat's Visit to Jerusalem

The new Prime Minister invited President Sadat of Egypt to come to Jerusalem. Menachem Begin wanted peace for Israel, and he hoped that through a talk with the Arab leader, peace with Egypt might be reached. In November 1977, for the first time ever, an Arab leader, President Anwar Sadat of Egypt, visited Jerusalem. Sadat spoke in the Knesset of his wish for peace between Egypt and Israel. The Jews hoped and prayed that Sadat's visit would begin a new era of peace and understanding. But many found it difficult to trust Egypt's promises. The Arab nations had never lived up to their promises of peace before.

Prime Minister Menachem Begin welcomes President Anwar Sadat of Egypt at Ben-Gurion Airport, November 21, 1977.

מְנַחֵם בֵּגִין

MENACHEM BEGIN (1913–)
Seventh Prime Minister of Israel

Born and educated in Poland, where he graduated from law school, Begin became head of the Betar movement before he was twenty. In 1936, when the British were not protecting Zionist settlers in Palestine from Arab attacks, Begin organized a mass demonstration near the British Embassy in Warsaw, the Polish capital. The Polish police arrested him. In 1939, when the Nazis conquered Poland, Begin went to Russia, where he was arrested because of his Zionist activities and sent to a Siberian labor camp. He was released in 1941 and went to Palestine the next year.

Thousands of Jews, struggling to flee the Nazi Holocaust in Europe, tried to come to Palestine. But the British rulers, giving in to Arab pressure, refused to admit the unfortunate Jewish refugees. Begin and his followers would not stand by while Jews were turned away from the shores of their homeland and sent back to certain death. Begin led the Jewish underground struggle against the British. To evade the British police who tried to catch him, Begin disguised himself as a bearded rabbi.

In 1948, the British Mandate came to an end and Israel finally became an independent state. Now all Jews could freely come to their homeland. Begin became active in political life. He founded the Cherut ("Liberty") party and ever since 1948 has been a member of the Knesset. From 1966 to 1970 he served as a Cabinet minister, and in 1977 he became Israel's Prime Minister.

A passionte speaker and Orthodox Jew, Menachem Begin is an articulate spokesman for the Jewish state. He speaks proudly of Israel as the God-given homeland of our people.

Camp David (place where a peace treaty was concluded between Israel and Egypt)

VOCABULARY AND CONCEPTS

| Camp David | קֶמְפּ דֵוִד |
| Anwar Sadat | אַנְוָור סָדָט |

The Camp David Agreement

On March 26, 1979, a peace treaty was signed between Israel and Egypt in Washington, D.C. Prime Minister Menachem Begin of Israel, President Anwar Sadat of Egypt, and President Jimmy Carter of the United States worked hard to bring about the signing of this historic agreement. It is called the Camp David Agreement, from the name of the place where the three leaders met with each other.

The other Arab states bitterly opposed Sadat's steps toward peace with Israel. They swore to have their revenge on him for having negotiated with the Jewish state. In October 1981, Sadat was killed by an assassin's bullet.

Hosni Mubarak

Hosni Mubarak succeeded the slain Anwar Sadat. Now, Mr. Mubarak is the target of Islamic extremists in part because he leads a government that maintains diplomatic relations with Israel. Equally important is Cairo's corrupt military government which no longer offers hope for a better life for the desperately poor Egyptian peasants.

Despite severe repression and countless death sentences, the fundamentalists wage a war of terror against the regime. Targeting government officials and Coptic Christians. On June 15, 1991, Hosni Mubarak escaped another assassination attempt in Ethiopia. The President has charged Sudan and Iran with supporting the miltant Islamic groups in Egypt.

ENTEBBE

•NATHAN NETANYAHU יְהוֹנָתָן נְתַנְיָהוּ
147–1976)
e hero of Entebbe

nathan Netanyahu is a very spe-
l hero in Israel's history. When
was seventeen, Yoni moved
th his family to the United
tes, where his father, a profes-
of Jewish history, was working
the *Encyclopaedia Judaica.* A
r later, Yoni returned to Israel
army duty, leaving his parents
d brothers in the States. Yoni
ickly impressed his fellow sol-
ers and his superiors with his
elligence, his sensitivity to
ers, his charm, and his per-
al strength and bravery. At a
ung age, Yoni began to move up
ranks of Tsahal. He was as-
ned to the most difficult, most
manding, and most prestigious
it of the army—the Tsanchanim
Paratroopers"), where he be-
me an officer.

A brilliant student and a tal-
ted writer, Yoni was an honor
udent at Harvard College and at
e Hebrew University. But he
ose to remain an army officer
ther than become a scholar or a
ofessor. In 1967 he fought coura-
ously in the Six-Day War; he was
dly wounded in his forearm and
quired several operations. In
173 he distinguished himself in
tion in the Yom Kippur War.

In June 1976, a terrorist band
jacked an Air France plane and
w it to the Entebbe airport in
ganda. While the world watched
d waited, Yoni went into action
save the lives of the unfortunate
wish hostages. The plan was
ubbed "Operation Yonathan" by
e army officers who were in-
olved in it. The Jewish prisoners
ere freed in the daring Israeli
aid. But tragically, Yonathan Ne-
nyahu himself was killed in the
rossfire.

Entebbe

On June 27, 1976, an Air France plane carrying 300 people was hijacked by a fanatic band of Arab and German terrorists. The plane was forced to land at the Ugandan airport of Entebbe, in the heart of Africa. The hijackers made a shocking demand—they would release the hostages if Israel would release the Arab terrorists imprisoned in Israeli jails, some of whom had murdered Jews in previous terrorist raids.

The terrorists divided up their hostages, separating the Jews from the non-Jews and allowing the non-Jewish prisoners to leave. This "selection" procedure conjured up bitter memories for the Jewish hostages who had survived the Nazi Holocaust. The terrorists held more than a hundred Jews prisoner in Entebbe, threatening them with death if they put up any sort of resistance. The Air France pilot, a French non-Jew, refused to leave his passengers and remained in Entebbe, but the Ugandan leader, Idi Amin, and his people cooperated completely with the terrorist gang.

Days passed and the helpless Jewish hostages were still held captive. No country made a move to help the Jewish prisoners; no international outcry arose to protest the terrorists' wanton violation of human rights or to decry the Ugandan cooperation in the crime. It looked as if Israel would have to release the murderous terrorists in its jails in order to save the lives of the Jewish captives.

The C-130 Hercules transport plane in which the Israel commando forces were flown to Entebbe.

Then, a sudden miracle, a freedom-rescue mission! On July 4, 1976, an Israeli raiding party flew 2,500 miles to Entebbe and rescued the prisoners. Transport planes swept into the African airport under cloak of night, and a hundred Israeli troops raced off the planes toward the building where the hostages were held. A blitz of gunfire exploded when the Ugandans and the terrorists realized what was happening and tried to gain control, but the daring Israelis had caught them completely by surprise and were soon victorious. After less than 90 minutes in Entebbe, the Israelis were flying back to Israel with the rescued hostages. Just imagine the atmosphere on that return trip—the tears, the joy, the relief, the prayers and the thanks.

Unfortunately, a few hostages were shot in the cross-fire, and one American Jewish woman, who had been in a Ugandan hospital at the time of the raid, was sadly never found. There was one tragic Israeli death—Lieutenant Colonel Yonathan Netanyahu. This brave and brilliant young man had engineered the entire Entebbe rescue strategy.

Yoni Netanyahu is buried by his comrades-in-arms. Can you find Moshe Dayan?

VOCABULARY AND CONCEPTS

Entebbe   אֶנְטֶבָּה

MISSION TO IRAQ

In 1980 the Israeli government grew very anxious over the growth of Iraqi military power, especially in the area of nuclear, chemical and biological weapons. Israel was especially concerned about the nuclear production facilities in the Iraqi city of Osirak, which French, German, and British scientists were building 10 miles from Bagdad.

Israel and Osirak

On June 7, 1981 Israeli fighter bombers attacked the factory. Eight Israeli bombers, escorted by fighter planes, flew about 600 miles through enemy air space and dropped sixteen 2,000-lb. bombs on the nuclear facility. The factory was destroyed and all the aircraft returned safely. The whole world condemned Israel, but secretly most of Iraq's neighbors applauded the raid.

There have been continual efforts by Iraq to produce nuclear, chemical, biological, and neurological weapons. Reliable sources report that the Iraqis have killed more than 50,000 men, women and children with these weapons in their wars against Iran and the Kurds. Some military sources claim that Iraq used biological weapons during the war.

After the Gulf War in 1993, U.N. inspectors identified numerous Iraqi nuclear and poison gas facilities.

What would have happened to the soldiers of the military coalition in the Gulf War if Israel had not destroyed Iraq's nuclear capabilities in 1981?

To this day no one has given Israel credit for saving the world from a nuclear Holocaust by a power-hungry dictator.

Saddam Hussein, President of Iraq, launched an ambitious program to modernize his arsenal of offensive weapons. He built chemical, gas and biological weapons and used them against the Kurds and Iranians. In addition he began building a nuclear weapons facility at Osirak. In 1981 an Israeli air attack destroyed the half-built reactor.

OPERATION "PEACE FOR GALILEE"—1982

An Al Fatah poster advertises its hate for Israel.

General Ariel Sharon commanded Operation Peace for Galilee.

The Palestine Liberation Organization (PLO) is an Arab terrorist group that seeks to destroy the State of Israel. It avoids fighting with the Israeli army and instead follows the tactic of conducting terror attacks against those who cannot defend themselves—innocent civilians, preferably women and children.

PLO Terrorist Attacks

PLO terrorists plant bombs in Israeli schools, buses, and marketplaces, hoping to kill as many civilians as possible and scare Jews away from Israel.

Israel Tries to Make Peace, But the PLO Refuses

On July 24, 1981, the PLO agreed to a cease-fire with Israel, but it never kept its promise of peace. From July 1981 until June 1982, during the supposed "cease-fire," the PLO killed 25 Israelis and wounded 250 more in a total of 150 sneak attacks in Israel and in European capitals.

Israel's government became deeply concerned about the situation. The Jews of northern Israel were living in dread of the next terrorist attack. They could not work or study. They had to leave their homes for underground shelters to seek protection from the PLO's rockets and shells.

The Israeli Army Moves into Lebanon

Finally, on June 6, 1982, Israel took action to defend herself against further PLO attacks. In Operation "Peace for Galilee" the Israel Defense Forces moved north into Lebanon to wipe out the PLO bases. Many members of the PLO were killed or captured, and vast stocks of guns and tanks and missiles, all supplied by the PLO's Arab and Russian allies, were captured.

IRAQ AND KUWAIT

On August 2, 1990 100,000 Iraqi troops invaded Kuwait and quickly took control of the country. Six hundred oil wells were set afire. Torture, killings, mass arrests, and stealing of anything of value continued without a stop.

On August 7, 1990 President George Bush set in motion Operation Desert Storm under the command of General Norman Schwarzkopf. A huge airlift of soldiers, arms and ammunition began flowing into staging areas in Saudi Arabia.

At the start of the war Israel had distributed gas masks to all of its citizens; Jewish, Muslim and Christian. Iraqi threats to use poison gas were no idle boast. They had already gassed 50,000 Iraqis and Kurds.

On the first night of the war, eight Scud missiles hit Israel, two in Haifa, two in Tel Aviv and four in unpopulated areas.

Saddam Hussein fired a total of 86 Scud missiles, 40 at Israel and 46 at Saudi Arabia. In Israel one person was killed and 250 were wounded. The most lethal Scud attack was on barracks in Saudi Arabia, filled with U.S. troops. Twenty-eight Americans were killed.

To deter Israel's response, President Bush sent two Patriot missile batteries. The Patriot missiles succeeded, as only one Scud landed in Tel Aviv and caused-property damage.

The ground combat phase of the Gulf War lasted a little more than 100 hours. The Iraqi army was easily destroyed by a combination of tanks, artillery and air power.

Iraqi cooperation in destroying its weapons of mass destruction is a condition for lifting sanctions imposed by the United Nations in 1990 after Iraqi forces attacked Kuwait. The removal of sanctions would allow Iraq to resume selling oil, its major earner of hard currency in the world market.

JERUSALEM AND THE ARABS

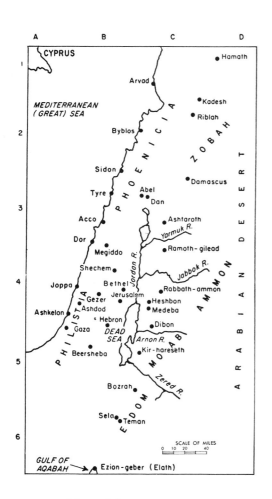

Map of the Israelite kingdom under David and Solomon.

To the Jewish people, Jerusalem has always been *the* holy city. As the capital of ancient Israel, where King David reigned and the wise King Solomon built the majestic Temple, where the biblical prophets spoke God's word and the sages taught the Torah, it has always been the focal point of Jewish prayers and Jewish hopes. According to Jewish tradition, God's sacred radiance—the Shechinah—dwelled in Jerusalem, and the city was the very center, or "navel," of the entire world.

Even during the two millennia of exile, the Jews never forgot their beloved Jerusalem. They longed to return there again, and no matter where they lived, they felt that they belonged to Jerusalem and that Jerusalem belonged to them. Throughout history, despite great dangers, pious Jews made the difficult journey to Jerusalem because of their intense love for the holy city. When the modern return to Zion began in the nineteenth century, Jews once again became the majority of Jerusalem's population. In 1948 the State of Israel made Jerusalem its capital, and in 1967, during the Six-Day War, when Israeli paratroopers captured the walled Old City of Jerusalem from the Jordanians, Jewish hearts everywhere swelled with pride and happiness.

Moslems also make a religious claim to Jerusalem, but their claim does not have the same spiritual intensity and solid historical basis as the Jewish claim. The two holy cities of Islam are both located in Arabia: Mecca, where Mohammed was born, and Medina, where he first preached the Islamic religion. Devout Moslems pray facing Mecca and try, at least once in their lifetimes, to make a pilgrimage to the city where their religion's founder was born.

Moslems praying in the yard of the Dome of the Rock.

Jerusalem played no role in the early history of Islam. It has special meaning for Moslems only because of its importance in Judaism. The early teachers of Islam accepted the Jewish belief that Jerusalem was holy and wanted to take over its holy status for themselves. To do so they developed the legend that Mohammed had been taken up to heaven from the Temple Mount in Jerusalem, and when the Arabs conquered the city in the seventh century, they built a mosque on the site where they said this had happened—the very place where the Holy Temple of Judaism had once stood.

Despite this claim, however, the Moslems never acted as if they felt Jerusalem was a very important place. In the Middle Ages Damascus, Baghdad, and Cairo were their glittering capitals; they left Jerusalem a neglected provincial town.

In modern times, though, the Arabs have tried to convince the world that they have a special right to Jerusalem and that Jewish control of the city is offensive to their religious doctrines. Anyone who is really familiar with Islamic beliefs, however, knows that this claim is just an attempt by the Arabs to gain by propaganda what they cannot gain by war.

Jerusalem and the Palestinian Authority

The peace process started in Madrid, commits Israel to discuss the final status of Jerusalem with the Palestinian Authorities. The Arabs insist they must establish their capital in East Jerusalem.

When the Declaration of Principles (DOP) was signed, Prime Minister Rabin stated, "Jerusalem is the ancient and eternal capital of the Jewish people."

The Labor Government, at least publicly, says that the status of Jerusalem is not for discussion. However, the Labor government has allowed the PA to establish their administrative headquarters in the Orient House in East Jerusalem. On July 10, 1995 the Palestinian Authority resolved to reconstitute the pre-1967 East Jerusalem municipality.

THE ARAB REFUGEES

In 1948, when the British Mandate ended and Israel declared its independence, seven hostile Arab countries—Syria, Lebanon, Transjordan, Iraq, Saudi Arabia, Yemen, and Egypt—massed their armies to attack the new state. They hoped to destroy Israel and annihilate the Jewish people.

The Arab leaders boasted about their bloodthirsty plan on radio and TV and in speeches to the Arab people. They told the Arabs of Palestine to get out of the area so that the Arab armies would be able to fight the Israelis more easily. As the Iraqi Prime Minister put it, "We will smash the country with our guns and obliterate every place the Jews seek shelter in. The Arabs should conduct their wives and children to safe areas until the fighting has died down."

Many Palestinian Arabs followed this advice. They left their homes and farms, hoping that Israel would be destroyed and all the Jews killed. Then they would return and take over the whole country, enriching themselves with the possessions of the annihilated Jewish people of Israel, just as the Arab leaders had promised.

But fortunately for the Jews, it didn't work out that way. Israel won the war, and the Arabs who had left their homes and farms lost everything because of their leaders' bad advice.

If the Arab states had been willing to make peace with Israel, the Palestinian Arabs would have been able to return to their former homes. But the Arabs refused to make peace.

At the same time, to avenge their military defeat by Israel, the Arab countries decided to get rid of all the Jews who lived among them. In North Africa, Iraq, Egypt, and Yemen, the Jewish communities dated back to ancient times. Now they came to an end, and hundreds of thousands of Jewish men, women, and children became refugees. Where would they find new homes? There was only one answer: Israel.

On May 28, 1948, after ten weeks of violent fighting following the establishment of the State of Israel, the Jewish quarter of the Old City of Jerusalem was in flames.

The pillar of black smoke marks the end of almost 2,000 years of Jewish residence beside the Western Wall of King Solomon's Temple, the famous Wailing Wall.

This is how the Arab press visualized the destruction of Israel on the eve of the Six-Day War, May 1967.

As a result, a huge population transfer took place, and the Jews expelled from the Arab countries poured into Israel, replacing the Arabs who had fled during the war. But while the Israelis welcomed the newcomers with open arms, the Arabs had a much different attitude toward the Palestinian refugees. No one wanted them, and no one wanted to help them. Many Arab countries had vast underpopulated areas with plenty of space available, but no one offered them the opportunity to make new homes for themselves. They were forced to live in refugee camps run by the United Nations and financed mainly by the generosity of the United States.

Why did the Arab leaders do this to their own brethren? The answer is simple: propaganda. They wanted to make Israel look bad, and what better way to do this than to coop up the Palestinian Arabs in dirty unpleasant camps, with inadequate food, medicine, and education, and then claim that it was all Israel's fault. To make the Israelis look even worse, the Arab leaders now pretended that they had never told the Palestinians to leave and claimed that the Israelis had forced them out—the very thing they had done to the Jews living in the Arab countries.

Hard as it may be to believe, the Arab propaganda ploy worked. Many people began to believe that Israel was responsible for the terrible plight of the refugees, and the world's anger was aroused against Israel. Because the ploy worked so well, the Arab leaders continue to keep the refugees homeless. Instead of helping them, they make them suffer, and they exaggerate their numbers to make the suffering seem even worse. The helpless refugees in the camps are victims—but not of Israel; they are the victims of the Arab desire to score a propaganda victory against the State of Israel and the Jewish people.

JUDEA – SAMARAI

The ancient Jewish cemetery on the Mount of Olives, destroyed by the Jordanians during their 1948–67 occupation.

In ancient times, the land now known as Palestine was called Canaan. As a geographical term, Canaan included all the territory from the Jordan River to the Mediterranean, as well as extensive territories east of the Jordan. When the Israelites, after the exodus from Egypt, conquered Canaan, two tribes—Reuben and Gad—were allocated lands east of the Jordan as their share in the national heritage.

The same geographical definition of Palestine prevailed throughout the Middle Ages and into modern times. The Turkish province of Palestine included the land on both sides of the Jordan, and so did the British Mandate over Palestine after World War I. Because the British followed a policy of appeasing the Arabs, however, they sliced off the section of Palestine east of the river and created a new Arab state. This state was originally called Transjordan and is now known as the Kingdom of Jordan. Its territory actually includes a much larger portion of historic Palestine than the area on the west side of the river.

Another slicing soon occurred, for in 1947 the United Nations decided to partition what was left of Palestine between the Jews and the Arabs. In this tiny territory there would be two independent states, one belonging to the Jews, the other to the Palestinian Arabs.

Of course it didn't, because the Arabs wanted everything for themselves. Seven hostile Arab states invaded Israel, but Israel won the war and preserved its independence. During the war, however, the Transjordanian army moved into the territory west of the Jordan. Thus the area that the United Nations had wanted to be an independent Arab state became a province of the Kingdom of Jordan. This area, sometimes called the West Bank, was made up of two regions, Judea and Samaria. Both of these regions had been part of the ancient Jewish state and had played a vital role in Jewish history ever since.

ISRAEL AND JORDAN

With Israel's Independence in May 1948, the Jordanian Arab Legion joined in the attack on Israel and illegally occupied East Jerusalem, Judea and Samaria. Jordan gave citizenship to the thousands of Arab refugees who streamed from Israel into the territories that it had conquered. After the 1967 war Jordan lost control of Jerusalem, Judea and Samaria to Israel

The Palestinians

Jordanian authorities have had many problems with the Palestinians. As a young man of fifteen, King Hussein witnessed the assassination of his grandfather, King Abdullah, by a Palestinian gunman. This murder took place in 1951, two years after Jordan annexed Judea, Samaria and Jerusalem.

In September 1970, Palestinian guerillas spearheaded by Syrian tank units attempted to overthrow King Hussein's pro-Western government. King Hussein called for help, but the United States did not have the capability to intervene. President Nixon realized that only Israel had the resources and power to save Jordan. Israel was alerted, and the threat of IDF intervention swiftly motivated the Syrians to retreat.

King Hussein's Arab Legion went on to crush the Palestinian guerillas. This attempt to overthrow King Hussein is known as the Black September War.

The Peace Treaty

On October 26, 1994, Prime Minister Yitzhak Rabin and Prime Minister Abdul Salam Majali signed a peace agreement between the State of Israel and the Hashemite Kingdom of Jordan.

The two countries are cooperating in the development of water resources, normalization of transportation, postal service and telecommunications, and have also agreed to alleviate the human problems caused by the Middle East conflicts. Israel and Jordan have exchanged ambassadors.

ISRAEL AND SYRIA

The establishment of the State of Israel initiated the war between Palestinians, Arabs and Jews. Hundreds of thousands of Jews and Arabs became refugees. As a result the situation of the Jews of Syria became highly critical. In 1947 violence broke out against the Jews of Allepo. All of the synagogues were destroyed and 6,000 Jews fled. By 1957 about 5,000 Jew were left in Syria. Jewish bank accounts were confiscated and many Jews were in prison without a trial. After the 1967 war, Israel occupied the Syrian territory of the Golan Heights. This strategic region overlooking the towns and kibbutzim of the Galilee, had been a staging area for terrorist attacks on Israel.

Israel's Druze population lives in several villages on the Golan Heights. After the 6-Day War Israel annexed the Golan Heights and as a result the Druze villages also became part of Israel.

The Golan is home to 50 Israeli kibbutzim, villages and 16,000 Israeli settlers.

Peace Talks Between Israel and Syria

Since 1991 Syria and Israel have been holding peace talks, in which Damascus has demanded full Israeli withdrawal from the Golan Heights. Israel has called for normalization of relations, open borders and diplomatic recognition. Prime Minister Rabin has indicated a willingness to withdraw from the Golan in states over a period of 8 years. The position of Syria is a full withdrawal or nothing. On July 12, 1995, Israeli-Syrian peace talks being held in Washington were terminated, and the delegates returned home.

President Hafez Assad of Syria is the last of Israel's neighbors to hold out against peace. Assad is a strong Arab nationalist, and has admitted that the 50-year war against Israel is over. He knows that in the near future, he will have to open the door to Israel and say: "Welcome back to your ancient and modern home."

The Peace Agreement /1993

The Middle East Peace Conference convened in Madrid, Spain in 1991. While further meetings were taking place in Washington in 1992, a tiny group of PLO and Israeli delegates met secretly in Norway. Their discussions continued for 15 months. On September 13, 1993, Prime Minister Yitzhak Rabin of Israel and Yasir Arafat, head of the PLO, signed a peace agreement in Washington.
Some of the terms were:

1. The PLO would have jurisdiction over the city of Jericho and the Gaza Strip.

2. The PLO would have jurisdiction over police, fire, health, water, and education.

3. Israel would have jurisdiction over borders, roads, and the protection of Jewish settlements in PLO enclaves.

4. A Israeli troop withdrawal would begin on December 13, 1993. Within nine months, Israel would withdraw from all West Bank cities. After that it, would transfer remaining land except the Jewish settlements to the Palestinian National Authority.

5. The final status of the territories would be settled at the end of five years.

On September 3, 1993 the Israeli Knesset, which has 120 members, approved the peace agreement by a vote of 61 to 50. Victory came, as expected, from the 44 members of Rabin's own party, 12 votes from the leftist Meretz party, and 5 votes from the Israeli Arab Knesset members. Without the Arab votes the agreement would not have been ratified.

The Withdrawal

As part of the agreement, Israel agreed to withdraw the IDF from six major Arab cities in Judea and Samaria: Qalqilya, Ramallah, Jenin, Bethlehem, Tulkarim, and Hebron. Israel has kept its part of the agreement, and has withdrawn from all these cities. As part of the agreement, there is a small detachment of Israeli troops to protect the 450 Jews who live in Hebron.

Prime Minister Yitzhak Rabin, and Yasir Arafat in Washington. President Bill Clinton negotiated a handshake between these two former enemies.

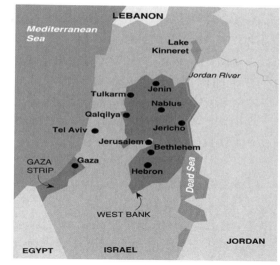

The Oslo Accords stipulated that Israeli troops would withdraw from all West Bank cities. Israeli troops have not been withdrawn from Hebron because of the fear of danger from the hostile Arab population.

The Assassination of Yitzhak Rabin /1995

Saturday night, November 4, 1995 was one of the most fateful moments in the history of modern Israel. On that darkest of nights, Yitzhak Rabin, Israels Prime Minister and one of its great military heroes, was assassinated.

That evening 100,000 Israelis had assembled in Tel Aviv to participate in a political rally. Rabin delivered a speech and joined in singing the "Song of Peace." After the rally, Rabin and Shimon Peres began to walk to their cars.

Lurking in the dark shadows of the night, a young assassin named Yigal Amir was waiting. As Rabin approached his limousine, Amir quietly stepped out of the shadows and from about a yard away, pumped three bullets point blank into the Prime Minister.

Rabin was rushed to a nearby hospital, where he died on the operating table. The shocked nation went into mourning, and the spot where Rabin was shot became a shrine filled with memorial candles, flowers, and posters.

The Funeral

Rabin's funeral was attended by President Bill Clinton, former Presidents Bush, Carter, and Ford, and the leaders of many other countries, including President Mubarak of Egypt and King Hussein of Jordan. Rabin was succeeded as Prime Minister by Shimon Peres, who vowed to continue his policies.

YITZHAK RABIN
(1922–1995) served his country both as a soldier and as a diplomat. Born in Jerusalem, he graduated from the Kadoori agricultural school. In 1940 he enlisted in the Palmach, and participated in numerous underground actions against the British Mandate. In 1946, he was arrested by the British and imprisoned for six months. During the War of Independence, Rabin commanded the Harel Brigade, which was active in the battle for Jerusalem. Appointed Chief of Staff in 1964, he led Israel's forces to victory in the Six-Day War of 1967. After serving as Israel's ambassador to the United States, Rabin became Prime Minister in 1974–77 and was reelected in 1992. On November 4, 1995 he was assassinated by Yigal Amir.

Among the foreign dignitaries paying their last respects to Yitzhak Rabin were *(from left to right)* President Bill Clinton, former Presidents Jimmy Carter and George Bush, Queen Beatrice of the Netherlands, Mrs. Peres and Prime Minister Shimon Peres, Queen Nur and King Hussein of Jordan.

The Election of 1996

On June 2, 1996 Benjamin Netanyahu (b. 1949), of the Likud Party, defeated Shimon Peres and became Israel's new Prime Minister. His victory was in large part due to public disquiet about the way the peace agreement with the PLO was proceeding.

While Israel had been fulfilling all of its commitments, the PLO was not. It had not modified its covenant to eliminate language calling for the destruction of the Jewish state. Even worse, terrorist attacks had become more frequent and brutal. While Israelis desperately wanted peace, a majority of voters agreed with Netanyahu that it was necessary to proceed cautiously and slowly, and with more concern for security than Peres had shown.

Benjamin Netanyahu addresses the U.S. Congress. In the background is Vice President Al Gore. Newt Gingrich, House Majority Leader, congratulates him.

Benjamin Netanyahu

Netanyahu was the first *sabra* Prime Minister of Israel. Although born in Israel, he lived for several years in the United States, and earned degrees in business and architecture from the Massachusetts Institute of Technology. In 1967 he returned to Israel to serve in the army. As an officer in an elite commando unit, he played an important part in the team that rescued hostages from a hijacked Belgian plane in 1972. He served as Israel's United Nations ambassador in the 1980s and was also Deputy Foreign Minister.

Political Manuevers

In a bold move to finalize the peace agreement, Netanyahu has proposed skipping the three stages of the Oslo Accord and moving straight into a final status negotiation. The Palestian Authority has resisted the suggestion.

The United States has suggested a withdrawal from 13% of the West Bank as a step towards peace. Israel has agreed to a 10% withdrawal with the remaining 3% be retained as a neutral barrier.

HOW ISRAEL CELEBRATES HOLIDAYS

Israel is the only Jewish homeland in the world, and only in this land are the holy days and festivals of Judaism not just religious occasions but also national holidays. Schools, banks, and businesses close down on Rosh Hashana, Yom Kippur, Sukkot, Passover, and Shavuot, as well as on other holidays. Nearly every citizen becomes a part of the holiday celebrations. Children are free from school, and grownups are free from work.

Holidays in Israel are very special times. Jews in their own homeland, celebrating their chagim, *feel a special closeness to their proud heritage. Jews celebrating Jewish holidays in a Jewish land rejoice in the wonderful return of our people to our beloved home, Israel.*

THE TEN DAYS OF REPENTANCE

The Bible says, "In the seventh month, on the first day of the month, shall be a solemn rest to you, a memorial proclaimed by a blast of shofrot" (Leviticus 23:24).

VOCABULARY AND CONCEPTS

e Ten Days of Repentance from
sh Hashana to Yom Kippur

עֲשֶׂרֶת יְמֵי תְּשׁוּבָה

The Talmud tells us that on Rosh Hashana, three books are open in heaven. One book names the righteous, the people who are completely pure and good. The second book names the evildoers who are completely bad. In the third book—the biggest one—are the names of people who are in-between, neither very good nor very bad. On Rosh Hashana, God inscribes the names of the saints in the Book of Life and the names of the total sinners in the Book of Death. But God does not write the names of all the others down in either book. According to Jewish tradition, God decides their fate during the Ten Days of Repentance.

Since Jews believe that at this time their fate is being decided by God, the Ten Days of Repentance are filled with prayer and seriousness. Jews strive for inner change, hoping that God will hear their prayers and grant them a year of health and happiness.

283

THE HIGH HOLY DAYS

A shofar-maker in Israel tries out one of his products.

VOCABULARY AND CONCEPTS

Days of Awe (the High Holy Days; includes Rosh Hashana and Yom Kippur)   יָמִים נוֹרָאִים

New Year   רֹאשׁ הַשָּׁנָה

Day of Atonement   יוֹם כִּפּוּר

An autumn chill is in the air, and the lemony greens of summer have changed to the russets, cinnamons, and burnished browns of leaves that crackle underfoot. People who had crowded the beaches have changed to more formal clothes and returned to their offices and schools. And the children are back in class, with shiny new notebooks, sharpened pencils, and full hearts. Autumn is a time of changes and beginnings.

But the most important change of autumn does not have to do with the weather. For Jewish people, autumn marks the holiest time of the year—the High Holy Days—a time of *inner* change.

During this season, Jews remember promises they made to God, to one another, and to themselves. They remember their promises to be honest and kind neighbors. They remember their promises to observe the laws of Torah. They ask themselves thoughtfully whether they have fulfilled their promises. They proudly remember their good deeds, and sadly too they recall their dishonesties, their sins, their acts of cruelty, great and small. They pray to God for forgiveness, and they struggle to change inside and to become better people.

The holidays of this solemn season are Rosh Hashana (the New Year) and Yom Kippur (the Day of Atonement). The ten days between these two holidays are called the Aseret Yemei Teshuva—the Ten Days of Repentance.

284

ROSH HASHANA

When we think of the civil New Year as Americans celebrate it, we think of drinking champagne, staying up all night at parties, singing "Auld Lang Syne," and screaming out "Happy New Year" at the dot of midnight on New Year's Eve. But Rosh Hashana, the Jewish New Year, is a very different sort of occasion. It is a serious time of prayer, thoughtfulness, and inner change. Rosh Hashana is celebrated each year, in Israel and the world over, on the first two days of the month of Tishrei.

Blowing the shofar at the Western Wall.

The Meaning of Rosh Hashana

On Rosh Hashana, Jews try to remember every detail about their behavior over the past year. "Was I as honest, as helpful, as loving as I might have been?" they ask themselves. They judge themselves strictly and they try to become better Jews. Another Hebrew name for Rosh Hashana is Yom HaZikaron, the Day of Remembering.

The Shofar

At the synagogue on Rosh Hashana, the cantor sings traditional, beautiful melodies as well as some by modern composers. The clear, resonant voice of the shofar, or ram's horn, is sounded many times. All over the world, it calls Jews to return to Torah and to inner change. The shofar's voice is such an important part of the holiday that Rosh Hashana is sometimes called Yom Teruah, the Day of Blowing the Shofar. Many religious people gather near Jerusalem's Western Wall to hear the shofar's call.

285

Rosh Hashana Greetings and Foods

Jews greet one another during this season with the blessing, "May you be written down for a good year." For during this time, according to tradition, God writes down all our names and decides what the coming year will bring for us. Hoping for a sweet new year, Jews traditionally eat sweet foods on Rosh Hashana. We dip apples and challah into honey. All over Israel and the world, Jews eat tsimmis—a mixture of carrots, meat, and honey—and tayglach—cake in a candy-like honey coating.

Tashlich

Jews group together on Rosh Hashana for the traditional Tashlich custom. Throwing small pebbles into a stream of running water, Jews say a special prayer. They pray that as the running water carries away the pebbles, so too will their own sins be carried away and forgiven by God. Many Israelis observe the Tashlich, or "Throwing," custom along the waters of the Mediterranean Sea or the Lake Kinneret.

Shabbat Shuvah

The Sabbath that comes out during these ten days is always called Shabbat Shuvah—the Sabbath of Return. For on this day, Jews feel a deep and special yearning to *return* to God and Torah. On this Sabbath day, they promise God and themselves to do their best to become better Jews.

Tashlich on the shores of the Mediterranean.

VOCABULARY AND CONCEPTS

New Year	רֹאשׁ הַשָּׁנָה
The Day of Remembering	יוֹם הַזִּכָּרוֹן
Ram's horn	שׁוֹפָר
"May you be written down for a good year"	לְשָׁנָה טוֹבָה תִּכָּתֵבוּ
Custom of throwing pebbles into a stream of running water, symbolic of throwing away one's sins	תַּשְׁלִיךְ
Sabbath of Return (Sabbath between Rosh Hashana and Yom Kippur)	שַׁבָּת שׁוּבָה

286

YOM KIPPUR

Israeli stamp with a Yom Kippur painting by the Jewish artist Maurycy Gottlieb.

On the holy day of Yom Kippur, the Day of Atonement, which is on the tenth day of the month of Tishrei, the final verdicts are sealed. God determines the future of every human being. On this solemn day, as the Bible commands, observant Jews do not eat a bite of food or drink a sip of water. They express in this way the seriousness of their prayers, their sorrow at their sins, and the intensity of their drive toward inner change.

Kol Nidre

The evening service of *Kol Nidre* includes slow, sad prayers with sighing, haunting melodies. A memorial prayer is chanted in the daytime for all those who have died and are remembered by their close relatives in the congregation. All day long the people pray to God for a peaceful year—especially in Israel, the Jewish state. Everyone still remembers the sudden shock of the 1973 war, when the Arabs attacked on Yom Kippur, the holiest day of the Jewish year.

287

The Message of Yom Kippur

As the day of Yom Kippur draws to an end, everyone looks pale and tired. The gates of heaven slowly close as God inscribes the final names in the Book of Life and the Book of Death.

A famous Yom Kippur prayer tells the story of the High Holy Day season:

> On the first day of the year it is written, and on the fast-day of atonement it is sealed and determined—how many shall pass away, and how many be born; who shall live and who shall die, who shall finish his given time, and who not; who is to perish by water, who by fire, who by the sword, and who by wild beast; who by hunger, and who by thirst; who by an earthquake and who by the plague; who by strangling and who by stoning; who shall be at rest, and who shall be wandering; who shall remain tranquil, and who shall be disturbed; who shall reap enjoyment, and who will suffer painfully; who will become poor and who will grow rich; who shall be cast down and who uplifted.
>
> But Penitence, Prayer, and Charity can turn aside the evil decree!

Kaparot ceremony in Jerusalem. The custom of Kaparot, meaning "atoneme[nt]" originated in Geonic times and became widespread in Eastern Europe. It consis[ts] swinging a chicken around one's head and praying that the life of the chicken substitute for the punishment due oneself. In very Orthodox homes this ritua[l] performed on the morning of the day before Yom Kippur.

VOCABULARY AND CONCEPTS

Day of Atonement   יוֹם כִּפּוּר
Evening service of Yom Kippur   כָּל נִדְרֵי
Closing service of Yom Kippur   נְעִילָה

SUKKOT

Five days after Yom Kippur, on the fifteenth day of the month of Tishrei, comes Sukkot, the Feast of Booths. All over Israel, little decorated booths spring up—in alleyways and on rooftops, on balconies and in the middle of front lawns. Children love to collect and arrange the green, leafy branches of the sukkah roof. It is fun to pick out luscious, colorful red apples, yellow bananas, ripe purple grapes, and golden ears of corn to adorn the sukkah walls. Colorful photographs of Israel, embroidered flags, and banners of the Twelve Tribes are hung up proudly. Everyone wants to win the sukkah-building contest held in every Israeli city. Families compete to decorate their sukkah with the most beautiful fruits, pictures, and flowers.

Blessing the *lulav* and *etrog* inside a beautifully decorated *sukkah*.

An Arab family gathering their harvest in the same manner as their ancestors, thousands of years ago. In the foreground is a sukkah built of branches and leaves to provide shade from the hot afternoon sun.

The Bible commands Jews to say special prayers over the lulav (palm branch) and etrog (citron) on Sukkot. In the marketplace, every customer haggles for the tallest, lushest, greenest lulav and the most fragrant, perfectly oval etrog. In the synagogues, the children proudly compare their families' lulavim and etrogim. Everyone strives to observe the commandments of the Torah with the most beautiful, glorious sukkah, lulav, and etrog.

The Meaning of the Sukkah

The ancient Israelites wandered in the desert forty years before they reached the Promised Land. Always on the move, these wanderers had no time to build permanent, solid shelters. Instead they lived in flimsy, makeshift booths, or *sukkot*. When we sit in our sukkot in modern times, we remember the struggles of those ancient Israelites as they traveled toward the land of freedom.

Helping to build a sukkah is a mitzvah.

The four kinds of growing things: etrog, lulav, hadas, and aravah.

Young Chasidim in Israel erecting a sukkah.

The sukkah also reminds us of the harvest season in the ancient Jewish state. Jewish farmers would build temporary shelters in their fields so that the crops were not left unguarded overnight. The fruits and vegetables with which we decorate our *sukkah* symbolize the rich harvest of the autumn months.

The Sukkah as a Reminder of the Exile

The rabbis of old gave detailed laws about building a sukkah. The booth must be sturdy enough to withstand an ordinary wind, but not a wind of unusual violence. The roof must be open enough so that stars can be seen. The rabbis saw the sukkah as a symbol of the difficult Jewish life in exile.

The Torah seems to be saying to the modern Israeli: "Now that you are settled down in your homeland, do not take everything for granted. For one week, live in a little tent—a sukkah. Remember how life was in the exile—flimsy, fragile, and subject to every ill wind. Remember how it was, and still is for many, and be glad that you celebrate your Sukkot holiday in freedom on the soil of Israel!"

A young girl puts the finishing touches on a richly decorated sukkah.

The Sukkot Pilgrimage

In Temple times, every Jew who could possibly make the trip journeyed to Jerusalem to join the gala Sukkot celebration there. Jerusalem was colored and scented with the rich, abundant autumn fruits and branches that adorned its streets, rooftops, courtyards, and gardens. Everyone streamed toward the holy Temple at the heart of the beautiful capital city. There a special water ritual would be performed, since it was believed that on Sukkot God decided whether or not to send the vital rainfall Israel needed to survive.

Silver trumpets sounded, a choir sang true and clear, and priests poured spring water from golden pitchers over the altar. All the assembled people joined in with the prayer: "We beseech thee, O Lord, to save us and make us prosper."

Three times a year, Sukkot, Pesach, and Shavuot, the Jews of ancient Israel would march on foot to the Holy Temple in Jerusalem. Today, in modern Israel, this age-old ceremony is reenacted. Here the pilgrims ascend Mount Zion to the sound of the blowing of the shofar.

Sukkot Observances in Israel Today

Many present-day Israelis go on a pilgrimage to Jerusalem on Sukkot, just as their ancestors in ancient Israel did on Sukkot and on the other two harvest holidays, Passover and Shavuot. Just as the ancient Israelites streamed toward Jerusalem, modern Israelis crowd the intercity Egged buses, laden with satchels of fruits and flowers, on their way to their beloved capital. They visit a big community *sukkah* on the top of Mount Zion and march in a special procession, led by rabbis who carry velvet-covered Torahs. On the way, the marchers stop for a ceremony and a memorial prayer for the six million Jewish victims of the Nazi Holocaust.

In modern Israel, some kibbutzim recall the ancient Temple water ritual of Sukkot by holding their own special water ceremonies. All the kibbutzniks come together, singing, dancing, and saying special prayers, as water is drawn from local springs.

Sukkot at the Western Wall in Jerusalem.

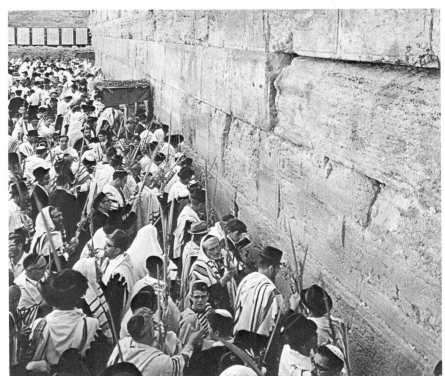

293

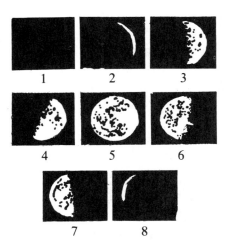

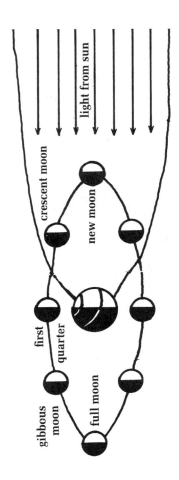

This diagram shows stages in the moon's journey around the earth. The diagram shows how the moon looks to us at each stage of its journey.

Why Are Sukkot, Passover, and Shavuot One Day Shorter in Israel?

In most respects Israelis celebrate the various holidays in the same manner as Jews in other countries. But there is one major difference that every visitor to Israel immediately notices. Sukkot, Passover, and Shavuot are one day shorter in Israel than in Jewish communities elsewhere. Why is this so? To answer that question, we must first learn a little bit about the nature of the Jewish calendar.

The Monthly Cycle of the Moon

Have you ever looked up at the moon in the night sky? If you have, you must have noticed how much the moon seems to change from night to night. One time it may be barely visible. But each night it will grow larger, waxing from a tiny, slender crescent to a round, full moon. Then it slowly wanes back down to a sliver again.

In ancient Israel, our ancestors noticed the moon's cycle, too. They measured how long it took for the moon to wax and wane (grow large and then grow small). They saw that each cycle took twenty-nine or thirty days, and they used the moon's predictable rhythm as a way to measure time. They called each cycle a *chodesh*, which means "month," coming from the Hebrew word *chadash*, which means "new."

Each one of the twelve yearly cycles, or months, had a different name on the Jewish calendar, and the Jewish holidays were scheduled according to these months: Tishrei, Cheshvan, Kislev, Tevet, Shvat, Adar, Nissan, Iyyar, Sivan, Tammuz, Av, and Elul. Sukkot always began on the fifteenth day of Tishrei. Passover always began on the fifteenth day of Nissan. Shavuot always began on the sixth of Sivan.

How Holiday Dates Were Calculated in Ancient Israel

In ancient times, when the Jews lived in their beloved homeland, they had no problem figuring out when to observe these holidays. To find out when the new month of Tishrei had begun, all they had to do was look up and watch for the moon. Once the new moon emerged and Tishrei had begun, based on Jerusalem observation points, the Jews all over Israel would simply count up the days until the day for Sukkot. The same system worked to determine when to celebrate Passover and Shavuot, in the months of Nissan and Sivan.

Why the Diaspora Jews Added on a Second Day

When powerful enemies conquered Israel, many Jews were exiled from their homes. Some Jews always remained, but those forced to leave the country often ended up in distant corners of the earth. They continued to celebrate the Jewish holidays. But now they did not know for sure when the new months of Tishrei, Nissan, and Sivan would emerge in Israel's night sky. These exiled Jews could not be positive just when to observe Sukkot, Passover, and Shavuot.

The Jews in the Diaspora communities were anxious to observe their holidays properly and on time. In order to make sure that they did not miss the correct dates of Sukkot, Passover, and Shavuot, the rabbis established a tradition of celebrating these holidays for an extra day in lands outside of Israel. Religious Jews all over the world began to observe eight days of Sukkot instead of the seven days observed in Israel, eight days of Passover instead of the seven observed in Israel, and two days of Shavuot instead of the one day observed in Israel.

To this day, Orthodox Jews living outside of Israel keep this rabbinic tradition alive. But the rabbis never established in Israel this tradition of an extra day of observance. Thus in Israel, Sukkot, Passover, and Shavuot are always exactly one day shorter than they are in communities outside of the Jewish homeland.

VOCABULARY AND CONCEPTS

kot	סֻכּוֹת
ooth made out of branches	סֻכָּה
ht day of Sukkot	שְׁמִינִי עֲצֶרֶת
ron fruit	אֶתְרוֹג
m branch	לוּלָב

295

SIMCHAT TORAH

Each week, we read another portion of the Torah. In the synagogue we go in order from the very first chapter of Bereshit (Genesis) to the very last chapter of Devarim (Deuteronomy). On Simchat Torah, the day right after Sukkot, the twenty-third day of Tishrei, Jews all over the world read the very last portion of the Torah's fifth book and then begin reading the Torah all over again, from the beginning.

Simchat Torah Observances

The Simchat Torah holiday is a festive, joy-filled time which marks this happy occasion. We show our pride in the precious Torah. We show our gladness in the study of God's words. The Torah scrolls in their brilliantly colored velvet robes are taken carefully out of the Ark and held lovingly aloft. Everyone dances around them, singing loudly.

All the congregation, even the most serious and formal people, loosen up on Simchat Torah, singing and dancing. The whole congregation circles the synagogue in processions called *Hakafot* in Hebrew.

How Simchat Torah Is Celebrated in Israel

Israeli *Hakafot* don't always stay in the synagogue. Carrying the Torah scrolls, Israelis dance through city streets, with happy children surrounding them, waving bright flags.

An early flag for Simchat Torah shows King David kneeling. The text reads: "David rejoiced on Simchat Torah."

In Jerusalem, whole congregations leave their synagogues and dance their way to the Kotel, the Western Wall, with their Torah scrolls in their arms. Oceans of people stream as one down the cobblestone streets. Everyone's heart seems to be bursting with joy, as if saying: "We have our beloved Torah and the freedom to learn and pray in our dearly loved homeland." The holiday's name, Simchat Torah, perfectly expresses the mood of the moment. It means, "Rejoicing with the Torah."

VOCABULARY AND CONCEPTS

oicing with the Torah"	שִׂמְחַת תּוֹרָה
h processions in the syna- e circling the Bimah	הַקָּפוֹת
esis	בְּרֵאשִׁית
teronomy	דְּבָרִים

Simchat Torah celebration in the streets of Tel Aviv.

297

CHANUKAH

Statue of Zeus (Jupiter) found at Caesarea. Throughout Israel Syrian overlords pressed the Jews to worship before such idols at public altars.

Alexander the Great, king of Macedonia (356–323 B.C.E.), figures prominently in Jewish legend.

When the Persians ruled over Palestine, from 536 to 336 B.C.E., the Jews were left in peace. The Persian rulers collected their taxes, and the Jews were allowed to study the Torah and follow its God-given teachings. Though a Persian official governed Jerusalem, he did not interfere with the Jewish community and the authority of the rabbis.

But Alexander the Great, a young and brilliant Greek general, changed everything when he conquered the Persian Empire in 336 B.C.E. Since the Persian Empire included Palestine, the Jews now had Greek rulers instead of Persians. After Alexander's death, his empire was split up among his generals, and Palestine fell into the hands of a Syrian-Greek family that did not have the same tolerant attitude toward the Jews as had the Persians. The new Syrian-Greek rulers tried to force all their people to follow Greek customs and worship.

The Conflict Between Greek Culture and Judaism

Some Jews did not mind changing their ways. Merchants who went along with the demands of the Syrian-Greek rulers could become very rich trading with other parts of the immense empire. Many Jews began to wear Greek-style clothes and sandals, to speak Greek rather than Hebrew, and to study Greek philosophy instead of the Torah. They even changed their Jewish names to Greek ones. Even Joshua, the High Priest of the Jews, called himself Jason.

Marble bust of Antiochus III. This bust was discovered in Italy and was acquired by Napoleon.

But many Jews, who loved their ancient Jewish heritage, disliked all this "Hellenizing." (Hellas was the ancient name of Greece. Since its culture was called Hellenism, "Hellenizing" meant "becoming like the Greeks.") These traditional Jews began to think of resisting the Syrian-Greeks, who sought to take away the Jews' religious freedom.

Matityahu and Judah Maccabee Lead the Resistance

One day the resistance against the Syrian-Greeks came to a head. It happened in Modi'in, the hometown of Matityahu, a member of a priestly family, the Hashmonaeem, and the father of five strong sons. Matityahu was commanded by some officers of Antiochus, the Syrian-Greek king, to appear in the town square. The officers had built a special Greek altar, where they commanded Matityahu to bow down and worship the Greek idol.

But the proud Jewish leader Matityahu refused to violate his Jewish ideals and values. Instead of bowing down to the idol, he called upon the Jews to attack the Syrian-Greeks and then follow him to the hills. Many Jews, full of pent-up rage at Antiochus, heeded his call,

This drawing shows Judah Maccabee and his soldiers fighting for the freedom of Jerusalem.

A Syrian war elephant.

Copper half-shekel of Simon Maccabee.

and the Jewish resistance had begun. When Matityahu died, his son Judah, who was so strong that he was called Maccabee ("the hammer"), took up the leadership. Soon Judah Maccabee and his courageous warriors were driving out the Syrian-Greek army from Israel.

In 164 B.C.E., Judah and his freedom-fighters defeated the army of Antiochus and were able to reclaim their beloved and holy capital city, Jerusalem. They had won the right to worship in their own way and to live their life as Jews once again.

The Miracle of the Oil

When the victorious Jews reached the Temple, they were sadly disappointed at its condition. Filthy, neglected, filled with statues of Greek gods, the Temple had to be purified. The eternal light had to be relit, but there was only one small flask of pure holy oil to be found, so thoroughly had the place been looted by the Syrian-Greeks. This was just enough to keep the light burning for one night. But by a miracle, the light burned on for eight days.

Full of hope and joy, the Jews rebuilt their altar, cleansed away the filth left by the Syrian-Greeks, and made new holy vessels. On the twenty-fifth of Kislev, they were ready to rededicate the Temple. On that day, Judah Maccabee announced an eight-day holiday for the Chanukah (Dedication) of the purified Temple—eight days for the miraculous burning of the holy oil. Jews everywhere keep alive the memory of the proud, courageous Maccabees and their triumph by lighting the Chanukah menorah candles. Each night of Chanukah, one more candle is added to brightly glow, until, on the final night of the holiday, all eight candles burn.

Israeli Chanukah Customs

Dreydel (spinning top) is a traditional Chanukah game. The draydl has a Hebrew letter on each of its four sides, each letter standing for a Hebrew word. Outside of Israel, the letters are *nun, gimel, hay, shin,* and the sentence they make, *Nes gadol haya sham,* means "A

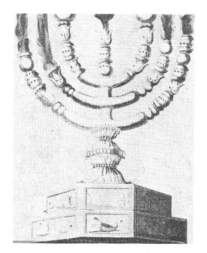
A picture of the seven-branched Temple Menorah. It was in a menorah such as this that the miracle of the holy oil was said to have occurred.

A giant electric menorah lights the skies of Israel for miles around. The Maccabee Forest in Modi'in is a living reminder of our glorious ancestors in days gone by.

great miracle happened there." In Israel, the letters are *nun, gimel, hay, peh*, and the sentence is: *Nes gadol haya poh*, "A great miracle happened *here*."

Every Chanukah, youngsters of the Maccabi Sports Club hold a torch-bearing relay race, celebrating the strength and the enduring faith and power of the Maccabee warriors of old. The first runner of the relay race begins from Modi'in, the town in which Matityahu fought against the Syrian-Greek tyrant Antiochus. After a ceremony at the graves of the five Maccabees, a torch is lighted and handed to the lead runner.

The torch is carried all over the country to light the menorot, finally going to the President, who uses the torch to light the Chanukah candles atop the Knesset building.

Passing the flaming torch on the way to Modi'in.

VOCABULARY AND CONCEPTS

Modi'in	מוֹדִיעִין
Chanukah	חֲנוּכָּה
Draydel	סְבִיבוֹן
Chanukah menorah	מְנוֹרָה

301

TU BESHVAT

The Hebrew month of Shvat comes when people in America and Europe are still shivering through winter's cold, dark days. Blustering winds and harsh blizzards make people stay home, wrapped in warm sweaters and sipping hot drinks. But in Israel, the weather of Shvat is entirely different. The heavy rains have almost ended, and a refreshing springtime fragrance lightens the air. The soil is moist and rich, the sun is bright and warm, and it is just the right time to plant new trees. There, on the fifteenth day of Shvat, Jews celebrate Tu Beshvat (*tu*, means "fifteen" in Hebrew). It helps to understand this holiday if we know its other Hebrew name, Rosh Hashana La'Ilanot—the New Year of Trees.

Carefully, the youngsters cover the fragile roots of the saplings. In years to come the wastelands of Israel will burst into foliage with millions of green trees.

This is the stately cedar. Its wood was used by King Solomon in building the Temple.

Tree-Planting on Tu Beshvat

Israeli children especially love this holiday, which is always a happy, exciting time, full of music, color, and the soft scent of trees, flowers, and fresh fruits. Schoolchildren in the villages and towns wear white shirts and blouses as they are led out of their classrooms by their teachers. Singing, dancing, carrying spades, hoes, and watering cans, the children carefully plant the delicate, tiny saplings in the ground and water them. In years to come, the land will burst into lush foliage, full of green, budding trees. Maybe the children love this holiday so much because they, too, are young and growing, one day to shoot up into strength, beauty, and vitality, just like the trees they plant!

People who live in countries far from Israel also want to participate in the planting of trees on Tu Beshvat. They do so by giving money to the Jewish National Fund, which plants trees in forests, parks, and gardens all over the Jewish homeland, beautifying the landscape and strengthening the soil. Whole forests of stately cypress trees, fragrant almond trees, rich and fruitful fig trees have been planted in Israel by people in faraway communities.

The Martyrs' Forest

One of the most unusual forests in the world has been planted in Israel by the Jewish National Fund. In the hills of Jerusalem, carefully tended saplings purchased with money contributed by Jews all over the world have become a forest woodland of six million evergreens. This forest, known as the Martyrs' Forest or the Forest of the Six Million, will stand as an eternal memorial to the six million martyrs who were murdered by the Nazis.

The tall, strong trees proudly declare the pride and the vitality of the Jewish people, who have returned to their homeland, Israel, and who have brought growth and green back to the barren, wasted soil. The Forest of the Six Million adds a new meaning to the ancient holiday of Tu Beshvat.

Tu Beshvat Customs

Trees are important to the economy of Israel. Young and old loving plant saplings, hoping to replenish the depleted forests of Israel.

Jews all over the world celebrate the New Year of the Trees by eating the fruit of trees that grow in Israel. In Europe, in America, in South Africa and Australia, everywhere that Jews celebrate Tu Beshvat, people munch almonds, raisins, figs, dates, and carob. They thank God for these fruits by reciting blessings.

Sephardic Jews have special, beautiful Tu Beshvat ceremonies honoring the seven species which the Bible tells us the land of Israel possessed since ancient times. Blessings are pronounced over wheat, barley, grapes, figs, pomegranates, olives, and honey. Four cups of wine symbolize the varying seasons of the Holy Land—the first cup contains white wine; the second, white wine mixed with a little red wine; the third, red wine mixed with a little white wine; and the fourth is entirely full of red wine. Children are presented with a *bolsa de frutas,* a bag of fruit, at Tu Beshvat parties.

The Kennedy Forest is dedicated to the memory of John F. Kennedy, a President of the United States who was a staunch supporter of Israel.

During the month of Shvat the almond trees embroider the landscape in a sea of snowy white blossoms.

Chasidim have a tradition that on Tu Beshvat, the fate of every tree and fruit is decided. Just as Rosh Hashana is the New Year for man, so the Chasidim believe that Tu Beshvat is the New Year for trees, and that God determines the future of each plant, tree, and shrub. Chasidim pray on this day that the etrogim may grow perfect and lovely, so that they can be used proudly to enhance the coming Sukkot holiday in the fall.

The Importance of Trees

The Bible commands the Jewish people not to destroy trees even when battling a city. "You may eat of them, but you must not cut them down." The rabbis said that when one chops down a fruit-bearing tree, the wanton destruction makes the tree's cry go forth from one end of the world to the other. Said Rabbi Yohanan ben Zakkai in the Talmud, explaining the great importance of tree-planting in Israel, "If you hold a sapling in your hand, ready to plant it, and you are told, 'The Messiah is here!'—first plant the sapling, and then go forth to welcome him."

The rains of Israeli winters can be strong and violent, washing away the soil. Rows and rows of trees help protect the land, keeping the soil of fields and orchards strong enough to withstand winter winds and rains.

Trees also provide luscious fruits which Israel can export, thus helping the country's economy. They give shade and lumber, and forests provide a place where animals can live. Trees help keep Israel's settlements secure, for they screen towns and villages from enemy attack.

Trees are also very beautiful! They are much nicer to look at than the concrete slabs of skyscrapers or a desert's blankness. Trees keep Israel strong, healthy, and beautiful. Happy Tu Beshvat!

VOCABULARY AND CONCEPTS

Tu Beshvat (fifteenth day of the Hebrew month of Shvat) ט״ו בִּשְׁבָט

New Year of Trees רֹאשׁ הַשָּׁנָה לָאִילָנוֹת

Martyrs' Forest (forest in memory of the six million Jews who were murdered by the Nazis) יַעַר הַקְּדוֹשִׁים

PURIM

Persian soldiers.

When Israel was part of the Persian Empire, a large community of Jews lived peacefully in the city of Shushan, Persia's capital. Haman, the chief officer of King Ahasuerus, was a very arrogant and wicked man. Drunk with power, he ordered everyone to bow down before him, but the Jew Mordecai, who worshiped only God, refused to bow down to Haman.

Haman's hatred for Mordecai became an intense fury. He decided to destroy all the Jews of Persia in revenge. Haman persuaded Ahasuerus that the Jews were a "problem people," and the king gave him a free hand to destroy them.

Haman's Evil Plan

The day chosen by the wicked Haman for the slaughter of the Jews was the thirteenth of the Hebrew month of Adar. He chose this day by casting *purim*, which means "lots" in Hebrew. Haman set up a special gallows where he looked forward to hanging Mordecai.

When Mordecai heard of the coming doom for the Jewish people, he became filled with dread. Mordecai's cousin, Esther, was the queen of Persia, but the king did

A wall painting from the Dura-Europos synagogue. Haman leads Mordecai's horse, and King Ahasuerus and Queen Esther are sitting on their thrones. Dura-Europos was an ancient city on the Euphrates River in the northern part of ancient Babylonia.

A Purim poster.

not know she was Jewish. Mordecai urged her to reveal her heritage and tell the king of Haman's wicked plot to kill the Jews. Esther was afraid, but Mordecai explained that the survival of the Jewish people depended on her alone. "Who knows," said the wise Mordecai to Esther, "if it was not for the sake of this moment that your destiny took you to the royal house?"

Queen Esther Saves the Jews

Queen Esther took the risk. She invited Ahasuerus and Haman to a banquet. There she told the king about Haman's evil plot to kill the Jewish people, explaining that she too was a Jewess and that her people were innocent of wrongdoing. The king was furious at Haman's wicked plot. He ordered his servants to hang Haman on the very gallows that had been built for Mordecai. Moreover, the king appointed Mordecai as his new chief officer, and honored Esther, his Jewish queen, above all other women in the land.

In memory of this event the fourteenth day of Adar, the day after the pogrom Haman had planned for the Jews of Persia, was made into the joyous holiday of Purim!

The Megillah Reading

The story of Purim is told in a special book called the Megillah, which means "scroll." The Megillah is read in the synagogue on the evening of Purim, but this is no solemn and serious occasion. Everyone is merry and full of fun, and a carnival mood prevails. People wear funny masks and dress in costumes. When the Megillah is chanted, the children listen carefully to the reading, for whenever the name of the hated Haman is mentioned, they try to drown out his name with the racket from their graggers, or noisemakers. No one tells them to sit still and be quiet. It is Purim, after all! Later, there are parties where all kinds of goodies are served—especially little poppyseed cakes called hamantashen.

rim is a time for merrymaking, th masks, graggers, haman-hen, and Megillah reading.

Purim Carnivals in Israel

Purim is the one day of the year when the rabbis encouraged people to get a little drunk! We are told to get so drunk on this day that we do not know the difference between the words "Blessed be Mordecai" and "Cursed be Haman." In Hebrew, this rabbinic advice uses the phrase *ad lo yada*—"Until one didn't know." Modern Israelis adopted these three words as the name for the jolly carnival that has become an Israeli Purim custom. Thus it is called the Adloyada.

In Tel Aviv, every Purim, an elaborate Adloyada parade proceeds with great fanfare through the city streets. Headed by mounted police, to the melodies of bands, colorful floats tell the story of Esther. There stands the beautiful young queen, in her shining golden crown and royal robes! There goes Mordecai, riding in triumph on a white horse! Oh! There is the villain Haman with his ten sons! Everyone is dressed in costumes and full of fun. People dance and sing in the streets.

An Adloyada float sponsored by the Children's Theater of Israel.

Two Israeli stamps with scenes from the Purim Megillah.

The Meaning of Purim

Purim started out as a holiday celebrating the delivery of the Jews from Haman during the time of the Persian Empire. But it is now much more. It is a festival on which Jews rejoice at God's protection of the Jewish people from any threatened evil. The name Haman has come to stand for any enemy of Israel. Mordecai is a name for every wise Jewish leader, and Esther for every Jewish heroine.

The State of Israel itself, like the holiday of Purim, is living evidence of Jewish survival. And in Israel, the wildly merry celebrations express the pride and joy of the Israelis in Jewish survival through the ages. Like the Jews in long-ago Shushan, modern Israelis also have enemies who are trying to destroy them. The Purim story gives them hope and faith that they too will triumph over their enemies and that peace will finally come to Israel for all time.

A Purim float featuring robots.

VOCABULARY AND CONCEPTS

he day on which Haman planned destroy the Jews; instead the ws were victorious	פּוּרִים
croll of Esther (read on Purim)	מְגִילָה
oisemakers (graggers in Yiddish)	רַעֲשָׁנִים
nding portions, gifts, candy	מִשְׁלוֹחַ מָנוֹת
until he would not know" ebrew name for Purim carnival)	עַדְלאִידָע
urim pastry	הָמֶנְטַאש
wish queen who saved the Jews Persia	אֶסְתֵּר
vil noble who wanted to kill all e Jews	הָמָן
ing of Persia	אֲחַשְׁוֵרוֹשׁ
usin of Esther	מָרְדְּכַי

PASSOVER

A Seder table set for Passover.

During a time of famine in Canaan, the Israelites settled in Egypt. For years they lived in peace and prosperity, but suddenly everything changed. A new Pharaoh enslaved the Children of Israel. Under the blazing sun, merciless taskmasters forced them to build palaces, cities, and pyramids for the cruel Pharaoh. Fearing that the Israelite slaves might rebel against him if their numbers grew, Pharaoh ordered all their newborn boys killed!

The Birth of Moses

An Israelite woman named Yocheved hid her newborn son, Moses, in a sealed basket and placed it among the Nile's reeds. The princess of Egypt found the baby and raised him in the royal palace. Moses learned from his mother, Yocheved, that he was a Jew. He learned the story of his people and of how God had promised that the land of Israel would become their home.

After killing an Egyptian taskmaster who had been mercilessly beating a Jewish slave, Moses had to flee. But he could not forget his people's suffering. One day, Moses saw a burning bush. When he came closer he heard the voice of God: "Go to the Pharaoh and tell him: 'Let my people go!' "

A painting discovered on the wall of an Egyptian tomb. The scene shows slaves taking care of cattle. Notice the slave being beaten by an overseer.

צְפַרְדֵּעַ · דָּם

עָרוֹב · כִּנִּים

שְׁחִין · דֶּבֶר

אַרְבֶּה · בָּרָד

מַכַּת בְּכוֹרוֹת · חוֹשֶׁךְ

Illustrations of the ten plagues, from a nineteenth-century Polish Haggadah.

The Pharaohs of Egypt left many monuments. They built temples, monuments, pyramids, and statues of themselves and their gods. This is a gigantic statue of a Pharaoh. It is about 40 feet tall and weighs many tons.

The Ten Plagues

Moses did as God commanded, but Pharaoh just laughed. Frightful things began to happen because of Pharaoh's refusal to let the Hebrew slaves go. All the water of Egypt turned to blood. Frogs swarmed over the country. Insects attacked the crops. Darkness, even in the daytime, cast everyone into confusion, but still the stubborn Pharaoh refused to let the Children of Israel go.

The last plague was the worst of all. All the firstborn children of the Egyptians died, but the firstborn children of the Israelites were left unharmed—"passed over." This is the source of the name "Passover"—Pesach in Hebrew.

The Miracle at the Red Sea

The Pharaoh finally released the Israelites. The Egyptian people were so anxious to see the end of the terrible plagues that they rushed the former slaves out of the land. But once the Israelites were gone, Pharaoh changed his mind. He sent his army to recapture them.

The Egyptians caught up with the Israelites at the Red Sea. The Israelites, frightened and bewildered, wondered how they would cross the sea to safety. Then God miraculously divided the waters so that the Israelites could pass through safely. Pharaoh's chariots charged after them, but the waters closed again, drowning the Egyptians.

The Meaning of Passover

Each year, on the fifteenth day of Nissan, we begin the celebration of Passover. This holiday reminds us of the escape from slavery in Egypt. Passover also stands for the beginning of Israel as a Jewish nation. With the Exodus ("Going-out") from Egypt, the Children of Israel came together as a people and readied themselves to accept God's Torah, the laws which bound them up into one community. Only as a proud, free people could they enter the Promised Land of Israel and claim their homeland.

Passover always comes in the springtime. The very

season, especially in Israel, seems to celebrate the delivery from Egyptian slavery and the birth of the Jewish nation. The flowers and trees are blossoming, the sky is clear and blue, and the sunlight sparkles over the Mediterranean.

The Passover Seder

All over the world, Jews celebrate the festival of freedom. At the Seder meal, many symbolic foods remind us of the history of the Passover holiday. The bitter herbs recall the bitterness of slavery. The shankbone recalls the lamb the Israelites ate at their last meal in Egypt. The charoset—a delicious mixture of apples, nuts, and wine— reminds us of the mortar that the Jews used to make bricks for Pharaoh. The roasted egg represents the special holiday sacrifice at the Temple in ancient Jerusalem. And the parsley represents spring and the new life that this lovely season brings to the land. It is dipped in salt water to remind us of the tears shed in Egypt by our enslaved ancestors.

On Passover, we eat matza instead of bread. It reminds us that the Israelites had to leave Egypt so quickly that their dough did not have time to rise, and they were left with flat unleavened bread like our matza crackers.

A Yemenite family at the Seder. Adults and children are dressed in costume and the table is set for the Seder.

"I know where the afikoman is hidden."

Page from a Haggadah issued for soldiers of the Haganah in 1948.

Present-day Samaritans in Israel, who claim descent from the tribes of Ephraim and Manasseh, have their own customs. Here they bake matzot for Passover.

...me out for matzah.

The Haggadah

At the Seder, we read the Haggadah, a book that tells the story of Passover with songs, stories, biblical quotations, and prayers. All Jews use the same Haggadah and celebrate the meal with customs and rituals that always follow the same order. *Seder*, in fact, means "Order." All over the world, on the night of the Seder, Jews thank God for delivering the Israelites from slavery and for protecting the Jewish nation from its enemies throughout the ages:

> Blessed be He who has kept His promise to His people Israel; praised be He.

> It is this promise that has stood by our fathers and ourselves. For not one enemy alone has arisen to destroy us—rather, in every generation, enemies rise up against us, seeking our end. And the Holy One, Blessed be He, always saves us from their hands.

The Message of Freedom

Israel celebrates the festival of freedom with a special joy. Not only do Israelis give thanks for the freeing of the Hebrews from their ancient bondage, they also rejoice that they are privileged to live as free people in their national homeland. In Israel they feel truly at home as Jews, truly free. Some Israelis have even written new parts into the traditional Haggadah, celebrating the rebirth of the independent Jewish state as a modern sequel to the Passover story of the delivery from Egypt.

VOCABULARY AND CONCEPTS

Holiday of Passover	פֶּסַח
Seder	סֵדֶר
Matzah	מַצָּה
Haggadah	הַגָּדָה

YOM HASHOAH

It is almost unbearable to think about the Nazi Holocaust, the most terrible event in Jewish history. Six million Jews were killed, for no other reason except that they were Jews. Innocent men, women, and children were cruelly beaten, tortured, and killed in ghettos and concentration camps. Six million Jews. The number is so big that it is hard to imagine.

Why We Must Never Forget

The events of the Holocaust are so horrible that we feel like crying when we think about them. But as much as we would like to forget the Holocaust, we *must* remember it. We must keep every pain-filled memory alive, so that we never allow something so awful to happen ever again.

Yom Hashoah, the Holocaust Remembrance Day, is

Two brave Jewish resistance fighters caught by the Nazis. They were executed on the spot.

Holocaust victims in a concentration-camp barracks.

לִיאוֹ בֶּק

LEO BAECK (1873–1956)
Rabbi and hero
—Leo Baech was one of the outstanding German-Jewish theologians and communal leaders of his generation. He wrote such notable works as *The Essence of Judaism* and *This People Israel*. During the 1930's, voluntarily staying with his congregation in Berlin even though he could have escaped, he was a great source of inspiration and spiritual strength for the persecuted Jews of Germany. He was later sent to a concentration camp and after World War II became chairman of the World Union for Progressive Judaism.

VOCABULARY AND CONCEPTS

Holocaust Remembrance Day יוֹם הַשּׁוֹאָה

Holocaust Memorial Center in Jerusalem יָד וָשֵׁם

observed in Israel and the world over on the twenty-seventh day of Nissan. On this day we remember the six million helpless victims of the Nazis, and we remember those who courageously resisted their attackers, even if only for a few proud days.

Yom Hashoah in Israel

On Yom Hashoah, a siren brings all of Israel to a halt. For a moment everyone in the country stops whatever he or she is doing, stands up quietly, and remembers. We force ourselves to remember all the terror and horror. We relive every wound of body and of spirit, and we vow never to let another Nazi Holocaust take place.

At the Yad Vashem memorial house in Jerusalem, special ceremonies are held. At this center, eternal candles flicker in the dimness, marking our remembrance of those who died in the Holocaust.

The Yad Vashem Memorial: "Ohel Yizkor"—Hall of Remembrance. The walls are built of large, unhewn black lava rocks. On the mosaic floor are inscribed the names of the twenty-one largest concentration camps, and near the wall in the west burns a light.

315

YOM HAZIKARON

Yom Hazikaron, the Day of Remembrance, is a day of great sorrow. On this day, we remember all the soldiers who were killed defending Israel and fighting to create a strong, independent homeland for our people.

The commemoration begins at sunset with a siren blast. A parent whose child died in the defense of Israel presents a torch to the President of the country, who lights a flame in memory of all Israel's fallen martyrs. Special prayers are said in the synagogue on Yom Hazikaron and on the Sabbath day which precedes it.

At mid-morning, on the fourth day of Iyyar, sirens are sounded throughout the country. Everything comes to an absolute standstill. Tailors put down their needles and thread. Bakers stop mixing batter. Teachers stop their

Monument on Mount Zion, Jerusalem, memorializing the heroic martyrs who rose up against the Nazis in the Warsaw Ghetto.

classes, and children put down their pencils and close their books. Cars pull over to the side of the road. Everyone stands silently at attention for a moment, sadly thinking of the brave men and women who gave their lives for Israel.

A special ceremony is held on Mount Herzl, where torches are lit, symbolizing the eternal memory of the dead. All day long, mournful music is played over the radio.

At seven in the evening, another siren goes off. This sound signals the end of the memorial day and the beginning of the Yom Haatzmaut (Independence Day) celebration.

Without the courage and self-sacrifice of the fallen soldiers, there would be no Israel today. Without Yom Hazikaron, there could be no Yom Haatzmaut.

In 1949, the remains of the visionary of the modern State of Israel, Theodor Herzl, were brought to Israel from Vienna, Austria.

Herzl's remains were buried atop Mount Herzl in Jerusalem.

VOCABULARY AND CONCEPTS

ınt Herzl	הַר הֶרְצֵל
⸱pendence Day	יוֹם הָעַצְמָאוּת
his day we remember all the ⸱ers who were killed defend- srael	יוֹם הַזִּכָּרוֹן

YOM HAATZMAUT

Israel stamp honoring Theodor Herzl, who dedicated his life to the establishment of a Jewish state in Israel.

In 70 C.E., the independence of ancient Israel came to an end. The Roman conquerors savaged the holy Temple in Jerusalem and exiled many thousands of Jews from their beloved homeland.

Some Jewish communities remained in Palestine, but large groups of Jews were forced to make their homes in different parts of the world. We call this time period the exile, for Jews were ousted, or exiled, from their land.

The Dream of the Return

Exiled Jews in Europe were often the victims of mockery and persecution. They did not have equal rights and they endured much suffering, just because they were Jews. It took all their faith in God and Torah to keep themselves and Judaism alive.

A military parade in Israel on Independence Day.

Celebrating Israel's Independence Day.

But through the centuries of exile, Jews in far-off lands kept up the dream of the return to Israel. Like a shining star in the distant sky, the dream of the return to Israel twinkled for them. Israel was a vision of hope that soothed their misery and suffering.

The Holocaust

Then came the final blow—the Nazi Holocaust. Europe became a terrifying, violent slaughterhouse. The Nazi murderers tortured and killed six million Jews—just because they were Jews.

Jewish people finally realized that they could not be truly free or truly safe in any country on the globe—only in their own homeland, Israel. And despite all the obstacles in their way, young groups of Zionist settlers rebuilt the land of age-old dreams and fulfilled the vision of return.

The Work of the Pioneers

The land of Palestine was swampy; epidemics of malaria struck the settlers; the Jews had little knowledge of farming; the Arabs claimed Palestine and attacked Jewish

An Israeli poster celebrating the thirty-fourth anniversary of the founding of the State of Israel.

319

Passage from Israel's Declaration of Independence

A JEWISH STATE

ACCORDINGLY WE, *the members of the National Council, representing the Jewish people in the Land of Israel and the Zionist Movement, have assembled on the day of the termination of the British Mandate for Palestine, and, by virtue of our natural and historic right and of the resolution of the United Nations, do hereby proclaim the establishment of a Jewish State in the Land of Israel—the "State of Israel" . . . from midnight the sixth of Iyar 5708, the fifteenth day of May 1948.*

settlements; the British refused to let more than a pitifully small number of Jews into the country. But the courageous and stubborn Zionist settlers refused to be stopped. They never gave up the fight for Jewish independence in their own land, and finally they succeeded.

Independence At Last

One of the most glorious days in the long history of the Jews came on the fifth of Iyyar, which in the year 1948 came out on May 14. After so many centuries of struggle and sorrow, Israel was once again the Jewish state. On this day, Israel made the formal declaration of its independence.

Every year, Jews all over the world—and especially in Israel—celebrate with excitement and joy the creation of the modern State of Israel. The Jewish dream of the return has finally come true.

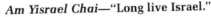

Am Yisrael Chai—"Long live Israel."

ۥᵣaeli Independence
ᵃy poster.

Independence Day Celebrations

Mobs of Israelis and tourists from other lands crowd into Jerusalem. The streets are decorated, blue-and-white flags are everywhere, and everyone's face—whether shopkeeper, doctor, schoolchild, or professor—has a special smile of anticipation. The holiday is celebrated out in the open, with singing and dancing in the streets, music playing, eating and drinking. There is a gigantic parade. Fireworks are displayed in brilliant color in the night sky. It is as if all of Jerusalem—and all of Israel—is having one big birthday party. The Israeli flag is waving all over the land. Happy birthday, Israel!

Parades are held in every city and town. Children wearing garlands of flowers and white shirts or blouses march happily through the streets. In Haifa, the symphony orchestra accompanies the celebrations. In Tel Aviv one year, a parade of military might was held. While supersonic jets and helicopters flew past overhead, tanks and armored units rolled down the streets of Tel Aviv to the cheers of the assembled crowds. Israelis are proud that their country has the strength and the arms with which to defend her people and her rights from all enemies.

Fireworks from the roof of the Tel Aviv Municipality Building on Israel Independence Day.

Israeli stamp issued to commemorate Israel Independence Day, 1972. The stamp pictures the Zion Gate in Jerusalem.

On Yom Haatzmaut, the finals of the Chidon Tanach (the International Bible Contest) take place. This popular contest attracts students from around the world. The first trials take place in local schools in towns and cities, and the finals are held in Jerusalem. When this exciting contest is shown on television, the people of Israel stay glued to their sets.

On this great day, Israel's birthday, the people of the State of Israel joyously celebrate because they are living in an independent nation that has the power to defend its freedom and way of life against all enemies.

Yom Haatzmaut Prayers

In synagogues in Israel and all around the world, special prayers in honor of Independence Day are added to the daily service. Just as on Purim and Chanukah, Jews celebrate on Independence Day the miracle of their redemption from enemies. On religious kibbutzim, Jews say the *Al HaNissim* prayer:

> Thou has delivered the strong into the hands of the weak, the many into the hands of the few, the impure into the hands of the pure, the wicked into the hands of the righteous, and tyrants into the hands of devotees of Thy Torah.

In Sephardic synagogues of Israel the congregation proclaims, "Hear ye, our brethren! Today, *X* [the number is called out] years have passed since the beginning of our redemption, marked by the establishment of the State." State."

Yom Haatzmaut in the Diaspora

The excitement of Yom Haatzmaut has caught on with Jews the world over. Jews everywhere celebrate the great day on the fifth of Iyyar each year. In New York, a big parade marches down Fifth Avenue. Children from schools and synagogues all over the city carry banners and ride on floats that rejoice in Israel's independence. Special groups dance and sing. Everywhere, onlookers wave Israeli and American flags and applaud the marchers.

VOCABULARY AND CONCEPTS

"For the Miracles" Prayer	עַל הַנִּסִּים
Pioneers	חֲלוּצִים
Israel Independence Day	יוֹם הָעַצְמָאוּת
International Bible Contest	חִידוֹן תַּנַ"ךְ

YOM YERUSHALAYIM

Israeli stamp to preserve the memory of those who died in the War of Liberation.

The newest holiday on the Jewish calendar is Yom Yerushalayim—Jerusalem Day—celebrated each year on the twenty-eighth day of Iyyar. On this day in 1967 (Wednesday, June 7, on the civil calendar—the third day of the Six-Day War), after bloody battle, Israeli forces broke through Jerusalem's dividing wall and reclaimed the Old City. Hardened soldiers wept as they neared the ancient Western Wall. United Jerusalem once again became the nation's capital.

Today Yom Yerushalayim is celebrated with joy and festivity. Special study classes about the history of Jerusalem are scheduled, triumphant psalms and prayers are sung, and special meals are prepared.

But Yom Yerushalayim is also a day of commemoration. We remember too the pain and struggle and sacrifice of Israel's soldiers. Eighteen torches are lit at the Western Wall, honoring the memory of those who fell in the battle to reclaim Israel's capital.

VOCABULARY AND CONCEPTS

Jerusalem Day (commemorates Israeli liberation of Old City of Jerusalem during Six-Day War)

יוֹם יְרוּשָׁלַיִם

LAG BAOMER

A nineteenth-century European omer calendar. The numbers, top to bottom, indicate that this is the thirty-third day of the omer (Lag Baomer), or four weeks and five days since the beginning of the seven-week period between Passover and Shavuot.

An ancient stone jug used for storing grain. It can hold an omer.

The Jews of ancient Israel were farmers. Their lives depended on their crops, for if the harvest failed, the coming year would be one of hunger and suffering. Passover was the time of the wheat harvest, and Shavuot was the time of the barley harvest.

The Counting of the Omer

The time between Passover and Shavuot became a time of seriousness and prayer for the Jews. The farmer prayed to God for a successful harvest and a year of plenty and gladness. On the day after Passover, the Temple priests would make a special sacrificial offering of a measure of grain, called an *omer*. The priest would mix the *omer* of grain with oil and frankincense and "wave" it up and down and from side to side in the Temple. This ceremony was interpreted as a prayer for God to protect the harvest from strong winds and harsh weather. Then Jews would count out the days between the waving of the *omer* and Shavuot.

We still call these seven weeks (or forty-nine days) the time of Sefirat Haomer, which means "The Counting of the Omer." Orthodox Jews, in Israel and the world over, consider these weeks a time of solemnity. People do not go to parties, and weddings are not held. Special daily prayers are said.

Lag Baomer Celebrations

But on the thirty-third day of Sefirat Haomer, the whole mood changes! On this holiday, Lag Baomer ("The Thirty-Third Day of the Omer"), everyone in Israel goes outdoors for a picnic. There is singing, dancing, sports, and general partying and fun. Lots of weddings are held on this day. People stay up late around bonfires, singing warm folksongs as they sway before the crackling logs.

RABBI AKIBA (50 C.E.–135 C.E.)
Rabbi and martyr

As a young man, Akiba tended the sheep of Kalba Savua, a wealthy Jerusalemite who had a beautiful daughter, Rachel. Akiba and Rachel fell in love and wanted to get married. But Rachel's father stubbornly opposed the match. He refused to see the young couple or to give Rachel a dowry when she left home to marry Akiba. Kalba Savua felt that Akiba, an un-learned shepherd, was not good enough for his daughter.

Soon after they were married, Rachel and Akiba had a son. When the boy was old enough to go to school, Akiba attended first grade along with him! So great was Akiba's yearning to learn the Hebrew alphabet and the Torah that he sat down with the small children to study. Along with the little ones, Akiba learned Hebrew, Bible, Talmud, and the commentaries. He progressed very, very quickly and soon became the best student in the school. With his wife's encouragement and bless-ings, Akiba left home to study To-rah at the great academy in Lydda. He was forty years old at the time.

In twelve years Akiba had be-come a great scholar. He even opened his own yeshiva in Bnai Brak. Now Akiba was a famous, revered rabbi whom others sought for advice.

The Romans ruled over Israel at this time, with harshness and cru-elty toward the Jews. The Romans issued strict decrees against the teaching of the Torah. But Rabbi Akiba defied the Romans and con-tinued to teach. Rabbi Akiba en-couraged the rebellion by the great Jewish hero Bar Kochba.

The Romans imprisoned him and condemned him to death by slow torture. Akiba, eighty-five years old, bore his torment with serene dignity. He was reciting *Shema* as his soul departed.

The Origin of Lag Baomer

Why is Lag Baomer so different from the rest of Sefirat Haomer?

On Lag Baomer we remember the faith and courage of the Torah scholars who lived in the land of Israel under the harsh Roman conquerors. The cruel Romans meant to wipe out Judaism, so they decreed: "Any Jew caught studying Torah will be killed!" This the Jews would not tolerate. The aged Rabbi Akiba, greatest teacher of his time, and a worker for peace all his life, was the leading spirit in the rebellion which now broke out.

The military leader, Simeon Bar Kochba, was a brave and loyal Jew who seemed like another Judah Maccabee to his people. He and his troops captured Jerusalem and built an altar on the Temple Mount.

Hadrian sent a powerful army, led by his best general. For two years they fought against Bar Kochba's troops, blocking supplies from reaching Jerusalem, and finally driving the rebels into the town of Betar. When Betar fell (135), betrayed by spies, thousands of Jewish fighters, including Bar Kochba, were killed.

To Rabbi Akiba, the life of Torah meant more even than his own life. When the Romans found out that the rabbi was still teaching Torah, they took him away and tortured him to death.

Rabbi Shimon bar Yochai

Rabbi Akiba's student, Rabbi Shimon bar Yochai, had loved and honored his teacher, and he spoke out against the brutal Romans. He, too, taught the Torah despite the Roman decree, and when the Romans found out, Rabbi Shimon bar Yochai was forced to flee for his life. He had grown up in Galilee, the mountainous, northern part of Israel, and so he and his son Eliezer escaped there. They hid in a lonely cave high on Mount Meron. The rabbi's loyal students traveled fearlessly out to the cave. They carried bows and arrows and pretended they were just going hunting in the country so that the Romans

Among religious Jews it is customary to give baby boys their first haircut on Lag Baomer.

REUVEN RUBIN · DANCERS OF MERON
ראובן רובין · הרוקדים במירון
1.30 ISRAEL ישראל
ל"ג בעומר
LAG BA-OMER

would not suspect them. But they were really going to study the holy Torah. For thirteen years, living mainly on the fruit of a nearby carob tree, Rabbi Shimon bar Yochai and his son Eliezer kept alive the knowledge of Torah on Mount Meron, far from the eyes of the Roman officials who sought to destroy the Jewish people by forbidding them to learn their beloved Torah.

Rabbi Shimon bar Yochai died on Lag Baomer, but on this holiday we remember not his death so much as his courageous and scholarly life, his faith, and his bravery. We have picnics, outdoor games, and bonfires, remembering the rabbi's students who journeyed through the countryside to the cave of their great teacher. We eat the fruit of the carob tree, remembering the hardships Rabbi Shimon bar Yochai and his son suffered for the sake of Torah. And in Israel on this day, many people travel all the way up to the high Mount Meron, where they visit the tombs of Rabbi Shimon bar Yochai and his son Eliezer. Everywhere in the land, people sit up late outdoors, singing songs about the great rabbi and about *his* teacher, the wonderful Rabbi Akiba.

The tomb of Rabbi Meir Baal HaNes, member of the Sanhedrin and pupil of Rabbi Akiba, in Tiberias. Lake Kinneret is in the background.

VOCABULARY AND CONCEPTS

Lag Baomer	לַ"ג בָּעֹמֶר
Sheaf, measure	עֹמֶר
Hebrew letter with the value of 30	לָמֶד
Hebrew letter with the value of 3	גִימֶל
Time of counting the omer	סְפִירָה
Leader of the Jewish revolt against Rome (132–135 C.E.)	בַּר־כּוֹכְבָא
Scholar, teacher, and student of Rabbi Akiba	רַבִּי שִׁמְעוֹן בַּר יוֹחַאי

326

SHAVUOT

Shavuot, which in ancient Israel was the time of the barley harvest, comes out exactly seven weeks after Passover, on the sixth day of the month of Sivan. This timing explains the name of the holiday, for Shavuot in Hebrew means "Weeks."

Shavuot, though, is much, much more than a time when happy farmers celebrated the successful barley crop. It also commemorates the giving the holy Torah to the Jews on Mount Sinai. Another name for Shavuot in Hebrew is Zman Matan Torateinu, which means "The Time of the Giving of Our Torah."

The Giving of the Torah at Mount Sinai

The Bible (in chapters 19 and 20 of the Book of Exodus) tells the vivid story of how God bestowed the Torah on the Jewish people:

> In the third month after the Children of Israel left Egypt, they came to the wilderness of Sinai. There they camped in front of the mountain. And Moses went up to God. And the Eternal called to him from the mountain, saying, "You shall say to the Children of Israel: 'You saw what I did to the Egyptians and how I saved you and brought you to Me. Now if you will listen to My voice and obey My laws, you will be My treasure from among all peoples.' "

And Moses told the people what God had said. And the people answered, "All that the Eternal has said, we will do."

All the people sanctified themselves and waited for the Torah. And there was thunder and lightning, and a thick cloud surrounded the mountain. Then the sound of a shofar blowing very loudly was heard and the people trembled. Soon the mountain was completely surrounded by smoke and flames, the shofar got louder and louder, and the whole mountain shook.

Wood carving of the Ten Commandments.

327

Israeli stamp in honor of Shavuot.

Then God spoke the words, saying:

1. I am the Lord your God.
2. You shall have no other gods before Me.
3. You shall not take the name of the Lord in vain.
4. Remember the Sabbath to keep it holy.
5. Honor your father and your mother.
6. You shall not kill.
7. You shall not be unfaithful to wife or husband.
8. You shall not steal.
9. You shall not bear false witness.
10. You shall not desire what is your neighbor's.

Chag HaBikkurim

A third Hebrew name for Shavuot is Chag HaBikurim—"Holiday of the First Fruits."

Just at this time of year in Israel, early summer, the first luscious fruits of the season start to ripen on tree and vine. All of the farmer's long, hard hours of work planting and tending the crop now begin to pay off in an abundant harvest. The Torah commanded that the Israelite farmer collect these first fruits and bring them to the Temple in Jerusalem. There the *bikurim* would be offered up as a thanks-offering to God.

In this way, our ancestors expressed their gratitude for a successful harvest. Farmers brought *bikurim* from each of the seven species described in the Bible as the rich crops of the Promised Land:

> For the Lord your God brings you into a good land, a land of brooks of water, of fountains in valleys and hills; a land of wheat and barley, and vines and fig trees and pomegranates; a land of olive trees and honey.
>
> (Deuteronomy 8:7)

In modern Israel, we still remember the *bikurim* brought by the Israelite farmers to the ancient Temple in Jerusalem. Baskets full of fruits and vegetables and bouquets of colorful flowers decorate the walls and tables of Shavuot celebrations. Special dances and murals recall the seven species of ancient *bikurim* offerings.

328

Shavuot Observances

In the synagogues, special prayers are said in honor of the great day on which God gave Jews the Torah. Many religious people spend the whole day and night of Shavuot in the synagogue, studying the books of the Torah and rejoicing in the sacredness of God's word.

At home, traditionally, Jews eat meals made with milk and cheese on Shavuot. Everyone is glad to join in this custom, although no one knows for sure what its origin is! There are crisp blintzes filled with soft cheese, and mouthwatering cheesecakes. Some rabbis quote a verse from the Bible in which the Torah is compared to milk and honey. Maybe that is why we eat these dairy foods on the day the Torah was given to the Jewish people.

These dancers are enacting harvest scenes in ancient Israel. Behind the dancers you can see signs enumerating the seven harvest fruits.

TISHA BE'AV

By the rivers of Babylon we sat and cried when we remembered Zion. We left our harps on the willow trees there. For those who led us as captives from our country asked us to sing. Our tormentors asked us to be happy and sing one of the songs of Zion.

How can we sing the Eternal's song in a foreign land? If I forget Thee, O Jerusalem, let my right hand forget its cunning. Let my tongue cleave to the roof of my mouth, if I forget you. If I do not set Jerusalem above my chief joy.

This sad poem, which is part of Psalm 137 in the Bible, was written about a terrible event in Jewish history—the destruction of the First Temple by the Babylonians in 586 B.C.E. The Babylonians came with a powerful army and forced large numbers of Jews out of their beloved homeland. The Babylonians conquered Jerusalem on the ninth day of the month of Av, or Tisha Be'Av, in Hebrew.

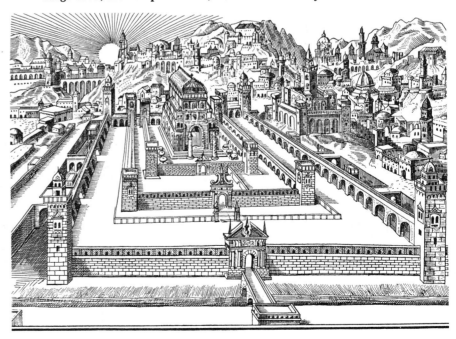

An artist's idea of the Bet Hamikdash, the Temple in Jerusalem. The large area, the Temple Mount, was surrounded by a wall.

A battering ram. Rams such as this were brought up to the walls of Jerusalem and used to punch holes in the stone wall. Once a hole was opened, enemy soldiers poured in and captured the city.

330

Years later, the Jews regained their independence in their own land and joyfully rebuilt their Temple. But once again tragedy struck. The Second Temple, too, was destroyed by savage enemies of the Jews. The Romans conquered Jerusalem in 70 C.E., and the marauding soldiers wreaked havoc throughout the city. This tragedy, too, came on the ninth of Av.

A Day of Mourning

Tisha Be'Av became a universal day of Jewish mourning. All over the world, through the ages, Jews remembered the degradation and shame that this sad day had brought. They recited special, mournful prayers, they fasted, and they hoped fervently that one day God would deliver them from exile and return them to their Promised Land.

The Western Wall in the Old City of Jerusalem is all that remains of the Second Temple.

Israeli stamp issued in honor of the dedication of the Knesset building in Jerusalem, 1966.

The Lamentations of Jeremiah

Lamentations, a sad book of the Bible, is read as part of the synagogue service on Tisha Be'Av. This book describes the sorrow of the prophet Jeremiah, who looked out at the ruined city of Jerusalem, which had once shone in splendor and radiated with pride. As Jeremiah looked upon the ravaged city, his heart cried out. He compared the sorrow and desolation of Jerusalem to that of a woman mourning her husband's death:

> How lonely sits the city
>   that was full of people.
> How like a widow has she become.
> She that was great among the nations,
> She that was a princess among the cities,
> Has become a vassal.
>
> (Lamentations 1:1)

Tisha Be'Av in Israel

In Israel on Tisha Be'Av, many people gather around the Western Wall in the Old City of Jerusalem. This wall is all that remains of the Second Temple that the Romans destroyed, long, long ago. Here people say prayers to God, and hope that Israel today can have the strength to withstand all enemies who seek her ruin.

VOCABULARY AND CONCEPTS

Ninth day of the month of Av	תִּשְׁעָה בְּאָב
Eleventh month of the Jewish calendar	אָב
Nine	תִּשְׁעָה
Western Wall, the last remnant of the Holy Temple in Jerusalem	כּוֹתֶל־הַמַּעֲרָבִי
Eternal Light	נֵר־תָּמִיד
The Holy Temple	בֵּית־הַמִקְדָשׁ
Lamentations	קִינוֹת

MODERN KIBBUTZ FESTIVALS

The grape harvest on a kibbutz in Israel.

The fifteenth day of the month of Av marks the beginning of the grape harvest in Israel. In ancient times, the maidens of Jerusalem dressed themselves in white clothes and went out dancing in the vineyards, celebrating the bountiful new crop of luscious, juicy grapes. In recent years the kibbutzim have revived a festival marking the beginning of the grape harvest. It is called Hagigat HaKeramim—the Festival of the Vineyards—and its celebrations include music, dancing, poetry, and songs about love.

At some kibbutzim which own flocks of sheep, the Sheepshearing Festival—Hagigat HaGez—is celebrated each year at the end of the sheepshearing season. As the last sheep of the flock is ceremonially shorn, everyone on the kibbutz sings and dances, rejoicing with the shepherd at the conclusion of the shearing.

The kibbutzniks are celebrating more than the grape harvest and the sheepshearing when they dance and sing at these special festivals. They rejoice that the Jewish people—persecuted for so long through the centuries of the Diaspora—have returned to their beloved Israel. Now Jews can till the soil and tend the crops and animals of their homeland.

We have finally come home!

A shepherd in Israel feeds his flock.

VOCABULARY AND CONCEPTS

Fifteenth day of Av (the festival of
the vineyards)   חֲגִיגַת הַכְּרָמִים

Sheepshearing Festival   חֲגִיגַת הַגֵּז

ROSH CHODESH

Sundial on a building housing a synagogue in Jerusalem. From the rooftop one can watch the sunrise signaling the time for morning prayers. The synagogue is named Zaharei Hama—"rays of the sun."

In modern times, the beginning of each new month no longer must be determined by the testimony of two witnesses; with the help of modern astronomical calculations, the date of Rosh Chodesh may be determined by computer, years in advance. But as the beginning of each new month on the Hebrew calendar, Rosh Chodesh is still a time of hope and prayer for the Jewish people.

Rosh Chodesh Prayers

Through all the long, dark night of the Diaspora, Jews hoped for redemption. Finally they saw a long-awaited glimmer of light with the creation of the State of Israel. In the same way, Jews each month search the night sky, seeking out the glimmer of the new moon. When we see the sliver of light, we proclaim the beginning of the new month—Rosh Chodesh. We say special blessings and prayers to enhance the moment.

On the Sabbath before Rosh Chodesh, we pray, "He who wrought miracles for our fathers and redeemed them from slavery into freedom, may He speedily redeem us and gather our exiles from the four corners of the earth, even all Israel united in fellowship, and let us say Amen." Sephardic Jews also recite Psalm 104 after the morning service and before the evening service. This psalm is a beautiful poem praising God as the Creator of our marvelous universe—its moon, its sun, and its marvelously diverse creatures.

Rosh Chodesh in Israel

In Israel, a special television program called "A Good Month" is broadcast on the Saturday night before Rosh Chodesh. In religious schools, Rosh Chodesh is marked by special assembly programs, where the students are reminded of all the Jewish holidays coming up in the new month.

VOCABULARY AND CONCEPTS

Beginning of the month	רֹאשׁ חֹדֶשׁ
Psalms	תְּהִלִּים

SHABBAT

The Sabbath day is a blessing of rest for all Jews. Men, women, and children who struggle at their labors all week long welcome the Sabbath as a day off. There is no cooking, no working, no school, and no housecleaning on this day. Wealthy people, on the Sabbath, rest from their concentration on money and business, and can open their minds and hearts to matters of the spirit. For everyone, rich or poor, it is a time of light and wine and gladness. On the Sabbath day we remember that God created the universe and rested on the seventh day.

How Israel Observes Shabbat

In Israel, where the majority of the people are Jews, the Sabbath is a countrywide holiday. All business stops. Theaters are closed, shops are locked, buses and trains go off duty. By mid-afternoon on Friday, one can already feel that the Sabbath is coming. People are rushing home to prepare for the Sabbath day. On the way they stop off at the florist to buy a beautiful bouquet. A delicious meal is being cooked, and challah is being baked. Many families attend synagogue services.

The Sabbath in Israel has a special quality of gladness that it can have nowhere else. The prayers in the synagogue are said in Hebrew, the national language. Everywhere people feel proud and happy that Jews have returned to independence in their beloved homeland. On this day, people visit friends and family, study Torah, have peaceful, pleasant discussions, and take leisurely walks through their lovely land.

This Israeli stamp was issued in honor of Shabbat. The quotation reads, "The Children of Israel shall keep the Sabbath, observing the Sabbath throughout their generations."

Inscription "To the Place of Trumpeting . . . to herald," uncovered below the northwestern parapet of the Western Wall. From here, a priest would proclaim the advent and end of the Sabbath.

Shabbat Shalom in a kibbutz dining room.

VOCABULARY AND CONCEPTS

The Jewish day of rest, spent in prayer, study, and resting שַׁבָּת

THE JEWISH CALENDAR

SEPT.-OCT.   תשרי תשד״מ

מולדו יום ד׳ שעה 2 21 מינוט 9 חלקים

8	T	א׳ דר״ה תשליך	חמישי	א
9	F	ב׳ דר״ה	שׁשׁי	ב
10	Sa	האזינו שׁובה	שׁבת	ג
11	S	צום גדלי׳ נדחה	ראשׁון	ד
12	M		שׁני	ה
13	Tu		שׁלישׁי	ו
14	W		רביעי	ז
15	T		חמישׁי	ח
16	F	ערב יוה״כ	שׁשׁי	ט
17	Sa	יום כפור הזכ״נ	שׁבת	י
18	S		ראשׁון	יא
19	M		שׁני	יב
20	Tu		שׁלישׁי	יג
21	W	ערב סוכות ערוב תבשׁילין	רביעי	יד
22	T	א׳ סוכות	חמישׁי	טו
23	F	ב׳ סוכות	שׁשׁי	טז
24	Sa	שׁבת חוהמ״ס	שׁבת	יז
25	S	ב׳ דחוהמ״ס	ראשׁון	יח
26	M	ג׳ דחוהמ״ס	שׁני	יט
27	Tu	ד׳ דחוהמ״ס	שׁלישׁי	כ
28	W	הושׁע״ר ערוב תבשׁילין	רביעי	כא
29	T	שׁמיני עצרת הזכ״נ	חמישׁי	כב
30	F	שׁמחת תורה	שׁשׁי	כג
1	Sa	בראשׁית מב״ח OCT.	שׁבת	כד
2	S		ראשׁון	כה
3	M		שׁני	כו
4	Tu		שׁלישׁי	כז
5	W		רביעי	כח
6	T		חמישׁי	כט
7	F	א׳ דראשׁ חדשׁ	שׁשׁי	ל

A page from a Jewish calendar. Notice the variety of information.

The Hebrew calendar — לוּחַ עִבְרִי

The beginning of the new month — ראֹשׁ חֹדֶשׁ

Year — שָׁנָה

Ancient Court which ruled on matters of Jewish religious law — סַנְהֶדְרִין

In ancient Israel, the calendar was created by direct observation of the moon. On the thirtieth day of each month, the members of the Sanhedrin (Supreme Court) would gather together and wait for two reliable witnesses to testify that they had seen the new moon in the sky. The Sanhedrin would then proclaim Rosh Chodesh—the first day of the new month. Rosh Chodesh was always a time of special prayers and hope that the new month would bring joy, peace, and fulfillment.

The Jewish year is made up of twelve months, just like the civil calendar. But the Jewish months have different names, and the beginnings of the Jewish and the civil months do not usually coincide. Thus, March 30, 1982, was the sixth day of the Jewish month of Nissan; May 30, 1982, was the eighth day of the Jewish month of Sivan.

The months on the Jewish calendar are:

Nissan (March–April)
Iyyar (April–May)
Sivan (May–June)
Tammuz (June–July)
Av (July–August)
Elul (August–September)
Tishrei (September–October)
Cheshvan (October–November)
Kislev (November-December)
Tevet (December–January)
Shvat (January–February)
Adar (February–March)

337

INDEX

INDEX

The page references in this index include illustration captions and sidebar material as well

Judea; Samaria
Western Wall, 13, 168, 214, 257, 258, 259, 280, 285, 293, 297, 323, 331, 332
Wilderness, sojourn in. *See* Desert, sojourn in
Wine industry, 53, 107, 109, 230
Wingate, Charles Orde, 237, 258
Wingate Institute of Physical Education and Sports, 134
Winter, 49
Wise, Stephen S., 241
Wolfssohn, David, 15
Women, 40, 41, 44, 73–74, 75, 76, 228
World Union for Progressive Judaism, 315
World War I, 152, 231, 232, 240
World War II, 15, 35, 36, 37, 171, 238, 243–244, 245–246, 258
World Zionist Organization, 38, 223, 225, 241, 248

Yadin, Yigal, 94
Yad Vashem, 169, 315
Yaffo, 104, 149
Yarkon River, 47, 48
Yavneh, 210, 211
Yehuda HaNassi, 211
Yemen, 273
Yemenite Jews, 60, 130, 137, 274, 312
Yemin Orde, 237
Yeshiva University, 85
Yeshivot, 78, 84–85
Yiddish language, 56, 125, 126
Yishuv, 74
Yocheved, 310
Yom Haatzmaut, 317, 318–322
Yom Hashoah, 244, 314–315
Yom Hazikaron (Memorial Day), 316–317
Yom Hazikaron (Rosh Hashana), 285
Yom Kippur, 64, 109, 279, 284, 287–288
Yom Kippur War, 31, 260, 261–262, 263, 267, 278, 287
Yom Teruah, 285
Yom Yerushalayim, 259, 323
Youth Aliyah, 37, 242
Youth groups, 79, 89–91, 231, 234

Zaharei Hama Synagogue, 282
Zeid, Alexander, 228
Zeus, 298
Zichron Yaakov, 107, 227
Zim Line, 103
Zion, defined, 20
Zion, Mount, 292, 316
Zion Gate, 322
Zionism, 36, 124, 169, 199, 222–225, 226, 230.

See also Zionist Congresses; World Zionist Organization
Zionist Congresses
First, 15, 223, 225
Second, 225
Zionist Organization of America, 241
Zion Mule Corps, 231
Zman Matan Torateinu, 327
Zodiac, 172
Zohar (town), 179